Community Participation and Empowerment in Primary Education

Community Participation and Empowerment in Primary Education

Edited by
R. Govinda
Rashmi Diwan

SAGE Publications
New Delhi/Thousand Oaks/London

First published in 2003 by

Sage Publications India Pvt Ltd
B-42, Panchsheel Enclave
New Delhi 110 017

Sage Publications Inc
2455 Teller Road
Thousand Oaks, California 91320

Sage Publications Ltd
6 Bonhill Street
London EC2A 4PU

Published by Tejeshwar Singh for Sage Publications India Pvt Ltd, typeset by Line Arts, Pondicherry in 11/13 Lapidary 333 BT and printed at Chaman Enterprises, New Delhi.

Library of Congress Cataloging-in-Publication Data

Community participation and empowerment in primary education/edited by R. Govinda, Rashmi Diwan.

   p. cm.

Includes bibliographical references.

   1. Community and school—India. 2. Education, Elementary—India. 3. Literacy—India. I. Govinda, R. II. Diwan, Rashmi.

LA1152.C67   372.954—dc21   2003   2002155676

ISBN: 0–7619–9673–7 (US-Hb)   81–7829–137–1 (India-Hb)
       0–7619–9674–5 (US-Pb)   81–7829–138–X (India-Pb)

Sage Production Team: Sam George, Ankush Saikia, Radha Dev Raj and Santosh Rawat

Contents

List of Tables, Boxes and Figures

Preface

The National Policy on Education (NPE) 1986 has had far reaching implications for reforming the educational system in the country in a wide range of areas. Consequently, the past decade witnessed an unprecedented level of activity in the field of primary education in the country. One of the major recommendations made by the NPE was related to empowering communities for the management of educational institutions at the local level. The NPE recommended the establishment of an appropriate institutional framework at the district and sub-district levels, such as the District Board of Education and Village Education Committees, in order to ensure that community members played an important role in the management of primary education. This move towards decentralization and empowerment of the community got a further fillip with the 73rd–74th constitutional amendments relating to Panchayati Raj institutions. Since then, tremendous amount of experience in the field has accumulated with respect to the involvement of the community in the management of primary education in different states. Simultaneously, very useful experiences on the involvement of the community have also emerged in other sectors of education and development. For instance, the lessons from the total literacy campaign for mobilizing the local community for educational action is valuable. Similarly, activities in the areas of watershed management and sustainable development present a wealth of experience and insight for the primary education sector.

The present volume, which documents the experiences on involvement of the community in the management of primary education in different states, is coming out at an opportune moment as the country is planning for the next phase of action with respect to primary education under the auspices of the Sarva Siksha Abhiyan. It is visualized that the illustrative case studies generated for different states of India would help understand the manner in which partnerships among civil society, government and non-government organizations function in the pursuit of universalization of primary education, and the dynamics involved in empowering the community for management of primary education. The volume consists of 10 chapters mainly focussing on the grassroots level efforts for community empowerment in Kerala, Rajasthan, Madhya Pradesh, Bihar and Karnataka, and their implications for provision of primary education for all in India. Beside state specific experiences, the book also presents additional papers on two other critical sectors, namely, literacy campaign and watershed management.

I understand that many of the papers in the volume were originally presented in a seminar on the same theme conducted by the National Institute of Educational Planning and Administration with support from the European Commission. I take this opportunity to thank the European Commission for offering financial support for conducting the seminar, which has resulted in this volume. I am also grateful to my colleagues Dr R. Govinda and Dr Rashmi Diwan who have ably edited the papers and put together this volume. I hope that the volume will be useful for teachers and researchers, as well as administrators concerned with the task of universal primary education in this country.

14 June 2002   B.P. Khandelwal
New Delhi   Director
                                        National Institute of Educational
                                             Planning and Administration

Acknowledgements

The genesis of this volume lies in a national seminar on the theme "Community Participation and Empowerment in Primary Education in India" conducted by the National Institute of Educational Planning and Administration (NIEPA). The seminar papers attempted to document the experiences of bringing communities and schools closer for improving primary education in different states of the country. The papers were since then further revised by the authors significantly. We are grateful to the authors for their valuable contribution. We are grateful to Ms Mervi Karikorpi and Ms Sabina Bindra of the European Commission not only for their active involvement in conducting the seminar, but also for ensuring that the volume reached its present shape. We are also grateful to Prof. B.P. Khandelwal, Director of NIEPA, who provided consistent support for the exercise and ensured that the arrangements for publication went through smoothly. We would like to thank the editorial staff at Sage Publications for their patience and cooperation.

1

Introduction: Emerging Issues and Practices

R. Govinda
Rashmi Diwan

Education policy makers all over the world have come to view active community participation as an effective means of promoting primary education, both in quantitative and qualitative terms. Further, community participation and empowerment in decision-making has commonly been understood and propagated as an attempt to counteract centralized actions. It is assumed that community participation and empowerment has the potential to make a major contribution towards educating people, increasing their awareness levels, improving their health and living conditions as well as enriching their life styles. The literacy campaigns in different parts of India have also, though not uniformly in all cases, demonstrated the potential role that community members can play for their own betterment.

Community participation in education is not a new concept in India. In the early years after Independence, it was viewed and promoted as part of the liberation rhetoric. In Gandhi's scheme of education, a school or any kind of educational setup was an integral part of the community. Therefore the question of community participation in school affairs was not to be a matter of debate and discourse. However, the post-independence years witnessed an altogether different phenomenon on the ground. With the virtual governmentalisation of primary education, schools became totally alienated from the community they served. Then, again, community participation became a major agenda of discussion in the country in the mid-1980s when decentralization began to be recognized as an important component of the educational reform and change processes. It was realized that responsibility should be devolved as far as possible upon the people involved in the actual task of schooling, in consultation with parents of the pupils whom they taught. The move, however, appears to have been prompted essentially by the utilitarian value of involving the community, which could possibly improve the deteriorating efficiency and effectiveness of the school system. The National Policy on Education (NPE) 1986 and 1992[1] recommended not only promoting participation of the community in primary education but also a movement towards empowering the local community to take major management decisions in this regard. The NPE and its Programme of Action suggested decentralized management of education at all levels (district, sub-district and panchayat levels) and involvement of the people in the decision-making process. It proposed adopting the Eleventh Schedule of the Constitution which provides, among other things, for entrusting with Panchayati Raj bodies "education including primary education and secondary schools, teachers' training and vocational education, adult and non-formal education, literacy and cultural activities". The subsequent 72nd and 73rd Constitutional Amendments passed in both the Houses of Parliament gave further fillip to this move towards decentralization and community empowerment in the management of education. It recommended the delegation of authority related to education, including primary and secondary schools, technical training and vocational education, adult education and non-formal education, and spread of literacy and cultural activities to Panchayati Raj bodies (Article 243 G of the 11th Schedule).

Alongside these developments at the policy level, the country has also witnessed major programmes of primary education in different states, particularly during the last 10 years. These programmes also have the promotion of community participation as a major thrust area in their activities. Some of them have tried to evolve special strategies for bringing community and the school closer, and also to involve community members in a significant manner for primary education development. Specifically, a variety of informal and formal structures have come into existence, such as mother-teacher associations under the District Primary Education Programme in Kerala, core team and women's group under Lok Jumbish in

Rajasthan, apart from village education committees in many states. Some states such as Madhya Pradesh are making a serious effort to link such groups with elected bodies of the Panchayati Raj. Community participation and empowerment for primary education is gradually acquiring a place of importance not only in education management discourse, but also in political reorganization measures in the area of public administration. Obviously, with varying formats being tried out in different states, the constitution and nature of participation of community groups vary significantly across different states.

Defining Community Participation— The Problematic

An increased use of the phrase does not seem to imply that community participation has acquired a more generalized connotation understood by everyone in the same way. Neither the theoreticians nor the practitioners seem to agree with any one definition of the term. Kantha and Narain consider that the idea of a community is based on a sense of identity, which also implies a difference.

Pre-modern or primary communities have set social forms, very intense, by which people are classified as similar or different. More importantly, these are communities which are not formed on account of the "convergence of interest" that underscores the identity of the other form of community. In contemporary discourse, the interest-bonded communities are those that are being structured and encouraged to participate in the development process. However, because the bonds are weak and uncertain, the picture of the primary community is sought to be evoked so as to draw on the strengths of the traditional community. Because of the newness of its form, the pretension involves taking the contemporary, interest-bonded communities to be immemorial, ancient ones. The earlier communities do not have a territorial identity—these are, for example, religious or caste communities. Larger collectives are now being constructed by creating linkages of common interest—from health to education. In this, the concept of the village as a community is fixed with a territorial identity and at the same time is placed above the traditional identities of communities existing in villages that transcend territorial boundaries (for example, linkages with castes or religious groups residing in other villages). Somewhere along the line, intrinsic to the concept in the formation of the interest-based community, is the idea of community advantage, both participatory and of the individual. So long as this advantage is apparent, the cohesiveness remains, but has to be continuously perceived.[2]

This issue is highlighted in all the articles in this book.

"Community" is obviously not a homogeneous notion. "It is either various communities unequally and differently placed within a society, or various groups in a community unequally placed."[3] Noronha further highlights this aspect of heterogeneity by pointing out that community could be viewed in two distinct perspectives: (1) "Local class-caste composition when parents, as the background for children, are taken into consideration." (2) "Elected representatives where their class composition influences the nature of involvement as well as the nature of conflicts arising from such involvement".[4] One can only carry a context-specific notion of the word "community". By implication, community participation has also to be viewed in a localized manner. The need for contextualised understanding of the notion is further illustrated by Ramachandran in her paper on Rajasthan.

"Community" in itself means very little—it is like saying "India" or "Rajasthan". Therefore, at the outset, it is important to define community participation in the specific context of primary education, that too in Rajasthan. Presumably, the reference is to the participation of those who are either left out or are participating from the margins.[5]

Acceptance of such a notion indirectly challenges the uncritical assumption that formation of such bodies as village education committees or parent teacher associations would ensure participation of people from all sections of the local society.

As in the case of community, "participation" has also to be perceived as a context-specific expression based on the degree of involvement of people, to bring certain systemic changes with a basic objective of ushering development and improvement in the quality of life of the participants. This involvement could be for health, education, social security, etc. When we speak of community participation in primary education, again it is the involvement of parents and community leaders as partners in supporting educational activities that contribute to improvement in their own lives. "Participation in itself provides an involvement with the system which can diminish alienation and also can serve to stimulate educational change; it is itself an educational experience."[6] Thus participation is an experience felt differently by different people in different circumstances, even in similar situations. This is because the benefits that flow from participation may not be the same for all. In the context of deep-rooted socio-economic stratification that characterizes our society, participation processes have to be orchestrated in such a manner that the benefits of participation are equitably distributed. "Participation would go hand in hand with safeguards for the poor and marginalized, which most often is a political task requiring active and sustained intervention of the state."[7] Therefore, the type of participation that makes the most sense will vary with the environment in which the school operates. The international literature, much of which is directed at the educational scene in developing countries, considers this issue in a somewhat simplistic manner. As Shaeffer summarizes, the various shades of meaning attached to the phrase are

(a) the mere *use* of a service (such as a primary health care facility); (b) participation through the contribution (or extraction) of resources, materials and labour; (c) participation through "attendance" (e.g., at parents' meetings at school), often implying passive acceptance of decisions made by others; (d) participation through consultation on a particular issue; (e) involvement in the delivery of a service, often as a partner with other actors; (f) involvement as implementers of delegated powers; and (g) most completely, participation in real decision-making at every stage—identification of problems, the study of feasibility, planning, implementation, and evaluation.[8]

The substance of all these propositions seems to lie in one or both of the two categories: (a) exhorting generally reluctant community members to take active interest in the education of their children; (b) liberalizing the otherwise rigid administrative framework to make way for participation of community members in educational management. The studies presented in this volume highlights the fact that the problem of community participation is much deeper and complex than its general conception presented in the available literature.

Some seem to consider that management by local self-government bodies could overcome this problem as it would apparently ensure more inclusive participation. In fact, such moves along the lines suggested by the 73rd and 74th Constitutional Amendments are already on the anvil in many states. But the issue does not appear to be that straightforward. One cannot rule out the possibility that the class and caste compositions of the elected bodies could influence their nature of involvement as well as the nature of conflicts arising from such involvement. The discourse becomes even more complicated if one moves from the question of "community participation" to that of "community empowerment". Will empowerment of the local political bodies ensure genuine representation of the traditionally excluded sections of the local community? This is a matter that needs to be studied more closely.

From Community Participation to Community Empowerment

It is obvious that mere participation, even if fully legitimized, need not lead to empowerment, particularly when the participation is used as a means of social transformation of culturally and economically diverse and hierarchical groups of people into a more democratic and egalitarian framework. One cannot undermine the ideological undertones of viewing empowerment for self direction in education as a basic right of the people, or merely as an instrument of improving the efficiency of the existing system, without correcting any internal anomalies of inequity and authoritarianism. In this context, "decentralization of educational governance" is often projected as the final means of community empowerment. But decentralization itself is a complex phenomenon. "It definitely requires a clearly developed governance structure: some functions are allotted at the individual school level, some at the district level and some at the state level. A balance of citizen and professional decision-making can then be outlined in each circumstance. Community participation implies redistribution of powers."[9] Further, it is also necessary to look at the way decentralization is being ushered into the governance system. "Involvement of the community was more natural or generic till the late 1960s. But now the changed scenario witnesses a more political involvement determined by a central mandate, and seen as a form of sharing of power and control rather than as partnership."[10] Also, as Raina points out, "the community participation efforts remain confined to decentralizing management and administrative responsibilities, with the clear understanding that the teaching–learning process would remain centrally controlled and closed for any kind of participation, even from NGOs."[11] Within the perspective of watershed management, he considers community participation as ill-defined and obscure regarding who is participating, how and in what, who has decision-making and regulatory powers, and who has access to resources and funds. But one thing is certain that a typology of participation taken together constitutes a set of political issues. While commenting on the tension between the state, market and community, and its operation in education, Raina also contends that

> though participation must begin at the local level with communities, a project cannot end there. Whether we like it or not, the state continues to be a major player, and we want it to be a major player if education is to be universalized or sustained livelihoods for the vast majority of poor have to be ensured. Local empowering action perhaps requires a strong state, particularly in times when the dominant market mechanisms can marginalize the poor further without state-mediated safeguards. If community participation is to advocate the social empowerment of the poor, it must also, therefore, advocate their political empowerment.[12]

Everyone would agree that the route to empowerment is through involvement and participation, usually taking place in communities with common self-interests. When people are entrusted with some power or given the opportunity to show their capabilities, participation becomes the means of empowerment leading people to feel and act empowered. Panchayati Raj could be viewed as a mechanism for promoting such involvement of people with common community interests. But as Kantha and Narain cautions, this cannot be naively assumed as a natural consequence of establishing the Panchayati Raj system. Though the process has the potential for leading the communities towards "empowerment", it can be understood only when one understands its relationship with "powerlessness".

Participation, which is also an intervention, has to be taken in all its seriousness, so that it does not become a tool for manipulation. The notion of empowerment is integral to the concept of participatory development. One begins with the presumption that one does not have the right kind of power, but also that somebody else has the secret of power to which the former has to be initiated. But people are not powerless, they have the power to resist. It has been pointed out later in this article that in Bihar there was a strong resistance to colonial education. The expression of power is different and it is constituted by thousands of centres and an informal network of resistance which people set up.[13]

It is the analysis of powerlessness that gives meaning to empowerment. It is the collective articulation that produces social energy, which leads to empowerment. As the paper on Rajasthan highlights, community participation implies, "participation of the disempowered". These include "those who have not had access as a community, as a geographic area or as a gender". Community participation in the specific context of Rajasthan leads to community empowerment only when the people who are involved are ideally those who have "little or no access to basic education".[14] One positive development that all the case studies indicate is that the movement for enhancing community participation in education has travelled a long way from a state of informal arrangement to a formalised policy intervention under the banner of decentralization through the Panchayati Raj system. Community participation as a means of power sharing and partnership in the formal sense is still at a nascent stage in the country. However, experiences from other countries indicate that participation itself increases only when more sharing of power is ensured. "Community involvement in education appears to be maximized by two specific but surprising factors—the distribution of money and power to the community. There emerges a situation where hierarchical relationships are minimized and genuine partnerships are maximized. Community involvement is most productive when handled as a joint exercise in communication and redistribution of power, responsibility and money."[15] Similarly, the move towards empowerment in education also gets influenced by the nature of interventions and programmes in other allied sectors. It is very clear that community participation seen as a means of empowerment in primary education needs

further empirical analysis. Certainly, the terrain from community participation to community empowerment is quite a difficult one, since it is
highly dependent on the readiness of decision-making authorities to
devolve power and money, and the preparedness of the community and
other personnel functioning at the grassroots to accept the challenge. One
can expect an empowered society where partnership and participation
proceed coupled with freedom to spend money and enjoy power with
accountability.

Review of State-Specific Experiences: Emerging Institutional Framework for Community Participation

Concrete measures for establishing a closer linkage between primary
schools and the community and providing a meaningful place for the community in primary education management have taken different shapes in
different states of the country. The models range from establishment of
Mother Teacher Associations in Kerala to community-based micro-
planning of the Lok Jumbish in Rajasthan. Efforts for decentralization
began in Andhra Pradesh and Karnataka even earlier and have taken a different shape with respect to primary education as compared to the more
recent structural changes that have been initiated under Panchayati Raj in
Madhya Pradesh. In essence, different strategies have been adopted by
state governments for enhancing the role of the community in the management of primary education. Needless to say that these efforts have brought
to the fore a variety of learning experiences as well as critical issues and
problems in empowering the local community in the area of primary education management. Further, experience has also been accumulated in several other sectors of education and development. For instance, the lesson
learnt from the total literacy campaign for mobilizing the local community
for educational action are invaluable. Similarly, activities in the areas of
watershed development and sustainable development of the environment
present a wealth of experience and insight for the primary education sector. Networking and collaboration with other sectors have strengthened
primary education in a number of states.

In order to facilitate effective community involvement and empowerment in primary education, different organizational configurations are
emerging or have emerged across the country. It is difficult to state with
certainty that local community empowerment will emerge as a major factor
in determining the future framework for primary education management.
Nevertheless, the experiences and lessons accruing from the initiatives
taken in different states are likely to guide the future course of action. Both
at the levels of policy and practice, several questions and issues need to be
carefully studied and documented. For instance, are community bodies
really being vested with powers and authority, or are they only being given
more responsibilities without full authority? Are the departmental personnel ready to share power with the community? Are the community members prepared to take on more powers and responsibilities? Will this really
usher in a new sense of accountability at the grassroots level for school
functioning? To what extent are the state governments ready to enact legislative measures to fully empower and legitimize the involvement of the
community in the management of primary education? There are no final
answers to these questions. But it is clear that various state governments in
India have started addressing these questions, though in different ways.

Reviewing the situation in different states, one can identify different
approaches towards establishing a system of local governance and community participation in education. The basic principle seems to be to transfer
the responsibilities of educational governance to the democratically elected local self-government bodies (Panchayati Raj bodies). But this also
depends on the seriousness with which the state governments have been
promoting local self-governments, which is quite uneven across the country. However, within the broad principle of governance by locally elected
bodies, four distinct trends can be observed.

Democratic Devolution of Powers
to Panchayati Raj Bodies

The first approach is illustrated by the experience in Kerala where a major
People's Planning Campaign was orchestrated with the help of an NGO,
the Kerala Shastra Sahitya Parishad, (KSSP). The campaign brought home
to the people their rights and responsibilities for self governance at local
levels. Subsequently, the state government adopted legislations transferring

wide-ranging powers and responsibilities to Panchayati Raj bodies in the area of education among several other social development sectors. The state government devolves about 35 to 40 per cent of the development budget to the local bodies. It is found that the panchayat development plans include 'school improvement planning' as an integral component and earmark a considerable amount of funds for this purpose. Parent teacher associations have been strengthened to take an active role in the implementation of school improvement programmes. Though the process of devolution of powers to Panchayati Raj bodies is not complete, the allocation of major part of development funds to these bodies indicate the direction in which the process of decentralization and community participation is moving. Reflecting on the significant moves made for democratic decentralization of public governance in the state, the Kerala Education Commission of 1999 described the state as being "on the threshold of a new era".

Combining Delegation of Authority and Devolution of Powers

The Madhya Pradesh government has recently completed an elaborate process of deciding on the powers and responsibilities for education governance at local levels through panchayat bodies. Unlike Kerala where most of the schools are under private management though fully supported by government funds, schools in Madhya Pradesh have all been established and managed at the primary level almost wholly by the state government. Therefore, the approach has been one of cautious and gradual transformation. Actions have been initiated through two sets of processes. On the one hand, significant powers and responsibilities have been delegated through executive orders of the state department of education to panchayat bodies at different levels—district, block and village levels. However, the state government is simultaneously moving ahead with a comprehensive legislation to transfer the school education system to the control of the panchayat system. This dual approach is being adopted as most of the personnel in the schools are legally employees of the State Government. This dual-track transformation is likely to continue till such time that the whole system comes fully under the legal control of the local self-government bodies. For implementing the local governance process, village education committees have been established involving the elected representatives of the local panchayat bodies along with other community and school representatives. Thus the Madhya Pradesh approach essentially consists of restructuring of the system by government bureaucracy through a gradual induction process.

Village Education Committees (VECs) as School Governing Bodies

Though it is a constitutional mandate to create elected panchayat bodies at local levels, within the federal structure of the country, it is for the state legislatures to decide on the actual powers and responsibilities that the panchayat bodies will be vested with. Most of the state governments have been slow to act in this direction. However, several states have created village education committees (VECs) to specifically oversee the functioning of basic education programmes at the village level. These village education committees are supposed to function as school governing committees. The experience in these cases is mixed. While some VECs function effectively, many tend to become dysfunctional in course of time. A major problem seems to be lack of a programmatic framework for their functioning on a regular basis. Also, local community members do not seem to fully understand the ways in which they could influence decision-making at local levels. Both the Bihar and Karnataka cases illustrate this model—a quasi-legal approach—of promoting community participation in management of primary education mainly initiated through State Sponsored Basic Education Projects. It is, of course, assumed that this is only a transitory phase finally leading to the merger of these bodies with Panchayati Raj institutions.

Lok Jumbish Experience of Building from Below in Rajasthan—Practice First, Principle Follows

Rajasthan, like many other states, has also been slow in implementing legal measures to transfer powers related to primary education governance to Panchayati Raj bodies, though management of primary education has traditionally been under the Panchayati Raj and Rural Development Ministry. Within this context, the Lok Jumbish project in Rajasthan broke new grounds by creating informal voluntary groups within the community in the form of a core team and a women's group in each village within the project area. These groups actively involve themselves in participatory planning for developing primary education in the village through systematic processes of school mapping and micro-planning. Through this process, Lok Jumbish has attempted to build a system of local governance for primary education from the grassroots level. The basic assumption is that capabilities for self management among the community members evolve through practice rather than prescription. Therefore, the project has started vesting in the community the responsibility of determining the demand and preparing local education development plans based on concrete empirical explorations. The state government, however, is yet to take full note of this practical move and legitimize the bodies through official recognition.

Some Emerging Issues and Lessons from State Experiences

Desirability of Dependence on Representational Politics of Panchayati Raj

Many contest the move being made by the state governments to vest all powers related to primary education in the elected bodies. They argue that these bodies are susceptible to political upheavals and intra-party power dynamics, and therefore may lead to parochial considerations in decision-making. The basic question raised is whether it will really ensure popular participation at the local level. Will primary education get due attention under these bodies? Or will it only result in decentralizing the existing problems of the system? While elected local bodies have legitimacy in a democratic representational sense, the issues raised above cannot be ignored. In fact, in many countries, the school governing boards are formed through independent election processes distinct from the local self-government bodies created for public administration. For instance, the KSSP which spearheaded the people's planning campaign in Kerala has strongly argued for integrating all moves towards decentralization of educational governance with the empowerment of Panchayati Raj bodies. However, Tharakan expresses reservations on such a move in view of "politically divided panchayats."[16] Similar apprehensions are expressed in the study analyzing the evolving situation in Madhya Pradesh.[17]

Recruitment of Personnel: Who will Control the Teachers?

Teachers have been quite apprehensive of the move to establish local governance systems. While some states continue to treat teachers as state employees even though they serve under local bodies, some others like Madhya Pradesh are explicitly creating district level cadres under the control of local bodies. The reservations among teachers need careful consideration. While treating teachers as employees of the district panchayat bodies has allowed for establishment of smaller systems facilitating increased management efficiency, the accompanying practice in many states of employing para-teachers with lowered qualification requirements and smaller salary packages has raised several issues. Referring to recent developments in Madhya Pradesh, Raina points out,

> "The perennial shortage of trained teachers has been eliminated in a single stroke by allowing panchayats to recruit from their areas 'lesser' teachers, shiksha karmis (SKs), for the job. They are different from regular teachers in terms of relaxation of minimum qualifications and do not require to have gone through any pre-service training. Consequently, their salaries are much less than that of regular teachers. With the recruitment of about 70,000 such SKs in one go, the state government has in fact abolished the post of a regular teacher and decreed that henceforth any teacher vacancy shall be filled only through the locally appointed SK."[18]

This highlights the inadequacy of transferring powers with respect to personnel-related matters without creating proper service rules to ensure that the local bodies do not create increased labour litigations for the state. In fact, if it is not carefully handled with a long-term perspective, the issue has potential to distort the basic orientation with regard to state policy on teacher background and qualification.

Political vs. Bureaucratic Control

Increased decentralization has also brought to the fore the issue of control over the system within the decentralized setup. Under the centralized system, the bureaucracy tended to have an upper hand, notwithstanding the complaints of political interference in decision-making. The new framework has created new tensions within the system in many states between the local bureaucracy and the political leadership.

Promoting Horizontal Communication across different Social Groups

In a hierarchically structured society which characterizes most villages in the country, and where the marginalized groups continue to remain outside the purview of education, political groupings and locally elected bodies may not fully solve the problem of educational governance. The effort has to be to go beyond the formal structures and create scope for horizontal communication across different social groups. The state has to initiate social mobilization processes which could change the existing power relations within the society. This is essential to make the local governance structures more inclusive and representative. As has been pointed out in the Bihar study.

> This dilemma brings into focus the basic questions: Which community are we talking about? Who will represent the community the best? How do we structure interest bonded communities and whose interest are we securing anyway? In the case of the fragmented and turbulent society of Bihar these issues assume acute significance. Caste identities are strong and of late quite aggressive, making it difficult to work out commonality of interests around which VECs could be structured. Further, in every village there are a few identifiable aggressive individuals or groups, and if they smell power and influence anywhere they are bound to chip in and assume a dominant role for themselves.[19]

Many contend that the state would be unable to orchestrate such a process of change without active involvement of the civil society. "NGOs have a definite advantage over the government functionaries on several counts. They are usually closer to the community, and the people's expectation from them is not that direct and big. They have greater operational freedom."[20] Building such a partnership between the state and the civil society needs careful consideration. However, the value of NGO involvement in orchestrating the voice of the community is not free from controversy and contestation. "Community participation being entirely facilitated by the intervention of NGOs and their status as externally funded agencies raise certain questions pertaining to the sustainability of such participation. If external resources are withdrawn, will the community sustain education programmes on their own along with other programmes? If the intervention ceases due to the NGOs withdrawing their operations in a specific geographical area, will the schools, non-formal education centres and resource groups become the responsibility of the community?"[21] A related issue is the frequently observed reluctance of the state to legitimize locally generated institutional practices. This is well illustrated by the case of Lok Jumbish in Rajasthan which successfully experimented with the creation of informal but fully functional local mechanisms for community participation not only at the village level, but also at the block level. The centre piece of this experiment was not so much of the structures as the programmatic activities for linking the community with educational processes. Yet unfortunately, these initiatives remain sporadic and peripheral, and never get fully integrated into the state system, as the state invariably refuses to legitimize such actions as integral to the standard functioning of the system and issues necessary legislations to that effect.

Transition from Project Mode to Programme Mode

It is significant to note that efforts for decentralization and community participation are often carried out under projects which are smaller in coverage and spread. Often, such projects attempt to put in place a new framework for governance. The critical question is: "Can such project-based efforts be considered as harbingers of system-wide reforms bringing in an era of decentralized educational management? Or will they remain mere show pieces of small-scale successes?" A frictionless, smooth *transition from the project mode to the programme mode* cannot always be assumed. At least two points have to be carefully examined: (*a*) A smooth transition from project to programme mode depends on the way the concerned policies, rules and regulations are re-oriented to accommodate the new initiatives; (*b*) Further, as long as we are operating within the framework of a project, it is not likely to be questioned by the stakeholders in the larger system. However, many components of such projects may become a bone of contention when they move to the mainstream. How do we minimise such frictions and human tensions within the management hierarchy? Can the integration process withstand the opposition from within the system posed by long-entrenched vested interests supporting the maintenance of the status quo? It is clear that mere short-term, project-based efforts will not do. Sustainability requires permanent transformation through legal measures.

Unfortunately, smooth transition through change in rules and regulations does not seem to be on the agenda of the state governments. For instance, though decentralized decision-making at block level involving the local stakeholders is operational under the Lok Jumbish project, the Rajasthan government has taken no steps to give any legal authority to the body.[22] In all probability, with the term of the project ending, the mechanism will also vanish. In fact, a general observation is that state governments have looked on projects only as efforts to overcome temporary problems with external financial support or as implementing an externally designed programme which does not have to seriously disturb the existing management set-up. It is very rarely that project initiatives are seen as harbingers of change processes to transform the existing system of educational management. Within this generally disappointing scenario, one could begin to see some positive shifts in the approach of state governments illustrated by the efforts in Madhya Pradesh to integrate project initiatives under District Primary Education Programme (DPEP), with system-level management changes to bring greater decentralization.

Conclusion

Answers to these issues obviously do not rest merely in procedural modifications in the way the education department functions. They have more deep-seated political implications. To bring about enduring changes in the framework, it is essential that they are incorporated into the basic framework of relationship between the state government and the local self-governing bodies; the changes also demand consistent action in modifying the age-old education acts that regulate the functioning of the government education department. This will also have to squarely address questions related to personnel recruitment policies and financial planning at the local government level. Though several such issues remain to be addressed, it is clear that a system of local governance is gradually taking root in the country. There are no standard solutions to the questions involved. Within the federal structure of the country, the situation is bound to vary from one state to another. Solutions have also to be found through local explorations, and not through top-down prescriptions.

The country has moved away from the goal of "power to the people" as an ideology to decentralization as a means of improving managerial efficiency. Yet any effort to decentralize and empower the local community is bound to disturb the existing power structure, whether it is a matter of empowering the Panchayati Raj bodies or the village education committees.

It is widely noticed that the members of the VEC or similarly constituted groups in other programmes acquire a sense of new found importance. A new power structure is introduced in the village, which may either remain broadly in line with the one that existed before or modify it somewhat. Usually the more articulate persons of the community are likely to gain influence. In a limited sense there is the empowerment of the community, but it remains debatable if it does mean empowerment of the community as an integral unit. On the other hand, given the apparent reluctance of the state and its functionaries to transfer real control and authority to the hands of VECs, it is at best a pressure group or a weak control mechanism. Perhaps community emerges as a rival site of authority, and the state authorities rather than working in tandem resort to a strategy of ignoring and sidelining them.[23]

Though such an assessment sounds too pessimistic and cynical, past experiences indicate the need for guarding against such eventualities if the new found enthusiasm for decentralization and community empowerment in education does not meet the same fate as has happened to such efforts in the initial decades after independence.

Though government and local bodies continue to be the main providers of primary education, one cannot overlook the contribution being made by several non-government bodies towards primary education. In fact, the common feeling is that the NGOs succeed in establishing a better rapport with the local communities and getting them more effectively involved in the education of their children. How does one capitalize on these experiences? Besides, an emerging phenomenon in many parts of the country is the increasing presence of private schools, many of which do not depend on government funding. This obviously adds a new dimension to the process of primary education management. Again, involvement of NGOs as well as emergence of private initiative is very uneven across the country.

There is a need, at this juncture, to understand the structure and mechanics created within the system and outside vis-à-vis community empowerment for improving primary education. It is in this context that the present volume attempts to present a critical review of the situation in selected states of the country. The review, it is envisaged, will throw light on the situation from varying perspectives—government, NGOs and people at the local level. The states selected are Madhya Pradesh, Karnataka, Rajasthan, Bihar and Kerala. Each of the selected states is characterized by a distinct set of efforts and experiences for community involvement and participation leading to community empowerment in primary education programmes. One underlying factor that is common to all these states is the unique effort made by the state from within or from outside through education projects for initiating participatory processes to reshape the education management scenario. It is visualised that these illustrative case studies would help understand the manner in which partnerships among civil society, government and non-government organisations function in the pursuit of universalisation of primary education, and the dynamics involved in empowering the community for management of primary education.

Notes and References

1. See GOI (1986), *National Policy on Education, 1986*, New Delhi: Government of India, and GOI (1992), *National Policy on Education (Revised), 1992*, New Delhi: Government of India. Also refer to the Plan of Action of these documents.
2. Kantha, Vinay K. and Daisy Narain, "Dynamics of Community Mobilization in a Fragmented and Turbulent State", article in this volume.
3. Saxena, Sadhna, "Community Participation and Literacy: Beyond Semantics", article in this volume.
4. Noronha, Anjali, "The Community in Charge: Shades of Experience from Madhya Pradesh", article in this volume.
5. Ramachandran, Vimala, "Community Participation and Empowerment in Primary Education: Discussion of Experiences from Rajasthan", article in this volume.
6. Gittell, Merilyn (1979), "Institutionalizing Community Participation in Education", in Carl A. Grant (ed.), *Community Participation in Education*, Toronto: Allyn & Bacon Inc.
7. Raina, Vinod, "Making Sense of Community Participation: Comparing School Education and Watershed Development", article in this volume.

8. Shaeffer, Sheldon (1991), "A Framework for Collaborating for Educational Change, Increasing and Improving the Quality of Basic Education", Monograph No. 3, Paris: International Institute for Education Planning.

9. Gittell, Merilyn, cited in note 6 above.

10. Norohna, Anjali, cited in note 4 above.

11. Raina, Vinod, cited in note 7 above.

12. Ibid.

13. Kantha, Vinay K. and Daisy Narain, cited in note 2 above.

14. Ramachandran, Vimala, cited in note 5 above.

15. Popkewitz, Thomas S. (1979), "Schools and Symbolic Uses of Community Participation", in Carl A. Grant (ed.), *Community Participation in Education*, Toronto: Allyn & Bacon Inc.

16. Tharakan, Michael P.K., "Community Participation in School Education: Experiments in the State of Kerala", article in this volume.

17. See Govinda, R, "Dynamics of Decentralized Management in Primary Education: Policy and Practice in Rajasthan and Madhya Pradesh", article in this volume.

18. Raina, Vinod, cited in note 7 above.

19. Kantha, Vinay K. and Daisy Narain, cited in note 2 above.

20. Ibid.

21. N. Shantha Mohan, Gayathri Devi Dutt, Piush Antony, "Community Participation in Primary Education: The Karnataka Experience", article in this volume.

22. See Govinda, R, cited in note 17 above.

23. Kantha, Vinay K. and Daisy Narain, cited in note 2 above.

Community Participation in School Education: Experiments in the State of Kerala

P.K. Michael Tharakan

The achievements of the state of Kerala in literacy and primary education are too well known. Kerala, with a total literacy rate of 89.81 in 1991, was one of the leading states in the whole nation in mass literacy. It apparently topped other regions of India in this matter at least from 1901, if not earlier.[1] The state has achieved near-universal enrollment. The drop-out rate in Kerala at the primary level is practically nil, while it is as high as 53 per cent at the all-India level. The percentage of enrollment of girls from I to X standards is almost equal to that of boys. There was one lower primary school serving every 4,575 people in Kerala in 1996–97. In the same year, the teacher-student ratio was as low as 1:29. The expense on education by different departments of the government as a percentage of total state budget was 29.9 and as a percentage of the State Domestic Product was 7 in 1990–91. This was clearly above the corresponding figures for all other major Indian states.[2]

There is hardly any urban bias in Kerala's educational development. But the 1991 schedule caste literacy rate was 69.38, around 20 percentage points below the general literacy rate. The schedule tribe literacy rate was as low as 48.62, which was nearly 40 percentage points below the general average. There are other depressed and "outlier" groups among the population of Kerala. Nearly 15 per cent of the job seekers in Kerala in 1996 were those who had education up to Secondary School Leaving Certificate (SSLC) level or above. There are schools with an alarmingly low student strength. If the student strength falls below 25, the school is considered "uneconomical" and in 1997, there were 1,407 schools belonging to this category. This may be partly a result of demographic change, but could also be due to the attraction of unaided English medium schools, which are on the rise.[3]

Many schools in Kerala have inadequate infrastructural facilities like buildings, laboratories, libraries, furniture, drinking water, latrines, urinals and girls' toilets. Even the statistics reported by the All India Education Survey do not tally with the concerns expressed by different village panchayats (at least in Thiruvananthapuram district), through their development reports prepared under the auspices of the People's Planning Campaign (PPC). More alarming is the fact pointed out by the base line study conducted in Malappuram district for the District Primary Education Programme (DPEP) by the National Institute of Educational Planning and Administration (NIEPA) that about 30 per cent of the children who complete primary school do not reach the necessary achievement level in literacy and numeracy. The Kerala Shastra Sahitya Parishad (KSSP), a people's science movement, found in a sample survey that in Thiruvananthapuram district, 30 to 35 per cent of standard VIII students have not attained the minimum level of language proficiency prescribed for standard II students. It is also well known that much less than the percentage of students that pass the SSLC examination in recent years (around 33) would have passed if it was not for liberal valuation and moderation. It was pointed out by the National Council of Educational Research and Training (NCERT), in a study in 1994, that Kerala stands 18th in the list of states in educational standards at the school level[4] and 11th on the basis of average levels achieved at the IV standard.[5]

The much acclaimed educational progress in Kerala has not resulted in the same level of progress for at least some of the marginalized sections. The commercialization of the agrarian economy could have resulted in the initial spurt of mass literacy.[6] The redistribution of incomes due to comprehensive land reforms resulted in "backward" Malabar catching up educationally with the "advanced" Travancore-Cochin area.[7] First, these developments did not help marginalized communities as much as the others. Therefore, their comparative educational backwardness persists.

Second, in the midst of quantitative expansion, which resulted in mass literacy and basic education, the quality of education seems to have suffered. Third, infrastructural facilities required for normal functioning of schools seems to be lacking widely. These three problems are faced by anyone who is genuinely concerned about education in Kerala.

One way to handle these problems is through greater community participation in the educational process. This is implied in the 73rd and 74th Constitutional Amendments which recommended the delegation of authority related to education to the decentralized Panchayati Raj institutions.[8] The DPEP, now implemented in different districts of India, including six districts in Kerala, has also been described as "an exercise in decentralised planning and disagregated target setting to encourage and promote local initiatives in primary education."[9] Even before the DPEP came into effect, under the auspices of the District Councils (DCs) which were in power for a short while in 1991–92, and under the initiative of the KSSP, there were at least four localized attempts at ensuring greater community participation in school education at Sivapuram, Madikai, Dharmadam and Kalliasserry, villages of Kasargode and Kannur districts. Now that the democratic decentralization process has been enchanced in the state through the People's Planning Campaign, more responsibilities are transferred to Local Self Government Institutions (LSGIs), both rural and urban. The 1999 Kerala Education Commission described Kerala as being "on the threshold of a new era" (p. 132) in this respect. Considering these, this study surveys: (a) how far decentralization or/and people's planning has resulted in greater community participation in school education, (b) how far such participation has resulted in greater local empowerment and (c) how far it has resulted in improvement of the educational process.

In a study conducted in 1980 in a cultural milieu far different from that of Kerala, it was found that in the context of changing school-community relationships, a variety of measures were tried, including (a) bringing resources and elements from the community into the school, (b) taking schooling out into other institutions in the community, and (c) building joint facilities with other social services.[10] Similarly, in response to the three important educational issues mentioned earlier—taking special care of the educational needs of marginalized sections, improving the quality of education through remedial teaching and providing infrastructural facilities through school complexes—several types of measures including seeking direct contribution from the immediate community are practised in Kerala too. Here, as it was found elsewhere,[11] the character of school-community relationships is likely to vary on the basis of the specific charac-teristics of the community. It is also dependent on the school's identification with its sorroundings, over and above its understanding of its own mission in society. Analytical discussions on these vital issues have already been ini-tiated by writings produced by the KSSP, literature by and on the DPEP and those brought out by the PPC. This study aims at contributing further to the ongoing discussion by essentially collecting information for docu-menting experiments found important.

Early Efforts

All the three problems mentioned earlier are widely perceived to particulary affect public schools in the state. It is on this basis that the Kerala Education Commission spoke with concern about the increasing number of public schools being declared "uneconomical" and the possible attraction of unaided (purely private) English medium schools playing a role in that development.[12] In the specific situation of Kerala, the public school system consists of, besides schools run by the government, schools run by non-governmental agencies with aid from public funds—the latter schools are run according to a common syllabus set by a state-appointed agency, with teachers being paid their salary directly from public funds. From various quarters of the Kerala society, concern was expressed over the setback to the public education system with the advent of private schools. Public schools being directly and indirectly subsidized, and there-fore cheaper, make education accessible to even economically marginalized groups. The apparent onslaught by the purely private, unaided school sys-tem could eventually lead to throwing open education to the vagaries of the market, thereby nullifying the chances of the poor to operate there effec-tively. In Kerala, which had undergone certain far-reaching changes like comprehensive land reforms,[13] the case was similar to the one faced by societies which were able to put an end to old barriers and privileges in education. The question of "whether we replace them [old barriers and privileges] by the free play of the market, or by a public education designed to express and create the values of an educated democracy and a common culture"[14] was found valid here as elsewhere.

In such a context, as early as the end of the 1980s and the beginning of the 1990s, there were attempts to rejuvenate the public education system in Kerala. Quite naturally, those who initiated such experiments turned to ensuring wider community participation because the history of education in Kerala clearly shows that the government schools as well as the aided private schools have gained immensely from community and local participation.[15] As mentioned earlier, the DCs gave legitimacy to some of these experiments undertaken under the initiative of activists of the KSSP, teachers' organizations, etc. At least four districts had different programmes under names such as *Aksharavedi, Aksharapulari* and *Gurukulam*. The districts which integrated local efforts into district-wide programmes under the auspices of the DCs included Kasargode, Kannur, Pathanamthitta and Thiruvananthapuram. Among them, four village-level experiments in Dharmadam, Sivapuram, Madikai and Kalliassery attained special attention. In these village panchayats, the educational reforms introduced were essentially that of establishing school complexes. This was a suggestion made by the Kothari Commission. But it was never tried out seriously anywhere in Kerala. The framework for sharing facilities was provided under the elected panchayat committees in association with school authorities, representatives of the public, and mother-teacher associations (MTA). The MTAs were a new innovation. It was based upon the particular interest shown by mothers in the education of their children. The initiative taken by the mothers provided a necessary fillip to the various programmes associated with the school complexes, and as long as these experiments lasted, it played a major role too.

What was most significant about these experiments was that the village panchayats proved capable of bearing the organizational and academic responsibilities of the school complexes. On occasion, when additional financial requirements arose, they also succeeded in raising such resources. LSGIs, which were the co-ordinating agencies, generally proved capable of effectively supervising even teachers' retraining.[16] Such successes were due to support from the local community—elected representatives, mothers of school children, school authorities and teachers. In 1989, in Kalliasserry, well ahead of the introduction of DCs, there were some initiatives introduced in the field of education, along with other developmental initiatives under the context of village-level resource mapping.[17] The school complex committee, having noted that the SSLC pass level in their panchayat in

1987–88 was as low as 29 per cent, took it upon themselves to better it to 100 per cent by the year 2000. In the academic year 1998–99, they managed to raise it to nearly 80 per cent. Though the "executing" organization has changed character now, much of the credit should be attributed to the community participatory efforts emerging from the Total Literacy Campaigns (TLCs) initiated in 1980–90 in Ernakulam district, and in the rest of Kerala in 1990–91.[18] The KSSP played a major role in the TLC as well. The school complexes helped interschool distribution of facilities. Schools in these panchayats without basic amenities like libraries and playground could let their students access these from schools that had them. With the backing of the MTAs and panchayat committees, school complex committees could find resources to supplement training programmes for teachers in the locality itself.

These local success stories got practically nullified with the adverse developments with regard to DCs, which gave much of the co-ordinating support to such experiments.[19] With the withdrawal of the DCs, much of the focus and spirit of such experiments withered away. Nevertheless, one good development emerged out of these experiments. Some officials of the state education department, as well as educationalists, were convinced that local-level community efforts harnessed by LSGIs are capable of making meaningful interventions even in the formal educational process. This was converted into a debating point by those who argued for greater community participation. In addition, at least in the communities around the villages which ran such experiments, the general public, and particularly parents or mothers of school children, put a lot of trust in such experiments. The reverse side of this was the widespread disappointment of the ordinary people in the loss of support for such experiments. It also raised one other important question. In the villages where these experiments were conducted well, there was considerable public support for them. What would be the fate of other village communities where due to various reasons, particularly political polarization, such public support was not forthcoming? This important question in the context of a highly politicized region like Kerala will have to be raised again in the course of this presentation. With the weakening of such experiments, the only factor which promoted the cause of community participation was the commitment of individual teachers and educational officials, and the abiding interest of the KSSP.

It is important to analyze closely a state-wide experiment conducted by the KSSP itself for many years, in upgrading pedagogical efforts in schools of Kerala. The *vigyanotsavam* was an examination conducted by the KSSP from 1990. It was an improved version of an earlier experiment of the KSSP called the Eureka competitive examination.[20] What this experiment aimed at was to present a better model of the education and examination system. It also tried to prove that people desire such changes, and that too in an active, participatory manner. The KSSP found that the formal education in Kerala had become too formal to reflect the real requirements of society. They wanted to demonstrate that a substantive change in the whole system can be brought about, particularly in examinations—an area considered the exclusive terrain of teachers and students. They wanted to prove this through public or community participation.

The organizational framework through which community participation was ensured for *vigyanotsavam* was committees convened at various levels. There were committees at the district and panchayat levels. The panchayat committee consisted of elected panchayat members, social workers, teachers and parents. These panchayat committees were entrusted with the task of carrying out the *vigyanotsavam* in their respective communities. The questions that the participants of this programme had to answer were meant to evaluate effectively the observational, discriminatory, and creative skills of the students. The questions were set by a state-level workshop involving KSSP activists and other experts. The wide community participation ensured through committees at every stage created a changed atmosphere at the grassroots level, particularly in the absence of any meaningful activity from the Parent Teacher Associations (PTAs) in schools. The students also found the interest taken by the local community encouraging.

Though the direct involvement of the community in setting questions was limited, the wide public participation in conducting them legitimised the *vigyanotsavam*. Not only that, the representatives of the public knew what went into the experiments and they generally welcomed them. If in 1991 the number of students who enrolled was 1.5 lakh, in 1992 nearly 6 lakh out of an estimated 56.2 lakh students in Kerala schools enrolled for the *vigyanotsavam*, through 1,124 centres. The experiment required only around 4,000 rupees per centre. But on the other hand, it required at least around 100 persons, including teachers and volunteers, to run it at each centre. This reflected the relative participatory nature of the programme, particularly through its high level of voluntary efforts. The most important outcome of this programme, apart from instilling a better learning environment, was community participation.

The DPEP was introduced in 1993, initially in three districts of Kerala. It was later extended to three more districts. First of all, DPEP attempts to alter the pattern of resource decisions, favouring local initiatives. It develops plans at the local level. It provides an area approach to planning that phases out sectoral plans which, in turn, allows bureaucratic controls. It is expected to result in convergence of services, interdepartmental co-ordination and public participation. The DPEP has learnt from the lessons of the TLCs, which proved that local initiatives can be mobilized to prepare comprehensive plans at the district level.[21] Though these possibilities exist theoretically in the DPEP, the implementation within Kerala has already drawn substantially adverse comments from the media representatives, teachers' organisations and even parents.

One may be tempted to dismiss such adverse comments as one of the many experiences of opposition to educational reforms in Kerala, due primarily to different political positions. However, it is not correct to dismiss it just like that. The criticism of DPEP in Kerala can be classified into three categories. One set stems from the opposition to the foreign agencies which are financially supporting the programme. The second set of criticism is directed against the actual way in which the programme is implemented in the state. The third is basically against the new textbooks and new teaching practices prescribed as part of the programme. Naturally, all these points come out mixed with others.[22] There is certainly a widespread apprehension of the new experiments envisaged by the DPEP, particularly in the context of these experiments being implemented only in the public school system. The fear is more specific to the possibility that students studying in the parallel system of recognized and unrecognized English medium schools with their additional coaching will make better headway in numerous scholarship and entrance examinations. Even if it is conceded that the DPEP aims at qualitatively improving the education available to the majority of students, the anxiety and concern in the hearts of a substantial number of parents about bettering the prospects of their own children cannot be overlooked.

None of these criticisms directly address community participation as such. Nevertheless, the general antipathy towards specific features of the

DPEP seem to overlap onto the community participation elements too. Otherwise, it is generally ignored in many debates on these issues, perhaps indicating a lack of interest in questions related to community participation. Therefore, it is important to understand the position of the KSSP which has consistently argued for qualitatively improving education through community participation. Their concern is also in saving the public education system in Kerala.[23] The KSSP approves certain important points made by the DPEP. But it offers its own criticism of the programme.[24] The KSSP argues that any attempt at improving the quality of education should be welcomed. Since it found some efforts in this direction in the DPEP, it was not ready to write off the programme completely. While most other critical discussions on the subject either totally or largely ignore community participation, KSSP gives it centre stage. It feels that the resources required can be found by the DPEP through community participation. For that, the implementation of the programme at the lowest level should rest with the panchayats. Its leadership should be taken care of by popular committees. The block and district committees should co-ordinate the activities of such committees and provide technical directives. Panchayats should become the centre of the DPEP and the village education committees (VECs) should be reorganized as panchayat committees. School committees, organized at the school level, should have complete authority to do micro-planning at both physical and academic levels for the schools in the respective panchayats. There will be no need of a bureaucratic state project office, etc., if the block- and district-level committees are democratically instituted. If the State Council for Educational Research and Training (SCERT) and District Institute for Education and Training (DIET) are strengthened, under their academic leadership, the physical implementation can be assigned to the panchayats.

The KSSP pointed out that the best method of solving problems existing in the educational sector is to introduce, along with other academic reforms, facilities for popular intervention. Not only can part of the resources required for additional physical facilities be raised by popular committees, but a model of popular monitoring in academic matters—where people's representatives and educational experts work together—can also be evolved. Since education is basically a social service, and the element of voluntarism is naturally high, the KSSP objected to some suggestions in the DPEP which it thought were trying to make teaching merely a paid job. It suggested that the participation of teachers in DPEP be made regular duty and the voluntary service at the village level be given preference.

The KSSP also found the lack of necessary interaction with all concerned at the stage of formulation of the programme regrettable. In a state like Kerala where it was proved that the TLC was successfully implemented through popular participation, it is paradoxical that a programme which was expected to take such participation to higher levels fell short of it. The KSSP felt that the VEC as it is envisaged now can end up as a mere mechanical appendage of the school. It is as if the importance of the teachers and parents, who are seen as mere implementors, is forgotten. With these criticisms, the KSSP, though supportive of the DPEP, opted to dissociate with some aspects of the programme. For it, the most important and immediate task was to integrate DPEP with the new Panchayati Raj system. They argued that apart from the international foreign funds made available, another important promotive factor for DPEP was the 73rd and 74th Constitutional amendments. Therefore, when an amount to the tune of Rs 1,025 crore was devolved upon the LSGIs[25], it turned out to be a great opportunity for activist groups like the KSSP to try to implement their own suggestions with regard to community participation in educational improvement.

Community Participation in Education under People's Planning Campaign

One of the important instruments used by the PPC in Kerala is a document called the Panchayat Development Report (PDR). This contains, for each of the panchayats, the felt need of the people and the local problems as identified at the Gram Sabha, which in the particular context of Kerala meets at the ward and not at the panchayat level. This document lists every project suggested by various village panchayats. Therefore, it is an important source to take stock of the actual number of projects in the educational sector taken up by the LSGIs. But very little progress can be expected on the basis of this source if an evaluation of the proposed projects are intended. Therefore, three other major sources of data generated by the PPC were explored. At the end of the second year of the campaign,

52 successful cases were reported from among various LSGIs and presented at a convention held on 16 August 1998. These reports were published by the State Planning Board (SPB).[26] Some of these included interventions based on community participation. Since they were reported as "successful" cases, they could not be accepted without further checking. Therefore, they were investigated independently.

One major problem that the PPC found in the functioning was with regard to the Gram Sabha. Even at the ward level, the Gram Sabha was found too unwieldy. For various reasons, there was a lack of attendance. One way out of such a situation was to work through structures smaller than the constitutionally provided organizational level of the Gram Sabha. Some panchayats, estimated to be 223 in number, went ahead and formed what came to be known as neighbourhood groups. Though they differed in many respects, they also shared many common characteristics. Such groups seem to have advanced the possibilities for real and direct participation by ordinary people in decision-making. Of 96 panchayats from which details were collected, 29 solicited attendance for the Gram Sabha through neighbourhood groups, with a reasonable amount of success. In addition to this, they help in identifying beneficiaries for various projects, and act as devices for monitoring and even for social auditing. Another related development was the organization of women into self-help groups. Through these, women's participation is also on the rise.[27]

Several of such neighbourhood groups reported on their experiences in a convention held in October 1999. Some of them have been selected to be published in two volumes.[28] There are some reports on educational projects with community participation. These were used only after proper checking, for obvious reasons. Another set of participants in the PPC who gave their reports were the beneficiaries. The SPB had instructed that the construction work under different projects should be undertaken by committees selected from among the beneficiaries and not by contractors. Though the habit was not wholly eliminated, there were many LSGIs which genuinely tried to operate through beneficiary committees. Around 250 of them reported on their experiences at a convention in November 1999 and these were published in three volumes.[29] Though such groups can go a long way in eliminating corruption, undertaking monitoring of public works in a transparent way, etc., their claims could also be controversial. Since they challenge an age-old system of contractors, which has generated corruption and facilitated a contractor–government official nexus, their position is certainly sensitive. Members of such committees can also be unnecessarily critical of others whom they suspect of wrongdoing. Therefore, their reports had to be seriously cross-checked. This could not be done for the simple reason that all the concerned parties in a public construction work could be met neither together nor separately. All that was checked was whether the work claimed to have been done was actually done or not. Nevertheless, the cases reported are of special importance since they give insights into how popular committees took necessary steps to construct or repair school buildings, playgrounds, etc. and raised additional funds when necessary.

The 1998 Report of successful experiments contains a very inspiring story from Athirapally panchayat in Thrissur district.[30] With the active co-operation of the local adivasi community, a one-teacher school was started in Adachilthotti. The lady teacher was selected by the adivasis themselves, whose children escort her back and forth at the beginning and end of every week from her home to the school. They have arranged a hut for her to stay. Fifty-one students are now studying in the school established with people's plan funds and inaugurated on 21 Feburary 1998.

Another case is reported by the Thodannur block panchayat in Kozhikode district. They learnt from the experiences of KSSP activists who had earlier organized effective intervention in education on the basis of community participation. They found that 35 per cent of the students in that block were lacking in proficiency in the minimum level of literacy. In the light of this finding, they devised a project to implement educational reforms which would make learning an enjoyable experience. They also aimed at increasing the SSLC examination pass percentage in the block. In order to implement this project called *Vijaya Redham*, they devised a four-tier organization starting with the block educational committee, followed by the village panchayat educational committee, and the cluster- and school-level committees. In addition to this, a block resource unit was also formed. Apart from activities in the academic sector and the co-curricular sector, they are undertaking several activities in the community sector too. Their main aim is to strengthen the relationship between school and society. For this purpose they are trying to strengthen the PTA, Mathru Sangam activities and popular monitoring. The activities that should take place every month in the schools is decided at the executive committee meeting of the PTA, in which all teachers are expected to participate, and the report is forwarded to the block and village panchayat committees. Further, a minimum pass scheme in which learning deficiencies of "backward students" are taken care of by group learning led by a peer master and tutor, comprehensive evaluation, documentation, and other co-curricular activities are also undertaken by the programme. The most impressive result is that in the seven high schools in this block area, the average SSLC pass percentage has increased from 26 per cent in 1996 to 41 per cent in 1998.

In Madikai in Kasargode district, a project to improve the learning experiences of primary school students studying in the 10 schools of the panchayat, called *Aksharapulari*, was already in place, inaugurated on 22 May 1993, under the auspices of the now defunct district council. This programme turned out to be quite promising, with children and parents appreciating the new teaching–learning practices based upon children- and activity-oriented programmes. Another interesting experience was that teachers willingly and voluntarily worked even extra hours for the programme. This programme eventually came to a standstill as a result of policy shifts at higher levels and the disbanding of the DC. What was realized later in the context of the advent of the PPC was that this could be revived effectively. What we can see in Madikai is an effort towards this goal. Similarly, in Mayyil panchayat of Kannur district, there were interventions meant to improve educational levels since 1995. In 1997–98 a new set of programmes were undertaken with the active co-operation of all 16 schools in the panchayat. Teachers' training, producing and distributing learning aids, preparing source books, coaching students for scholarship examinations, celebrating nationally important days, helping libraries work better, conducting educational exhibitions, distributing lab equipments wherever necessary, giving umbrellas to students of first and second standards, and distributing furniture to *anganwadis* are some of the activities undertaken by these programmes. The education sub-committee of the development committee (a registered parallel body with the panchayat president as chairperson) visited all schools to check whether any change was required in the learning–teaching aids distributed. The committee had retired headmasters, social activists and elected representatives as its members. In addition to all this, neighbourhood groups were formed and a special education sub-committee was also organized. This sub-committee monitors developments in each student household. It has already undertaken a survey to identify educationally backward students, and a special programme has been devised to help them.

In Kayyoor-Cheemeni village panchayat in Kasargode district, the people raised an amount of about 3.5 lakhs of rupees through donation in kind and cash from the locality and built a school building through voluntary labour for the Kayyoor government high (VHSC) school. This was done under the auspices of the PTA and a special group of the parents. The students played a major role in instilling the necessary sense of need in the local population. They also started pre-primary classes attached to eight government lower-primary schools. Further, they undertook the preparation of a new pre-primary curriculum, and organized awareness programmes for mothers, training for teacher–ayahs and youth festivals at the panchayat level. The additional funds required for the youth festivals were about 2 lakhs of rupees and that was raised by the respective educational welfare committees. They are now planning to extend the programme to the aided schools in the area. Another project is being implemented to improve the SSLC pass percentage. Students who are found backward in the three high schools of the panchayat are located and helpful learning notes are distributed among them. Volunteers give remedial training for them at neighbourhood group meetings.

A similarly interesting case is reported from the Kumarakom panchayat in Kottayam district. The students found wanting in pre-testing are offered remedial training during early morning as well as after-school hours by - voluntary workers assigned for the purpose by the educational sub-committees of the neighbourhood groups. They have facilitators for every four students of each neighbourhood group, studying from I to VII standards. They are also convening special sessions of parents of the "backward" students to ensure their support. The educational sub-committee has already collected information on the students from their homes as well as from schools. In addition, all students are presented with school diaries given by the panchayat. Madikai, mentioned earlier, has once again reported progress in their activities with reference to neighbourhood groups. The fact that the neighbourhood group has taken over the drinking water project for Keekankottu LP school, which was earlier taken up and dropped by the PTA, is worth mentioning.

Vithura Panchayat in Thiruvananthapuram district has already organized 96 balawadis attached to neighbourhood groups. A committee consisting of two parents, three activists, two representatives of the children and the person in charge of the educational sub-committee of the neighbourhood group are appointed to run them. Their activities, among other things, also help children's education. Similarly, the Kodumon panchayat in Pathanamthitta district is planning intervention in the educational sector through neighbourhood groups. Amarambalam panchayat in Malappuram district has already organized 17 remedial teaching centres along with neighbourhood groups. The physical facilities for these centres, including temporary sheds, have been already provided. In their plan, which is well prepared, activities are included to control children of school-going age, facilitate group learning and organize reading groups at remedial centres, promote non-formal education of students through *bala sauhruda vedi*, distribute midday meals in schools, and intervene in syllabi- and curriculum-renewal activities through PTAs and MTAs.

Aryad panchayat in Alappuzha district reported a limited exercise of improving the SSLC pass percentage of the only high school in that panchayat. Koppam panchayat reported on their efforts at improving physical facilities, activating PTA, and enrolling students in the "uneconomical" government welfare school through neighbourhood groups. Unfortunately, these claims could not be checked at the field level. Kuttiattoor panchayat in Kannur district talks of the role being played by neighbourhood groups in implementing the earlier *Gurukulam* project and in the current efforts at improving the quality of education. Sreenarayanapuram panchayat in Thrissur district reported that the educational subcommittee of the neighbourhood group is intervening in the learning activities of the local LP school. The Thrikkovilvattom panchayat has identified the possibilities of intervening to change the conditions existing at the household level blocking children's education, through neighbourhood groups. What these groups have reported are the beginnings of a few ambitious projects. Nevertheless, they look encouraging because most of such interventions are planned to suit the prevailing perspectives on community participation.

Let us now review the reports submitted by the beneficiary groups. The corporation of Thiruvananthapuram reported considerable progress in building a two-storey building of 20 rooms for the Manacaud government technical training institute. The school authorities and the PTA had given several memoranda to the government requesting the building. The city corporation agreed to finance the project on the request of the ward convention in 1997 under the PPC. A school development committee was formed in a meeting presided over by the ward councillor, in which the teachers of the school, parents, ward committee members and local people participated. They took up the initial responsibilities of the construction. When the first instalment of the financial allocation was granted by the corporation, a separate building committee consisting of 19 members was created. A retired superintendent engineer agreed to serve as the chairperson and the PTA president himself was appointed convenor. A number of teachers, engineers, government officers, retired persons, ordinary labourers, merchants, socio-political activists, etc., did voluntary work for the construction. The committee signed the agreement with the secretary of the corporation. A significant gain was that there was hardly any long waiting period for the fund allocation. Under the provision of the People's Plan, the popular committee was able to get permission for the project and the necessary permit for construction from the local corporation office. The project received voluntary services from technically qualified people. According to the report of the committee, they were able to maintain a high level of quality in their work.

A similar two-storey building for the Manacaud VHS school in the Thiruvananthapuram corporation area was built by a committee selected at a meeting of parents, local leaders, educationalists and people from voluntary organizations. The construction was supervised by the PTA and the committee. In the Pattom government model girls school, the higher secondary school section was also built by a committee selected in a meeting of the ward-level committee. It had the ward councillor as chairperson, school PTA president as convenor, headmistress as secretary, and five representatives of the PTA, two leading citizens of the locality and two representatives of voluntary organizations. Though this committee took charge of overseeing the work, a 11-member committee with a retired industrial training centre officer as chairperson and a public activist as convenor was formed for the sake of convenience. Three women teachers were also included in this committee. In order to oversee technical aspects of the work, a retired chief engineer (civil) of the Kerala state electricity board and an assistant engineer from irrigation department were available. An effort along the same lines at constructing a building for the Sree Moolavilasom government model higher secondary school in Thiruvananthapuram corporation is running into problems due to lack of support from the people of the concerned corporation ward. But the teachers and students are highly supportive and Rs 700,000 has already been collected as the beneficiaries' share through their efforts. Nevertheless, the progress of the building, estimated to cost Rs 50 lakhs, is not moving well.

If the experiences from Thiruvananthapuram are mixed, there was a promising story reported from a panchayat in Kozhikode district. The Anthita Government UPS, catering to the poorer sections of the society, was allotted a building under PPC in 1997–98. In a meeting where 518 people, including the local MLA, representatives of educational, social and cultural organizations, trade union representatives, and the head of the Sri Ramakrishna Madom participated, an 11-member committee taking into consideration women and scheduled caste representation was formed. They managed to raise one lakh rupees that was to be the beneficiaries' share from the very deprived neighbourhood. As reported, the role played by the headmistress of the school in all these was indeed great. Puthrika panchayat in Ernakulam district reports that the Kakkattupara LP school building was constructed with the utmost co-operation of government officials concerned. Since it was found out that it would be impossible to raise the beneficiaries' share from the parents of children coming from lower middle class families, their contribution was estimated in terms of voluntary labour.

Elanji village panchayat faced difficulties in renovating the Elanji Government LPS building through a committee selected from the PTA. First of all, local community participation was not as forthcoming as expected. The only exception was 12 activists of the non-gazetted officers union offering their voluntary services. The lack of experience of the PTA members in building matters also seems to have adversely affected their efforts.

From Mukkom village panchayat in Kozhikode district comes the report of the completion of a road linking the Chendamangllur high school with Pattasserri. This vital road, which benefited the staff and students in no small measure, was built by raising the beneficiaries' share in quick time, supervised by an 11-member committee including 4 women members elected by a ward-level meeting. Kodakara panchayat in Thrissur district reports on the PTA committee undertaking the construction of the Kodakara government higher secondary school building. Even though the block panchayat president was directly involved in the effort as the chairperson of the development committee, the building efforts had to face quite a lot of problems, stemming from non-cooperation of the officials. But then, we have not been able to hear the officials' version. Similarly, the report from Parasala panchayat of Thiruvananthapuram district regarding the efforts of a beneficiaries' committee to take up innovation schemes including provision of drinking water, construction of classrooms, plastering and separation of classrooms in Dhanuvachapuram Neelakandaru Krishnaru Memorial school is replete with complaints. All of them are with regard to non-cooperation of the officials.

The Perinthalmanna municipality reports on the construction of a higher secondary building by an 11-member beneficiary committee consisting of the PTA president, teachers and school welfare committee members. They also faced difficulties from the non-cooperation of officials. Nevertheless, they claim that the facilities provided by their school are the best in the district. What seem to have stood them in good stead are the co-operative efforts of trade unions, service organizations, clubs, youth movements and student organizations. In Punalur municipality of Kollam district the only government high school in the region was upgraded to a higher secondary school. Almost every facility—classroom, laboratories, urinals, toilets, furniture, etc.—needed to be built. These needs were prioritized and taken up one by one by the municipality with the co-operation of PTA, MTA, students and the general public. In this success story everybody, including the officials, co-operated to the utmost extent possible.

The Kadayirippu government higher secondary school felt the need for more infrastructure in 1996. It had impressive results in the SSLC examinations. The local people and the PTA offered a helping hand by even donating land to build the new building. Kadakkarapalli panchayat, in Alappuzha district, took up extension of the playground for the Kottaram UP school through a popular committee. Through an extensive publicity campaign, all political parties, and youth, cultural, and community-based organizations in the area were attracted to this task. The Pattanakkad block-level expert committee member was the chairperson and the secretary of the Kottaram KSSP unit was the secretary. Members of various organizations worked along with the beneficiaries. When they completed the playing field, a considerable portion of the estimated fund was found unspent, which they used with the permission of the panchayat to further extend the playground. Nevertheless, they also faced the problem of non-cooperation of the officials which, according to their report, led to loss of enthusiasm for such work among the local people.

Reports on such local-level experiences may be wound up with a story from Valiasala ward of Thiruvananthapuram Corporation. The Chala government boys school in this ward faced extinction nearly 10 years ago. There were less than 150 students, with an SSLC pass percentage ranging between 10 and 15 per cent. The students coming to the school were from the poorest of the poor families of Thiruvananthapuram. Some teachers decided to end such degeneration and offered extra classes, including extra studying facilities at the school during after-school hours, the like of which could not be expected at the homes of the poor students. Several organizations including merchants of this busy trading zone of Thiruvananthapuram helped. The Thiruvananthapuram district council also helped during its time and now there are around 800 students. This caused a strain on physical facilities and the current ward convention took the initiative to build a new building with 12 rooms, protected water supply and toilet facilities.

Conclusion

The three sources of data referred to in this study—the 1998 reports of successful experiments, the 1999 reports of neighbourhood groups, and the 1999 reports of the beneficiaries' groups—provide a range of educational experiments with community participation which is not so extensive. Some of these stories are encouraging. Having built a school for tribals, and that too with the active co-operation of the tribal community concerned, and having extended both academic and physical facilities for children of the poorest sections in Thiruvananthapuram are both remarkable achievements. In both these cases, the potentialities inherent in the PPC for community participation have come in handy. Most of the success stories are from regions that had a history of educational intervention mainly by KSSP and teachers' organization activists. Other areas that report similar activities are only entering the field anew. Naturally, they have very little success to report. But the fact that they are taking care to make use of the potentialities of neighbourhood groups to monitor the academic requirements of students even at homes, and are providing remedial facilities, are likely to result in substantial gains in the long run.

Their support for reform-oriented interventions is highly dependent upon their closeness with reform-minded experts, particularly from the KSSP.

Similarly, the few instances of successful community interventions for facilitating physical facilities are also encourgaing. One problem reported in this context is the lack of local support. More important is the non-cooperation of officials. Though the reports are not complete, this points to two major problems that public intervention based on community participation will have to face in the context of decentralization in the particular circumstances of a state like Kerala. Nevertheless, the three type of interventions possible within the PPC—one for providing educational facilities for the marginalized sections, the other for qualitative improvement of the educational process and the third for facilitating physical facilities—are all addressing basic problems of the education system in Kerala. The only problem is that these experiments are highly limited. They are yet to form into a movement. But they also show how the PPC's facilities can be used in an organized manner for such concerted intervention in future.

One abiding factor in all stages is the strong presence of the KSSP. One wonders whether the idea of community intervention would have survived but for the consistent presence of KSSP activists. But even the KSSP activists could not effectively withstand problems emanating from earlier policy changes, like dismantling of the DCs. Even now, different regions with different backgrounds and varying affinities towards reforms are behaving differently. As pointed out, the individual reports of KSSP intervention "showed considerable variation among themselves in the evolution of the educational sector, local leadership, and local participation in educational development, educational environment, and current performance". In consequence, "the intervention strategies that KSSP followed also differed from one locality to the other."[31]

There are still regions in Kerala where the advocacy for educational reforms as well as for community participation is practically nil. In addition, education has become a contentious issue in Kerala. Therefore, even with the facilitating role of the PPC, the reform agenda will find itself difficult to be pushed forward. The PPC has shown the possibilities for furthering educational reforms with community participation. To realize such potentialities, a lot more people and institutions have to be gathered behind the reform agenda. As it was said in the European context, "the more the school and its operation is to be attuned to the whole range of the needs of its community, the broader could be the framework of reference for school facilities."[32] In such a context, local and community participation in favour of the school and its educative mission can be expected to be forthcoming. Though in a different historical context, it was found that the "early modern schools" were "popular schools" which responded to the needs of parents and local communities, and that while the early reformers "were appalled by the boredom and cruelty of the popular class room" the parents were satisfied with the individual method of instruction prevailing in 18th century Europe.[33]

One important thing should not be ignored. Once the features of the same reform agenda that became controversial at the state level were presented at the local level through the PPC, there was hardly any resistance. On the other hand, when the DPEP version was presented at the state level there was bitter polarization of opinions. KSSP had argued that the DPEP experiment would have a better acceptability if it is integrated completely with the objectives of decentralization and the three-tier Panchayati Raj system. This seems a strong argument in the context of the experiments that have been reported in this study. Nevertheless, as already hinted earlier in this article, it will be difficult to implement such experiments in politically divided panchayats.

It would be difficult to state with definiteness whether this increased participation has led to effective empowerment of the local community, and if it has resulted in improving the educational process significantly. One can conclude, however, that the people's planning campaign has the potential for furthering local empowerment, and it is resulting in such developments. It is too early to say whether the specific experiments in the field of education reported here have contributed to the same. Similarly, if we go by the limited evidence of SSLC pass percentages, some of these experiments have resulted in qualitative improvement of the educational process. However, more evidence will be required to confirm such an observation. Here also, the potential inherent in these developments is the exciting prospect.

Notes and References

1. See Tharakan, P.K.M. (1984), "Socio-Economic Factors in Educational Development: Case of Nineteenth Century Travancore", *Economic and Political Weekly*, vol. XIX, nos. 45 and 46, November 10 and 17.

2. See Mitra, A. et. al. (1999), *Report of the Kerala Education Commission*, Kochi: KSSP, p. 159.

3. See Mitra, A., et. al. cited in note 2 above; Tharakan, P.K.M. and Navaneetham K. (2000), "Population Projection and Policy Implications for Education: A Discussion with Reference to Kerala", *Review of Development and Change*, vol. 5, no. 1, January–June.

4. See Ramakrishnan, C. (1999), "Educational Environment of Schools", in *Quality of School Education in Kerala: Dimensions and Determinants*, Thiruvananthapuram: Kerala Research Programme on Local Development (KRPLD), Centre for Development Studies (CDS), p. 18.

5. See Ganesh, K.N. (1997), "Puthia Pada Pusthakangal: Vivadam Arkuvendi", (Malayalam), *Sasthragathi*, August, pp. 25–29.

6. See Tharakan, P.K.M., cited in note 1 above.

7. See Tharakan, P.K.M. (1998), "Socio-Religious Reform Movement, the Process of Democratisation and Human Development: The Case of Kerala, South-West India", in Lars Rudebeck and Olle Tornquist with Virgilio Rojas (eds), *Democratisation in the Third World: Concrete Cases in Comparative Perspectives*, London: Macmillan, pp. 144–72.

8. See the Constitution of India, Article 243, 11th Schedule.

9. Varghese, N.V. (1996), "Decentralisation of Educational Planning and the District Primary Education Programme", Occasional Paper No. 22, New Delhi: National Institute of Educational Planning and Administration (NIEPA), p. 13.

10. See OECD (Organization for Economic Co-operation and Development) (1980), *School and Community, Vol. II: The Consequences of Some Policy Choices*, Paris: Centre for Educational Research and Innovation (CERI).

11. Ibid.

12. See Mitra, A., et. al., cited in note 2 above.

13. See Raj, K.N. and P.K.M. Tharakan (1983), "Agrarian Reform in Kerala and Its Impact on the Rural Economy: A Preliminary Assessment", in Ajit Kumar Ghose (ed.), *Agrarian Reforms in Contemporary Developing Economies*, London: Croom Helm, New York: St. Martin's Press; Tharakan P.K.M. (1982), "The Kerala Land Reforms (Amendment) Bill, 1979, A Note", in Sheo Kumar Lall (ed.) *Sociological Perspective of Land Reforms*, New Delhi: Agricole Publication Agency.

14. Donald, J. (1992), "Dewey-eyed Optimism: The Possibility of Democratic Education", (Review) *New Left Review*, March/April, p. 101, referring to James Donald and Jim Grealy, "The Unpleasant Fact of Inequality", in Ann Marie Wolpe and James Donald (ed.) (1983), *Is There Anyone Here from Education*, London: Verso, pp. 133–44.

15. See Tharakan, P.K.M., cited in note 1 above.

16. See Parameswaran, M.P. (1995), "Pradhamika Vidyabhyasam: Vibhava Samaharanavum Managementum", (Malayalam), *Sasthragathi*, vol. 29, no. 7, September, pp. 21–26.

17. See Tharakan, P.K.M., cited in note 7 above.

18. See Tharakan, P.K.M. (1990), *The Ernakulam District Total Literacy Campaign, Report of the Evaluation*, Thiruvananthapuram: CDS.

19. See Raj, K.N. (1993), "Some Thoughts on Decentralisation of Development Planning and Implementation", Paper presented at the Seminar on Decentralization, Thiruvananthapuram: CDS; Nagaraj, K. (1999), "Decentralisation in Kerala: A Note", Discussion Paper No. 2, Thiruvananthapuram: KRPLD, CDS.

20. Very little has been published on this experiment. For ready reference, see Antony, J. (1996), "For a Better Tomorrow", *Down to Earth*, 15 February, pp. 38–9.
21. See Varghese, N.V., cited in note 9 above, pp. 19–20.
22. See Ganesh 1994, p. 25.
23. See Raveendran. P.K. (1995), "Pothu Vidhyabhyasathe Rakshikkuka", (Malayalam), *Sasthragathi*, vol. 29, no. 8, November, pp. 21–26.
24. Ganesh K.N., (1997), "DPEPum Kerala Vidhyabhyasa Parishkaranavum" (Malayalam), *Sasthragathi*, vol. 32, no. 7, September 1997, pp. 6–12, 27.
25. See Issac, T.M.T. (1999), "Janakeeyasoothranavum Ayalkootavum: Anubhavangal, Padangal", (Malayalam), *Ayalkootta Sangham 99, Part I*, Thiruvananthapuram: State Planning Board (SPB), p. 15.
26. See SPB (1998), *Janakeeyathayude Ponkani*, (Malayalam), Thiruvananthapuram: SPB.
27. See Issac 1998, cited in note 25 above.
28. See SPB (1999a), *Ayalkootta Sangham 99*, (Malayalam), Part I and II, Thiruvananthapuram: SPB.
29. See SPB (1999b), *Gunabhokta Samithikalude Anubhava Padangal*, (Malayalam), Part I, II and III, Thiruvananthapuram: SPB.
30. See SPB, cited in note 26 above, pp. 69–172.
31. Nair, P.R.G. (1999), "School Education in Kerala: Performance and Problems", in *Quality of School Education in Kerala: Dimensions and Determinants*, Thiruvananthapuram: KRPLD, CDS, p. 4.
32. OECD, cited in note 10 above, p. 42.
33. Maynes, M.J. (1985), *Schooling in Western Europe: A Social History*, Albany: Suny Press.

3

Community Participation and Empowerment in Primary Education: Discussion of Experiences from Rajasthan

Vimala Ramachandran

Ground Reality

"Savitri's family is anything but well off. But when she dropped out of school here in Viraatnagar, it wasn't because of poverty. Her own class-mates—and teacher—made it impossible for the 15-year-old to continue. 'The moment I enter the room in school, the other children make faces. They start singing *"bhangi aayee hai, aayee hai, bhangi aayee hai!"* (The *bhangi* has come.) The words of the song are foul and insulting.' Savitri is from a family of manual scavengers. A group that's among the most vulnerable within Dalits. The official label for them is '*bhangi*'. Many here are from the Mehter caste. And quite a few of these groups now call themselves Balmikis. With even other scheduled castes practising untouchability towards them, they end up pretty close to the bottom of the social heap. Women scavengers cleaning dry latrines tend to draw their pallu over the noses and grip it in their teeth. That offers them some protection in their unsanitary work. The children at the school mimic this when Savitri enters. 'They bite a side of their collar, push their noses up. Sometimes put a hanky on their faces. I would start crying, but it didn't matter to them.'[1]"

"When we did the household survey we were amazed to note that the number of girls in the total was very low. We inquired further, went over the survey forms and met families that had 'missed out' the girls. They said they did not count them as children, these young ones were married! 100 per cent of girls in Bapini Village of Phalodi Block of Jodhpur District did not attend school. This was revealed when school mapping was done.[2]"

These descriptions are not unique. They do no shock people in Rajasthan. These real-life situations have been narrated over and over again in the past 50 years. Almost any discussion on educational access and educational backwardness of Rajasthan invariably begins—and often unfortunately ends—with stories of unequal access, persistence of caste prejudices and the situation of women and girls. These snapshots of the situation on the ground are often used to argue for more investment in the education of girls and also for more foreign aid to the state.

Rajasthan has made considerable progress in the last 50 years, especially in providing primary schools within 1 to 3 km radius. Yet, it remains one of the most difficult regions of India with regard to ensuring universal access to basic education. According to the 1991 census of the seven million primary-age children (6–11 years) in Rajasthan, the proportion attending primary schools is 52.8 per cent (3.7 million). Only 37.4 per cent of primary-age girls attend school. The drop-out rate in primary schools (between class I and V) is around 55 per cent and under 30 per cent of children complete education to an age of over 14. Though there has been substantial progress post-independence in the number of educational institutions, enrollment and literacy rates, the overall picture remains bleak. At the beginning of the last decade (1991), around 6,200 villages and 20,000 small habitations did not have primary school facilities. Dalits, especially those belonging to communities like the Balmiki, tribal communities like the Garasia, and people living in remote areas and in the margins of society have almost no access.

A significant number of the out-of-school children are girls. As can be seen from table 3.1, the literacy rate among women from scheduled castes is 9.10 per cent and scheduled tribes is 7.50 per cent. Formal primary schools are still not within the reach of children from disadvantaged communities and remote areas.

Table 3.1
Literacy status in rural Rajasthan

By land size group:	Landless	Marginal	Small	Medium	Large
Male	44.70	52.60	61.70	63.70	65.90
Female	5.70	14.50	17.90	19.80	21.40
By occupational group:	Agriculture	Salaried	Wage earners	All others	Total
Male	57.20	83.30	44.90	70.40	60.40
Female	14.60	42.10	6.00	29.20	19.00
By social group:	ST	SC	Other Hindus	Minority	Total
Male	39.10	51.80	66.40	45.90	60.40
Female	7.50	9.10	23.90	7.80	19.00

Table 3.2
Enrollment rate in rural Rajasthan

By per capita income:	Up to 1,500	1,501–2,500	2,501–4,000	4,001–6,000	> 6,000
Male	76.00	69.60	75.50	87.90	89.70
Female	31.80	32.10	40.10	55.90	65.40
By land-size group:	Landless	Marginal	Small	Medium	Large
Male	63.10	73.80	76.60	83.60	80.00
Female	15.02	36.40	41.80	45.20	47.00
By social group:	ST	SC	Other Hindus	Minority	Total
Male	57.10	58.40	76.80	71.90	68.50
Female	42.90	46.40	64.80	58.40	55.80

Source: NCAER/HDI Survey, 1994.

What does Community Participation mean in this Context?

"Community participation" is perhaps the most misused and misunderstood word in development jargon today. "Community" in itself has no specific meaning—it is like saying "India" or "Rajasthan". Therefore, at the outset, it is important to define community participation in the specific context of primary education, that too in Rajasthan. Presumably, we are referring to those who are either left out or are participating from the margins. This article focuses on two important initiatives in Rajasthan, namely Shiksha Karmi project and Rajasthan Lok Jumbish. It also draws upon the experience of the women's development programme in Rajasthan, which was a learning ground for many people involved in conceptualizing, designing and implementing the above educational projects.

P. Sainath's travels around Rajasthan reveal that Balmiki children are made to sit on their own mats, often outside the room or at the door. Participation in education is very low, and is worse among girls. Untouchability is still a reality that Balmiki children have to deal with. The situation of girls is disturbing. As we have seen in the opening paragraphs of this article, school mapping brings out the "invisibility" of girls. Parents and their in-laws do not count them as children! Over two thirds of children who are not in school are girls—their participation is critical.

Therefore, in the context of Rajasthan, community participation implies the participation of the disempowered. Ideally, it would involve people who have little or no access to basic education—as a community, geographical area or gender. However, this is easier said than done because it is these very people who are the most difficult to reach out to.

Being the poorest in the society, they are caught up in the daily battle for survival. From their perspective, a kind of education that does not lead to any tangible or intangible gain could be dismissed as being irrelevant in their struggle for survival. They do not readily participate in larger societal forums and bodies—whether it is the panchayat or the VEC or the village women's health committee. Even if they are made mandatory members, they rarely speak out—if they attend in the first place. Being at the bottom of the social ladder, their interaction with the rest of the society is from a position of disempowerment. In a patriarchal society like Rajasthan, women shoulder the additional burden of gender-based discrimination. Women in poor communities have problems of sexual abuse and oppression added to their list of woes.

Apart from the "target population" for community participation—given the social and economic status, gender inequality and also given that an overwhelming proportion of the poor are illiterate—the mechanisms and processes used for it need to be appropriate. Systems that succeed in Kerala, Tamil Nadu or West Bengal are not likely to be effective in Rajasthan. Similarly, processes in Rajasthan are likely to be more human resource intensive than in areas that have a history of popular participation in social reform movements or struggles.

Rajasthan Shiksha Karmi Project[3]

The Shiksha Karmi project of Rajasthan was initiated in 1987 to improve access to basic education in remote areas where existing primary schools were plagued with teacher absenteeism, non-functioning schools, and community despair and cynicism. The accent was on removing the inaccessibility due to remoteness and the terrain. This programme has its roots in Social Work and Research Centre (Tilonia) night schools. The concept of the shiksha karmi (SK) is based on the supposition that a change agent, especially in the field of education, can work effectively if he/she belongs to the same locality. The concept is particularly important for remote and backward villages where it is difficult for an outsider to stay or be accepted. This unique project started by acknowledging the problem of teacher absenteeism and dysfunctional schools. This in itself was a major step forward.

The Main Features of the Project

1. Villages/hamlets are identified where primary schools are nonexistent or dysfunctional, or where a significant proportion of children are out of school.
2. The community is made aware of the need to have a functioning school and energized to act.
3. An SK school is established after two local residents, preferably one male and female, with educational qualifications of class VIII and V respectively, are identified with the help of the community, and appointed as SKs after specific, intensive training.
4. Training to Shiksha Karmis is regarded as a continuous process designed to upgrade qualifications, improve and promote teaching abilities, reinforce solidarity among them to act as social activists, and provide motivation and support. Regular annual training, and two-day monthly review and problem solving meetings follow an intensive 41-day pre-service training.

5. The project operates three different kinds of schools—shiksha karmi day schools; *prehar pathshalas* (schools of convenient timings) to cater to children unable to attend day school; and *aangan pathshalas* (courtyard schools), which are non-formal schools mainly to prepare girls for entry to regular day schools or *prehar pathshalas*.

6. The project has evolved a structure of training, support and monitoring by involving shiksha karmi *sahyogis* drawn from both the formal school system and NGOs. In addition, the project has created a category of *mahila sahyogis*, part-time workers, mainly to escort girl students.

7. To address the gender imbalance in the appointment of SKs, the project has set up *mahila prashikshan kendras* (residential training schools) for women SKs.

8. The project involves a process of regular school mapping and continuous monitoring through specialized institutions, NGOs and VECs. This permits regular feedback and mid-course correction. More than basic research and evaluation, the focus is on problem solving.

The project seeks to combine the openness and flexibility of NGOs with the legitimacy accruing to the official government system. A key element of the Shiksha Karmi process is its emphasis on consensual functioning, with all decisions related to schools (selection of SKs, location of *prehar/angan pathshalas*, mapping, etc.) taken in VEC meetings. The pace of the project is related to the contextual need. The project also seeks to adhere to a spirit of partnership. Decision-making and control over critical issues such as selection of personnel, pace of expansion, forums and strategies for problem solving and generating approvals have not yet become bureaucratized. They also do not pass into the hands of government officials or experts. Slow reformism to ensure sustainability rather than radicalism marks the project's style.

Community Participation in Shiksha Karmi Project

The process and extent of community participation in the Shiksha Karmi Project is outlined below.

1. As a first step, dialogue is generated around and about the school, within the educational administration and amongst the teachers.

Table 3.3
Shiksha Karmi project—status as of March 1998

Unit	Achievement
Districts covered	32
Blocks covered	140
Block/Unit	200
Day schools (DS)	2,600
Prehar pathshalas (PP)	4,335
Upper primary schools	20
Aangan pathshalas	105
Shiksha karmis	6,085
Male	5,390
Female	695
Mahila prashikshan kendras	13
Resource units	9
Village education committees	2,137
Shiksha Karmi sahyogi	188
Master trainers (after training)	798
Male	757
Female	41
VEC members	19,917
Male	13,244
Female	6,673
Mahila Sahyogis in	331
Day schools	53
Prehar pathshalas	178
DS + Prehar pathshalas	100
Enrollment	2,02,000
Boys	1,18,000
Girls	84,000
Participation DS	85%
Participation PP	80%
Retention DS	65%
Retention PP	55%

Source: 17th Report, SK Board.

Then a decision is taken to go to the concerned village and explore the possibility of opening an SKP school.

2. Second, the SKP workers initiate a dialogue within the village, with the panchayat, local leaders and/or concerned persons. A group from the village is taken into confidence. At this stage there is no specified pattern in the composition of this group.

3. Third, the village identifies two people of the age group 18–33—the men should have cleared class VIII and women class V. In the early years, the SKP did not insist on women because of a very low literacy rate among women. The criterion of selection is important. The project looks for people with a positive attitude, high energy levels and excitement about new opportunities to learn and be a teacher. There is also a clear focus on local youth, sense of belonging, identification with the community and willingness to work together. Where there is a choice, preference is given to candidates from the local community. This is done because the project has good back-up, academic support and supervision, thanks to the SK *sahyogis*.

4. Intensive training follows the selection process. Trainers are drawn from among school teachers, local unemployed graduates, NGOs, etc. The training also focuses on subjects, teaching methods, keeping in touch with the families of children, keeping the dialogue open, eliciting the support of families/leaders to ensure attendance, etc.

5. There is one VEC for every Shiksha Karmi school. This has 11–15 members representing all castes, minority groups, educationally deprived groups and women. This has had a positive impact on school environment and facilities. Encouraged by the positive response to Lok Jumbish, in 1994 SKP introduced school mapping and formed village-level forums to generate demand, educate the community, and monitor and support SKs.

6. Given the project's aim to improve the access of girls to primary education, women are identified and trained in *mahila prashikshan kendras*, over and above the regular training programme. These *kendras* function as a condensed education programme where girls with little or no education are brought up to class VII or VIII level before they are sent for selection as SKs. There are 14 such *kendras* today.

7. Another interesting aspect of the project is that NGOs are involved at the block level for training, educational support, monthly meetings, etc. As of now, there are 28 NGOs involved in SKP, and in addition to their specific responsibilities, they participate and initiate mobilization activities.

Community participation in SKP started with the official acceptance of the problem of dysfunctional schools and the need for an alternative means of creating and running a functional school. The community was involved in the selection of SKs, providing support in enrolling children (with an evident focus on girls), day-to-day support and monitoring, etc.

Does Getting into the Mainstream Lead to Less Community Participation? SKP started as a "people's problem". Originally, the driving force was the community. Today, it seems to have become a "government's problem". The present project leadership argues that the government has enough baseline data to enable them to plan the opening of new schools and also identify dysfunctional schools. Therefore, school mapping and micro-planning is not necessary, or so the argument goes. It is indeed interesting to note that phase III of the project, scheduled to have started in 1999, focuses more on the success of the "alternative model". The document does not say much about community participation in school mapping, it is possibly assumed. Now that the SKP concept has been accepted by the educational system, government officials dealing with this project seem to be more preoccupied with the model of "para-teachers", and not so much with the local youth who are drawn from the community and identify with it. Project functionaries admit that there was greater reliance on community support during the early years. Now there is a greater reliance on "systems"—management, training, supervision, etc.

Rajasthan Lok Jumbish

Rajasthan Lok Jumbish was launched in 1992 by GOI and the government of Rajasthan, with support from the Swedish Agency for International Development (SIDA). The main objective of Lok Jumbish is to develop, demonstrate, catalyze and transform the mainstream education system with the objective of ensuring that every child has access to basic education (class I to VII). The starting point was a recognition that the real problem is not one of supply alone, but also of unutilized capacities as indicated in low enrollment and participation rates. Even after 50 years of independence, very few literate men and women are found among the poor in the villages. The problem of non-participation is chronic. Therefore, Lok Jumbish was started with the mission to mobilize, motivate and energize.

Community mobilization is at the heart of Lok Jumbish, followed by acknowledging the importance of sensitive management and improving the quality of education. The document states that it is not enough to create delivery mechanisms—providing access includes creation of demand. The parents and community should acknowledge the availability of facilities and utilize them. An environment must be created where parents feel motivated to send their children to school. Special needs of children have to be acknowledged, and arrangements made for children engaged in work, girls who cannot attend formal schools, children of migrant families, nomads, tribal children and those with disabilities.

It is quite interesting to note that at the very beginning there was a recognition of the need to involve not only the community, but also the "teaching community". Respecting the teacher and supporting her/him through training, motivation and encouragement was flagged as a very important area of focus. Project leaders acknowledged that this was not going to be easy. Therefore, the motto was to learn by doing and progress gradually by reviewing processes continuously. This hinged on the ability of the project to be vigilant, and maintain open channels of communication and dialogue. There was also a commitment to uphold transparency and accountability.

Community Involvement in Lok Jumbish

From the very beginning, there was an agreement on who constituted the community. The project workers were explicitly asked to involve those who had been left out of educational processes—this was to be initiated through debates on the problems of education and that of their children. There was also the recognition that community participation could not "happen" unless the project developed and refined techniques to facilitate participation. As a result, in the first two years of Lok Jumbish a great deal of time and effort went into fine-tuning techniques for school mapping. Similarly, the composition of the VECs and the core groups (*prerak dal*) was also decided in the early years. Finally, Lok Jumbish developed village education registers, retention registers (for each class) and also the concept of a forum for building maintenance and school environment called the *bhavan nirman samiti*.

The above process went hand in hand with some tenets followed in Lok Jumbish, which are outlined below:

1. Engage the community—as represented by a group that comes forward or is created—in analyzing the information generated, and explore ways and means to make education available to all children.

2. Empower the disempowered to participate—create a *mahila samooh* to help women gain information, knowledge and the confidence to participate in a larger forum.
3. Make demands on the community—commitment to sending and maintaining children in schools, participation in improving school environment, etc.
4. Respond sensitively to the demands made by the community for more teachers, buildings, *sahaj shiksha kendras* (non-formal education centres), etc.
5. Make the functionaries, teachers and others accountable to the community.

School Mapping and Micro-Planning

School mapping and micro-planning form the core of the community participation in Lok Jumbish. In the beginning, there were no precedents and there was no guidance in terms of experiential knowledge. The International Institute for Educational Planning, Paris had brought out a document, but most of the literature available was on spatial planning. These were essentially top-down, a mapping exercise done by the state. Therefore, Lok Jumbish decided to learn by doing—and this took almost three years. The pioneers started with an emphasis on conducting diagnostic assessment, treating each village as the basic unit of analysis. Gradually, they built their experiments on PRA techniques. The focus was on mapping all children of the school-going age and the exact reasons for absence. The challenge was to present this information in a form in which the people—literate and illiterate—could understand. Depicting the physical condition of the school, rooms, water, playgrounds, etc., and developing a visual database using symbols was indeed an exacting task. The core principle was "rely on the people to diagnose the problem and articulate their demand". There was a confidence that once this happened, everything else would start falling into place.

After the first survey, the registers are to be updated every year. The VEC and *mahila samooh* are also expected to meet regularly. This has not always been smooth, and problems have been reported. Data from all villages are first collated at the cluster, then at the block and finally at the state level. Then, the block data is collated and sent to the headquarters. This is

---

Box 3.1: Illustrative sequence of school mapping activities

- Environment building—house to house contact.
- Formation of *prerak dal* and *mahila samooh*, and their training.
- Confidence and skill building of *prerak dal* for school mapping through training and other activities.
- Village meeting to introduce the concept and elicit participation.
- Household survey, followed by compilation of the data and cross-checking (where feasible) with school records.
- Preparation of school map.
- Preparation of village education registers.
- Village meeting to discuss results, followed by planning and demand articulation.
- Enrollment day.
- Preparation of proposal for *sahaj shiksha*, additional teachers, repairs of building, construction of additional rooms, etc.
- Establishment of the *bhavan nirman samiti* to monitor and support building repair and maintenance, tree plantation and other inputs.
- Organization of water for children.
- Taking care of seating and other logistics.
- Starting *sahaj shiksha* and enrollment of children.
- Formation of PTA and VEC.

---

an alternative database—because it is not always possible to match this with the one generated by the education department. Matching the data generated from school mapping with the database of the department is another area of concern. Further, given that Lok Jumbish (LJ) is an autonomous body that was till recently seen as being outside the government, legitimacy of this data in the eyes of the government was also a contentious issue. Notwithstanding these problems, the authenticity of this data in the eyes of the community was what mattered—and part of the effectiveness of the LJ strategy is attributed to this legitimacy.

Once the data is collated and the village-level plans are brought together, the block education management committee acts upon village-level proposals. Till recently, it was empowered to sanction *sahaj shiksha kendras*, schools, additional teachers, etc. The Block Steering Group (BSG) is the principal level for planning and implementation. Again, there have been delays because sanctioning a primary school or appointment of additional teachers was not within the purview of Lok Jumbish. Building repair, construction of additional rooms, etc., also takes time. Comparatively, it was easier to establish *sahaj shiksha kendras*.

Decentralization goes hand in hand with community participation. Recommendations, reviews and changes were till recently initiated from the cluster level upwards. The cluster-level Review Planning Meeting (RPM) is a forum where information is shared and the project functionaries take stock of the situation on the ground. This is fed to the block-level RPM. The recommendations of the BSG are taken up at the state-level RPM. Essentially this implies that the planning system flows upwards from the cluster level. The database used at the cluster level is generated at the village level—the cycle is set in motion by school mapping. This process developed over the years, and was fine-tuned and adjusted with experience. Its implementation has not been smooth everywhere, but reports from the field are quite encouraging. "People" are the most precious asset of Lok Jumbish and finding the people with the right aptitude and attitude is not easy. Finding women workers is even more difficult. *Mahila shikshan kendras* are partly a response to this problem. Hearteningly, almost all the major policy decisions of the project drew their inspiration and also their strength from below.

Spin-off of Community Empowerment and Participation

Community participation and involvement threw up many challenges. It also opened up many new avenues, which were not part of the original project design. These spin-offs really made Lok Jumbish very different from other projects. Some of these intended and unintended spin-offs are listed below:

1. The problem of girls who suffer due to dearth of opportunities was brought into focus. LJ workers, under pressure to respond to the educational needs of adolescent girls and young women, responded by setting up *mahila shikshan vihar*. These residential condensed courses for adolescent girls and young women also became a means

to identify and train women workers—a rare opportunity in Rajasthan. This is indeed a direct product of community demand and would not have been possible without the involvement of parents.

2. In 1995 the *sahaj shiksha* teachers realized that adolescent girls needed a lot more than the three R's—Reading, Writing and Arithmetic. Building their self esteem and confidence, giving them information about their body, health and hygiene, and just letting them discover the joys of childhood was considered important. *Kishori manch* was thus born.

3. *Balika shikshan shivirs* (short-term adolescent girls' education camps) that help girls bereft of opportunities to catch up and join the formal schools, and build self esteem and self confidence were started. This also would not have happened without the active support and involvement of parents. Winning the confidence of the community to send their girls to a camp speaks for itself. 1,495 girls participated in these camps till April 1997.

4. School preparedness camps for children with disabilities was organized. Again, the problems of such children were brought home through school mapping and through the experience of working with children having moderate to mild disability in Kama Block.

5. Reaching out and working with girls from the *Garasia tribe* (Abu Road camp) was another challenge. Educational processes had totally bypassed this community. Again, bringing girls from this community was possible because of continuous dialogue with parents.

6. *Muktangan pathshalas* are yet another innovation. These "open" schools with flexible timings, where the teacher is available for eight hours to tribal children who come according to their own convenience, were also inspired by the needs of tribal children who wander with their parents collecting minor forest produce.

7. The initiative for surveying buildings, creating committees to oversee repair and maintenance or even new construction, etc., was transferred to the people. When the community became ready, women were trained to supervise construction and the levels of enthusiasm rose high due to the absence of delays. This aspect of LJ is a significant achievement. It also challenges conventional development projects to build infrastructure through people's participation.

Unfortunately there are too many vested interests—especially in the brick and mortar levels of development.

Box 3.2: Statistics at a glance–Lok Jumbish, December 1997

- Blocks covered: 58
- Revenue villages: 9,755
- Environment building done: 5,683
- Core teams formed: 4,420
- *Mahila samooh* formed: 2,816
- School mapping completed: 4,006 (70.49 per cent)
- New primary schools opened: 383
- New Shiksha Karmi schools opened: 454
- Upgradation to upper primary schools: 227
- Additional teachers recruited—primary 752, upper primary 559
- *Sahaj shiksha kendras*: 3,703 (April 1997)
- As of December 1997 14,691 boys and 31,148 girls were studying in *sahaj shiksha kendras*
- Number of *balika shivirs*: 11; number of girls participating: 1,495
- Number of new primary school buildings: 125
- Number of school buildings repaired and rooms constructed: 773
- Cost for repairs were much lower than PWD estimates.
- Worked with minorities to make arrangements for education of girls.

Has Community Participation happened in Lok Jumbish?

The existing evidence, at least up to June 1999, is encouraging. The results in the box above are quite self-explanatory. This does not mean that everything was fine and that there were no problems. Some issues have been taken note of in the annual reports and others have been discussed widely in the project. The issues that came up are outlined below:

1. It is said that all the poor were not involved—some village leaders and families on the fringes were left out. Project documents highlight the need to make school mapping much more inclusive. Lok Jumbish has been working with the middle tier of the society, and it would have to work harder to include the lowest ends of the spectrum.

2. While almost every visitor and evaluator will agree that the village community and the children were energized—a very important factor in an environment of despair—this cannot be said about the formal school system. Evaluations point out that the impact of Lok Jumbish on the teachers and administrators in the formal system has been, at best, patchy.

3. Building a consensus and initiating meaningful consultations is important. But in an unequal society as ours, with unequal access, power and information base, this kind of consensus building is not easy. It is not possible to involve everyone—the powerful, the disempowered, teachers, administrators, etc. Lok Jumbish did make a conscious choice, and in many areas (including the state capital) they alienated powerful people in powerful positions. High-caste leaders and some powerful (again upper-caste) administrators were not very happy with Lok Jumbish's social agenda. It may be recalled that a similar fate befell the women's development programme in Rajasthan. This project, which involved hundreds of very poor women, was not welcomed by upper-caste patriarchs. As a result, it was neglected and left to decay after foreign funds were withdrawn in 1992–93.

4. Lok Jumbish was not able to create the supportive environment highly necessary for girls' participation. The "empowerment" agenda of Lok Jumbish was challenged time and again. Today, in the new phase of the project, this component has been withdrawn.

5. Generating information that is universally accepted, and is legitimate in the eyes of all, is also a contentious issue. Data generated by Lok Jumbish was not accepted by all parties concerned. This led to friction and tension, undermining the efficiency of the project.

Can a Poor, Backward State Afford such Cumbersome Processes?

One of the questions asked in Rajasthan today is "Can a poor, backward state afford such cumbersome and time-, energy- and resource-intensive processes?" Fifty years of experience has shown that there are no short cuts. We have been in so much of a hurry that we have not had the time to plan and move systematically. The initial investment in process-oriented projects may be high, but the returns have been encouraging. Shiksha Karmi and Lok Jumbish workers argue that there is really no other way to ensure the deprived have access, leave alone the ones who are in the margins like Balmikis, Garasias, etc.

Community participation is not a one-time affair. Sustaining meaningful participation demands vigilance. We also need to organize activities and develop mechanisms for continuous involvement, year after year. This needs a very high level of commitment and there is no space for cynicism or despair. The administration has to play a proactive role in sustaining the momentum. Where there is complacency, processes are reversed quickly.

Seven years of experience in Lok Jumbish has shown that community participation is human resource intensive. It needs people with commitment and vision. It needs a supportive environment. In the present scenario, a few NGOs can surely help sustain the momentum, but we have to recognize that not all NGOs have the aptitude or inclination for such processes. If people are the most precious resource, demoralization through administrative red tape, suspicion and disrespect has the potential to kill their initiative.

Another question asked is whether the community needs to be involved in building construction, repair and maintenance? Despite millions of dollars spent on building Primary Health Centres (PHCs) and sub centres under various family welfare projects, the actual quality of buildings is there for all to see. Poor-quality buildings, corruption, lack of ownership—these are familiar pictures in the development chronicles. Unfortunately, the bricks and mortar of development have become ends in themselves. Vested interests of administration linked to the "contractor raj" have opposed any transparency in this field. They have fought tooth and nail against community participation. The village community, which has a stake in good buildings, are the ones who suffer due to this.

Yet another contentious issue that has drawn wide attention in Rajasthan is the need for a women's development component in Lok Jumbish, and *mahila prashikshan kendras* and similar inputs in the Shiksha Karmi project. Government officers, on the other hand, raise the question of the need for *mahila samooh?* The universalization of elementary education will be impossible unless girls are encouraged to participate. Women need space to discuss and gain confidence to articulate their needs and aspirations in a larger forum. They cannot participate effectively in the VEC or even the panchayat unless they gain the confidence to speak and have access to information beyond their immediate present. The experience of the women's development programme has shown that individual leaders get isolated and are not as effective. Therefore, any project or programme that seeks to involve women has to work towards building and sustaining a group. This programme has also shown that rural women have the ability to critically assess their own strengths, and plan and take initiative. The question is not really whether we need a women's group in Lok Jumbish— the actual question is why senior and responsible people in the Rajasthan government do not want women's groups.[4]

Sustainability has remained a big issue in Rajasthan. Programmes and projects have a tendency to be identified with the founders. Given the overall administrative and political environment in the state, societal commitment for basic education, women's development, empowerment of dalits and other backward/disadvantaged classes and communities, etc., cannot be taken for granted. Top-level political or across-the-board administrative commitment is not visible for the above issues. As a result, individual administrators with personal zeal/commitment introduce programmes with an agenda of equality and empowerment. These projects are often relegated to the sidelines by those in power. The rest of the mainstream is at best dismissive. In a feudal social, political and administrative climate, commitment to individuals is given precedence over commitment to an idea or a goal. As a result, such out-of-the-way projects tend to get caught in conflicts.

The women's development project failed to inspire confidence in Rajasthan, even though it was proclaimed a major breakthrough across the country and even in the world. The then prime minister, the late Rajiv Gandhi, hailed it as a landmark in India. This project inspired similar initiatives in other states. However, the bureaucracy and political leaders in

Rajasthan were not impressed. The very fact that a high-caste person was challenged in a rape case was cause enough for the upper-caste leaders of Rajasthan to refuse support for the project. Unfortunately, this feeling ran across party lines.

The Shiksha Karmi project has, thankfully, survived for the last 15 years. The challenge today is whether the community participation dimension of the project will survive in an environment where the very rationale of involvement of the community for promoting primary education is being questioned. Evidence suggests that in phase III of the project systems are being given more attention than participation. Participation could become mechanical where formulas and forms take precedence over content and process. But it is too early to say which way the wind will blow.

However, the same cannot be said about Lok Jumbish—it has been caught in the seven-year jinx. There are many danger signals from above. Despite positive evidence, there is still little appreciation among political leaders and mainstream administrators of the importance of community participation and empowerment in primary education in Rajasthan. These are seen as NGO processes that do not have a legitimate space in the main-stream. Community participation is at the heart of democracy and decen-tralization. Commentators argue that nothing short of a social reform movement will shake the Rajasthan society from its feudal mindset. And this remains the most formidable challenge.

Rajasthan has the distinction of being the home of a range of highly visi-ble innovations in primary education and women's development—the women's development programme of 1984, Shiksha Karmi project of 1987 and Lok Jumbish project of 1992. As mentioned above, all these innovative projects have been entangled in bureaucratic and political bat-tles. The Shiksha Karmi project has managed to survive. The other two have been reduced to a pale shadow of their former image. Sustainability of innovation has remained a problem in the state.

It is in this context that a study of community participation and empow-erment in primary education has to be viewed. On the one hand, the ground situation in Rajasthan is crying out for more decentralized and people-centred approaches to education, women's development and sus-tainable livelihood. On the other hand, there is little evidence—at least among the majority of the political and administrative elite—of commit-ment towards such people-centred processes. Most recently, a senior official of the government who is in charge of Lok Jumbish, the Shiksha Karmi project and DPEP asked,

> What has gender got to do with primary education? Why should an education project waste time on *mahila samooh*, training of women and things like that? This deflects attention from the main business of education.... Similarly, we have a lot of data—district-wise and even school-wise. We can plan with the data we have. Is school mapping necessary to justify opening primary schools and/or Shiksha Karmi schools? A lot of energy, time and money is wasted on these processes.

Having emerged from a predominantly feudal system in 1950, democratic processes and democratic culture are yet to take root. Caste, community and other forces continue to exert a lot of influence in the Rajasthan society. Unlike the ongoing debate in Madhya Pradesh, Andhra Pradesh and Kerala, the debate on community participation and empowerment in primary education and the relationship between women's status and the education of girls has unfortunately been caught up in the rhetoric of personalities and political parties. There is little public debate on these issues in newspapers, in government circles and among the lay public. Travelling around the districts of Rajasthan, one cannot but notice that it is only the very poor who resort to government schools in rural and even in urban areas. Anyone with even a little bit of money prefers to send their children to private schools. Within poor families, also there is a gender dimension—girls, if they are sent, go to government schools. Therefore, the political and the administrative elite of Rajasthan have no stake in improving the quality and outreach of basic education.

People across the country are today asking about the sustainability of innovations, especially when the bureaucracy does not wholeheartedly endorse such innovations. Rajasthan seems to be more susceptible than other regions of the country. Is it because the administrative culture of the state is still feudal and rooted in individual charisma and loyalty? Is it because democratic processes have not taken root? Or is it because no social reform movement has churned up the society enough to make people question age-old values and customs? The answer probably lies in a combination of the above factors. But the fact remains that India has a lot to learn from Rajasthan. However, is Rajasthan willing to learn from the rest of India?

Notes and References

1. Sainath, P. (1999), "This is the Way they Go to School", *The Hindu*, 28 November.
2. Lok Jumbish Worker, 1999.
3. This section of this paper draws upon Vimala Ramachandran and Harsh Sethi "Rajasthan Shiksha Karmi—an overall appraisal"; Desk study commissioned by Sida, Embassy of Sweden, New Delhi, February 2000.
4. The Government of Rajasthan, Director of Lok Jumbish, made the following declaration on 17 January 2000 in the High Court of Judicature of Rajasthan (SB Civil Writ Petition No. 113/2000; Mrs Vijay Laxmi Joshi versus Lok Jumbish and Others): "The petitioner was working in the unit of Women's Development. The same has been abolished and the reason being that because of financial constraint every effort was made to see that the project should be reduced to such an extent that there may not be an excessive burden on the project and also to see at the same time that the very object of the project may be achieved which was related to universalisation of primary education, providing access to primary education for all children upto 14 years and accordingly a decision was taken to abolish the Unit of Women's Development in the project and the same has been done so for the Phase III of the project. The First Phase of Project ended on 30 June 1995. The Second Phase was from 30 June 1998 to 31 December 1999. However for the purpose of transferring the balance fund available with SIDA the latter agreed to pass this fund upto December 1999. The Parishad under such financial constraints was required to restructure itself and exhaustive exercise was carried out in this regard and the following decisions were taken which are as under: (*a*) The Unit of Sahaj Shiksha should be merged into Education for Children of deprived section. (*b*) The School Mapping Unit should be merged into planning, monitoring and evaluation; and (*c*) The Unit of Women's Development to be abolished."

4

Community Participation and Literacy: Beyond Semantics

Sadhna Saxena

The focus of this paper is, in a way, very specific and narrow. The main agenda is to understand the meaning of community participation in the context of mass education, i.e., literacy and primary education. "Community participation" is the latest buzzword in the context of education programmes in particular and development programmes in general. Its arrival on the scene is a bit paradoxical as well. During the last 50 years or so, the grassroots-level groups and people's organizations have criticized the state policies for their elitist bias and the denial of right of participation to the people in framing these policies. And now it is the state which is taking upon itself—at least on paper—the responsibility of ensuring this through Panchayati Raj institutions. More importantly, since the beginning of the process of liberalization, it is not only the government agencies, but also the foreign funding agencies and the World Bank that are talking about community participation loudly.

Community participation has a peculiar glamour and aura attached to it. However, its legitimacy comes primarily due to its acceptability in the progressive arena. More than the aura, it's this air of political correctness and legitimacy that prevents a thorough debate even on the timing, origin and meaning of the *sarkari* and international, top-down notions of community participation. So much is the power of the undefined terminology that within a short time it has come to dominate the discourse on education and development, and has become an essential part of the vocabulary of policy makers, funding organizations, media and NGO activists alike, emerging contradictions and conflicts notwithstanding.

The key words "community" and "participation" remain undefined in any of the documents. There seems to be little concern, even in progressive circles, about how such a longstanding but "unacceptable" demand of the people's organizations, considered too radical hitherto, acquired centre stage in the circles of national and international power. In this context, equally important is the complete marginalization of contentious issues like the purpose and content of education, definition of knowledge, the use of local language or dialect as medium of learning and, of course, the issues of control and decision-making from the education discourse.

Unfortunately, what is missing from the discourse is a critical, constructive and organic analysis of what decentralization and community participation means in a deeper sense—a unanimous understanding is presumed. In a recent article, Shilpa Jain has posed the issue rather sharply:

> The truth is, the Development circle as a whole does not want to "rock the boat" by seriously challenging or changing the underlying power structures, notions of roles, responsibilities, and relationships, or the vision of Development that suffocates our humanity today. They fall into the trap of viewing the decentralised political or educational structures as, at their best, vehicles for making the delivery of State/Market goods and services more efficient, and thereby ensuring an expedient achievement of development. They fail to see "decentralised participation" as little more than a form of insidious manipulation, to ensure that all the world's people succumb to a uniform vision of human beings, human knowledge, human relationships, and human progress.[1]

It is no coincidence that the notion of community participation is being propagated vigorously when the public sector is being condemned for its "inefficiency", privatization is being generally promoted and, under the World Bank–IMF conditionalities, the social sector is experiencing major cuts. It has also to be kept in mind that the government schooling itself is considered a vast, badly managed and inefficient system needing managerial intervention. Community participation, in the long term, envisages the community to not only appoint teachers through village-level committees, but also mobilize resources for running the schools and continuing education centres. Permanent posts of teachers are being replaced with contractual appointments and intensive teachers' training with short-term in-service training.

The process of gradual privatization has to be looked into along with the talk of community participation and international funding coming for quality improvement in primary education. How should these changes be interpreted? At one level primary education is seen as a crucial social sector and it is the responsibility of the state to provide resources for this, and at another level, the state is abdicating from this responsibility in the name of community participation. The moot question is, does the community have the resource to support its children's education and, if yes, what exactly is this community? It certainly cannot be the community of the deprived, which is itself struggling hard to survive.

Total Literacy Campaign (TLC), as the nomenclature suggests, is based on the massive mobilization of people during the environment-building phase. There is a lot of unevenness across the country on how much of this mobilization could be transformed into a sustained programme of adult education or literacy. However, now when the mass-based approach of TLCs seems to have lost its fervour and appeal, community participation is being projected as an answer to most of the problems hindering universalization of literacy and primary education. At such times, it has become important to deconstruct the key words "community" and "participation", both in the light of theoretical and sociological understanding as well as previous experiences in the field.

This article is divided into three sections. In the first section I have tried to trace the place and role assigned to community participation at the policy level and its articulation in actual practice in the (TLCs). This is closely linked to the interpretation given to the term "empowerment" by the TLC leaders. The analysis would be incomplete without including the Post Literacy Campaign (PLC) and Continuing Education (CE) programmes within its ambit.

The second section tries to explore the theoretical underpinnings of the key words "community" and "participation" and the specific connotations they have acquired with reference to classical understanding of communities and their unequal status in a society. It is important to understand how and why they stand defined differently from terms like "people's initiative" or "people's movement", particularly in their relation to the state. This probably circumscribes their effectiveness as tools of social engineering and development.

The third section concludes the argument with an attempt to define the parameters that "community participation" will have to address even as a state-sponsored activity, where mobilization of the public is used as a strategy to build a conducive environment for launching an education programme. We also need to locate literacy and universalization of elementary education movement in the context of the existing movements, political and social, and to recognize the inherent dangers in a simplified, unarticulated approach.

Community Participation in the Literacy Campaigns: Policy and Implementation

From Adult Education Centres to Campaign Mode

Literacy movements or campaigns on a limited scale have a long history in India. Whether it was the widespread library and literacy movement of Andhra Mahasabha in the pre-independence days in Telengana region or the Gram Shiksha Moheem of 1959 in Satara district, Maharashtra, people's participation in the campaigns was the life of these movements. The literacy campaigns were in-built in many political and socio-economic movements and struggles as in the *akil akharas* of the Jharkhand movement, the night classes of the Warli movement of Thane district led by Godavari Parulekar, or the literacy efforts along with fighting for minimum wages in the agricultural labour movement in Chinglepet area of Tamil Nadu or by Bhoomi Sena and Kashtkari Sangathana again in Thane district, Maharashtra.

In spite of this varied history, the governmental efforts have taken a long time to come anywhere near appreciating the crucial role played by people's involvement in such campaigns. In spite of strong recommendations for this approach by the Education Commission (1964–66) and the National Board of Adult Education (1970), the governmental policies plumbed for the functional literacy approach within the framework of the "Community Development Programmes". Among the notable features of this phase was the emergence of the concept of "village community" as the focus of developmental inputs. Placed in the immediate context of facilitating widespread introduction of the Green Revolution technologies, the programme was heavily supported by international funds.

The upheavals and social turmoil of the late 1960s and 1970s, culminating in the post-emergency upsurge, paved the way for the formulation of the "Draft Policy Statement of Adult Education" followed by the launching of the National Adult Education Programme (NAEP) on 2 October 1978. Ostensibly inspired by the writings of Paulo Friere about his work in Latin America and Guinea Bissau, the NAEP professed a people-centred approach to adult education. Some of us who had the privilege of having "a ring-side seat" on the process of formulation of the policy and programme documents, saw to our consternation the gradual dilution of this perspective even as the policy and programme documents were being finalized. As with many other formations that emerged in the post-emergency euphoria, the NAEP also lost its fizz within a couple of years.

However, the NAEP made significant gains on some fronts. The Government of India for the first time committed substantial amounts of funds from its budget for adult education. Further, for the first time the focus of adult education was shifted from the earlier functional objectives to conscientization. With a long-term perspective, institutions and structures to organize and support adult education were set up from national down to district and block levels. A major role was designed for voluntary organizations within the programme.

Perhaps the most significant lesson from the NAEP effort lay in its failure to mobilize the people for literacy and adult education. Bureaucratic delays in releasing funds to small organizations that were running the centres also played a crucial role in the failure of this ambitious programme. With the issue of people's active involvement emerging as a central concern, reports about the Nicaraguan Literacy Crusade of the early 1980s rekindled the discourse on literacy efforts. Along with the Chinese and Cuban success stories, the efforts of Father Fernando Cardenal and his literacy brigades implanted the idea of an intensive, nationwide mass campaign for literacy in many minds.

In this scenario came the National Policy on Education, 1986, followed by its "Programme of Action" that led to the formation of the National

Literacy Mission (NLM). The NLM was conceived as a "societal mission" to demonstrate that "there is a political will at all levels for the achievement of Mission goals...a national consensus...for mobilization of social forces, and mechanisms...for active participation of the people". Mass mobilization and people's involvement were identified as one of the key issues for the success of the NLM.

The potential of organizing a nationwide mass campaign was first demonstrated very effectively by the Bharat Jan Vigyan Jatha (BJVJ) of 1987, albeit on the slogan of "Science for the People". The All India People's Science Network (AIPSN) emerged from the BJVJ of 1987 with the Kerala Shastra Sahitya Parishad (KSSP) playing a leading role. The realization that the prevailing high levels of illiteracy could be a major impediment to building up a people's science movement led to adoption of literacy as a major agenda. This coincided with the NLM's search for a vehicle for mass mobilization, eventually leading to the formation of the Bharat Gyan Vigyan Samiti (BGVS) as a major collaborator of the NLM in organizing a nationwide literacy campaign. The *kala jatha* of 1990 took the message of literacy far and wide, linking it to many livelihood problems. It succeeded in an unprecedented mobilization leading to literacy getting placed as a national agenda.

The environment thus built up had to be channelized into an effective programme of literacy learning. The model for this was provided by the KSSP through the TLC of Ernakulam district, which sparked of a host of TLCs in many other districts in a phased manner. The rest is history, even if not very distant. The challenge of moving from the already high-literacy-level districts of Kerala and other South Indian states to the more backward North Indian states was taken up with enthusiasm. The race between districts to declare themselves totally literate was seriously joined. In the initial heady days it was almost "anti-literacy" to ask for a critical appraisal of the model adopted. But now as the dust has settled and more authentic versions of the experiences are emerging, a sober analysis of the entire experience seems feasible.

TLC Model and the Post-TLC Scenario

There can be many dimensions to such an analysis, but given the scope of this paper, I would attempt to focus on the issue of people's mobilization or community participation and its contribution to the post TLC scenario. It was realized very early that the gains of the TLCs must be consolidated immediately in order to prevent their disappearance into thin air. The Post Literacy Campaign (PLC) and the Continuing Education (CE) programme were designed keeping precisely this in mind. Assuming successful mobilization of people's initiative in the TLCs, the PLC and CE have been designed basically as community-sustained initiatives. The state of PLC and CE in the TLC districts is a good indicator of the extent and quality of community participation in the TLC phase. But before we proceed to report and analyze the experiences let us look at the elements of community participation incorporated in the TLC model.

The initiation of the TLC through a massive environment-building campaign was a strong step towards mobilizing people, both literate and illiterate, for the cause of eradicating illiteracy. This mobilization was further organized by the formation of Zilla Saksharta Samitis and similar subordinate structures right down to the block, town, panchayat, village, *basti* and *mohalla* levels, involving community leaders and representatives at various levels. The house-to-house survey to identify illiterates and using that information to organize learning groups, with the teaching responsibility entrusted to a volunteer, was also meant to mobilize local initiative. Training-and learning-material preparation were two areas where varying degrees of centralization were envisaged. These along with evaluation seem to have emerged as strong areas of centralization with rigorous enforcement of IPCL (Improved Pace Content Learning) norms at the central level.

By its very nature, the model has heavily relied on the leadership of the district-level bureaucracy with the Collector as its powerful, hierarchical head. In effect, then, all efforts at people's participation de facto depend on his or her benevolence and the good work done by committed Collectors could always be undone by their successors. This has been in direct contradiction with a basic premise of the TLC model—"the community with its reservoir of innate wisdom, idealism and voluntarism should be allowed adequate space in owning and supporting the programme", along with the intended strategy of "de-linking the implementation machinery from Government bureaucracy to increase dynamism and flexibility, and at the same time, ensure strict accountability by stringent monitoring by the people themselves."[2]

NLM took almost four to five years to formulate its strategies and guidelines for the post-literacy and continuing education programmes. The approach to continuing education envisages involvement of the community at four levels. These levels are:

1. Raising critical awareness, enhancing functional capabilities and facilitating organization of neo-literates for collective action within the larger perspective of empowerment.
2. Formation of popular committees, especially at the block and village levels, to provide leadership and direction and take management responsibility of the PL and CE centres and the programme itself. This role also envisages resource mobilization, including financial resources from the community itself.
3. Involvement of the community in determining the nature of learning and skill upgradation or vocational training programmes.
4. Promotion of voluntarism and assigning roles to volunteers in various aspects of community life.[3]

The revised Programme of Action (1992) had spelt out the three important learning objectives of PLC as redemption, continuation and application, and declared that the role and function of the PLCs would be to ensure that the community is fully involved in planning and implementation of the post-literacy programmes, the ultimate objective being to organize the unorganized. It was perceived that the PL and CE centres would function more efficiently under the direction and guidance of the people's committees set up at the village level instead of getting directions from the district level. They would work through a culture of solidarity building and group formation among the neo-literates, and collective action around worthwhile economic or common well-being-oriented activities like health, environment, vitalization of community forums, etc.

While in the TLC phase the overriding concern has remained the achievement of literacy norms in quantitative evaluations, the working group for the ninth five-year plan document in 1996 emphasized a shift towards qualitative processes—activities, structures and mechanisms aimed at strengthening the people's movement character. It was also envisaged that the PL programmes would be supported by the government for two years after which they would gradually transform into self-reliant, community-supported education centres. The Continuing Education

Centre (CEC) is perceived as a permanent, institutionalized arrangement to meet the learning needs of the neo-literates. It is also seen as a people's institution with its management and ownership in the hands of the people. The financial assistance extended to the CEC is made conditional upon the financial and material resources mobilized by the community.

Thus the community is supposed to play a vibrant and active role in sustaining and consolidating the achievements of the TLCs. The success of the PL and CE schemes hinged on the hope that the mobilization initiative and participation generated during the TLC phase could be consolidated in setting up centres of sustained learning. Though at the policy level there was a change in the conception of PL, according to Mathew: Prior to 1998, the PL programmes were regarded and implemented as a continuation of the TLCs, implemented essentially in a mission mode and with a campaign approach. This changed after 1998. Now the post literacy endeavour is not to be regarded as a campaign but as a programme.[4]

The problems with such a scheme are manifold. Apart from the "community" itself being a problematic notion, in a village society there is not one but many communities which are unequally placed. When any policy document emphasizes community participation, which community is being talked about?

The PL and CE schemes were endorsed almost five years after the Ernakulam declaration and completion of several TLCs in other districts. This was the phase when the literacy movement was on the decline, as has been recorded in various studies. So whatever potential for consolidation of community mobilization that may have existed in the post-TLC phase was also eroded due to the time gap.

So far CE programmes have been sanctioned for 60 to 70 districts and it may be too early to say anything about their fate. Field reports indicate a highly uneven CE scene across the country, not only between different states, but also among different districts within a state. According to Mathew, "PLC perspective was turned upside-down since 1998 and there is no trace of any people's character left either in conception or design and implementation."[5] About the dilution of the people's movement character, he writes,

What made the dilution of the movement character, as evident in the conceptual evolution, particularly adverse was its simultaneity with the hectic pace of expansion. With TLCs becoming almost history by 1998–99, and PL having been turned into a bureaucratic programme as any other government programme or as the NAEP, with the *Prerak* replacing the community involvement oriented PLC, it made little sense to locate CE at the heart of the community in terms of their involvement and support. The serious deviation in NLM policy has irretrievably turned the programme into the old disreputed tract of target orientation.[6]

TLC: People's Movement or Mobilization?

People's movement character of TLCs was also highly uneven across the country as is evident from the range of accounts available, for example, from Pudukkottai[6] to Rohtak.[7] Recent studies from some of the front-runner districts in their TLC phase—Ernakulam, Pudukkottai, Ajmer, Dumka and Bilaspur—also do not present an encouraging picture. Ajmer district, which the author visited recently, seems to have no remnants left of a once very energetic TLC.

It is interesting and probably not unexpected to note that the focus of mass education shifted from adult literacy to universalizing elementary education from the early 1990s. This was the time when the euphoria generated over the dramatic achievements of literacy campaigns—including empowerment of women—was on the decline. Even Sudha Sundararaman, herself a very active leader of the TLC in Pondicherry, did admit decline by raising questions such as: "Why are literacy movements collapsing today? Why has the Total Literacy Campaign been a nine day, or to be precise, a five year wonder only? Why could these campaigns not be sustained?" She also observes that "today literacy campaigns appear to be largely losing their transformatory potential and are increasingly degenerating into routine governmentalised schemes."[8]

Despite this, it was probably too early to engage in any kind of in-depth analysis, for even in 1996 any questioning of, or discomfort with, the tall claims of achievement of total literacy led to immense resentment, if not outright contempt and condemnation. The situation obviously was much more so when this author wrote the first article questioning the total literacy declaration at Narsinghpur district in Madhya Pradesh in 1993.[9]

Undermining the hard work of individuals, especially the grassroots volunteers, was never the objective—the effort has always been to look beyond that and engage in a critical appraisal. The concern has been about the future and disillusionment of the unpaid literacy workers—the volunteers, the representatives of the community. Generally, after the TLC phase, the volunteers at the grassroots level were left disillusioned and directionless. This sentiment has been expressed very strongly in recent studies in some TLC districts. Even in Nellore, famous for its anti-arrack agitation, in 1996, BGVS activists had expressed their sense of being let down.[10] We must remember that it was the neo-literate women in Nellore who interpreted the anti-drinking messages in their primers into a full-blown anti-arrack agitation, which shook the roots of the state government. The subsequent response of the state was to crack down on the literacy campaign, leaving the motivated volunteers in a daze. Such actions arose out of a fundamental opposition to the literacy campaigns transgressing the boundaries of caste, class and gender, despite the claims of community mobilization and participation. Nellore was a transgression of the boundaries of awareness laid down by the state and crossing them jeopardized the legitimacy of the seemingly progressive agenda of literacy.

However, the euphoria of state-managed total literacy could not be sustained for too long. The disconcerting voices became too loud for the state to ignore. The turning point came with the harsh comments of the Arun Ghosh Committee, especially on the method of quantitative evaluations and claims of total literacy, and with the TLC's entry into northern states. Unlike some of the districts of the southern states such as Pudukkottai or Nellore or Pondicherry, this expansion was not accompanied with success stories. In the southern states also there were no more shining stars and the eastern successes of Midnapore and Barddhaman faded soon as well. Of late, studies in Ernakulam, Dumka, Ajmer, Pudukkottai and Ganjam are also not coming up with very encouraging findings. Relapse into illiteracy is almost universal and quite understandably also. There are stories of dashed hopes of the volunteers, along with a lack of evidence of political awareness. On the contrary, individuals often continue to see poverty as a condition of their own making or as given. The TLC efforts at awareness raising at times seem to have sold dominating social myths and ideologies quite effectively.

Bureaucratization, loss of voluntary spirit, discredited internal and external evaluations, delay in starting post-literacy and continuing education programmes, etc. are impediments that are widely talked about. Not so widely discussed, however, is the disillusionment of the people, which is expressed in form of symbolic rage at times. This brings us to another point which needs attention. As stated before, literacy was provided as the solution to all the problems of the underprivileged and this is repeated in various government documents in different ways. One such document states, "The mass literacy programme will include, in addition to literacy, functional knowledge and skills, also awareness among learners about the socio-economic reality and the possibility to change it."[11] And also, as the first Director-General of the NLM states, such programmes would make learners "perceive and internalise their plight and predicament, correlate that plight to illiteracy and innumeracy, and discover the wherewithal for liberation through literacy."[12]

The important political underpinnings of such statements are not to be missed. The illiterate people are deemed responsible for their plight due to illiteracy, and not the oppressive social, political and patriarchal structures. Literacy documents are replete with such expressions, which suggest the onus of their plight is on them. Oft-repeated statements such as "Devdasis of Andhra Pradesh and Karnataka started correlating their own predicament to the illiteracy, and innumeracy and resolved that they would not allow this to happen to their supporters", and "thousands of contract labourers in the steel plant at Durgapur in Barddhaman district of West Bengal began to perceive the roots of their plight and predicament in illiteracy and innumeracy and resolved to become literate and numerate to put an end to that plight"[13] reveal a strong ideological thrust in the attempts at awareness raising or "conscientisation."

It is worth noting that one of the major achievements of literacy programmes is cited as the bringing of mass education on to the national agenda. People demand and struggle for minimum wages, land, employment, rights to forest produce, food at subsidized rates, drinking water, etc. None of these issues have been brought on the national agenda through literacy programmes or through massive mobilization of volunteers. These are issues of survival of the marginalized and deprived people. However, the politics of literacy campaigns manages to push them back from becoming issues of national urgency by ignoring them. These issues have no doubt come up in some of the districts either because of a history of people's movements, or the special efforts of one or two individuals. However, the national policy and agenda do not highlight minimum wages or effective implementation of the public distribution system. In a country where nearly one third of its population is forced to live under sub-human conditions, the reason for the nationwide mass mobilization not bringing survival issues on the national agenda can only be political. With the same population forming the majority of the illiterate, they fail to perceive the literacy campaign as involving or concerning them.

Are any of these outcomes of a state-sponsored, high-profile campaign surprising or unexpected? Could there have been empowerment of the people, as hoped by some, without disempowerment of the powerful elite? And could all this happen without struggle and confrontation? There is an inherent contradiction between the state and the community. However, this contradiction is not as apparent in the context of literacy as it is in the context of women's issues. The state and its patriarchal character stand exposed due to the presence of a strong and autonomous—not funded or sponsored by the government—women's movement.

Despite this difference, during literacy campaigns, in some of the districts, mobilization of the people by grassroots-level volunteers—themselves rooted in the same social reality and sometimes also victims of exploitation and cultural oppression—led to a kind of social and political upheaval. Consequences of such upsurges precipitated the contradiction between the people and the state and created a situation of conflict. Much as we would like to celebrate such sporadic "successes" the short-lived nature of these cannot be overlooked. Unless there is a base of strong political movement or mobilization, larger forces always manage to overcome such spontaneous movements and diffuse the community's involvement. This is what happened in these districts as well. Without the engagement of the people in a political struggle, can there really be a sustained process of mobilization and community participation? This also depends on how we define the community. TLCs are often referred to as literacy movements or people's movements. And sometimes, peoples' mobilization is used interchangeably with people's movement.

All the boundary conditions for literacy programmes are laid down by the state to the last detail. Though Nellore happened in spite of this, no stone was left unturned—including threat of punitive action, ban on distribution of post-literacy books, transfer of the Collector who helped postpone the auction of arrack outlets a number of times, and so on—to diffuse the upsurge. The literacy programme in Nellore district did not start in a political vacuum, as a host of reports seem to suggest. Nellore and the surrounding districts have had a decade-long history of anti-arrack agitation. The naxalites are also stated to have led it. This history was the bedrock of the anti-arrack agitation, which surfaced during the literacy mobilization. The women of the district were pushed to the wall with the state's arrack policies in the 1970s and 1980s when the arrack packets were despatched to the village houses through the henchmen of the liquor contractors turned politicians and politicians turned liquor contractors. The role of the various state governments in Andhra Pradesh was clearly anti-poor and pro-liquor-lobby. It actually taxed the poor through the sale of liquor to collect revenue instead of taxing the rich. All this is lucidly brought out by the articles that appeared in the columns of *Economic and Political Weekly* during the anti-arrack agitation.[14] The TLC leadership at the state or national levels did not take a clear stand vis-à-vis the punitive actions.

What is this literacy movement then? Where does it lead a genuine movement of women's empowerment to? The world over there have been political and social movements with workers and peasants as vanguards. The last three to four decades have seen the emergence of new social movements such as autonomous women's movements, environmental movements and civil rights movements. A question worth pondering is, where does one situate the literacy movement in this context?

Roughly, the pattern which has emerged in India is that TLCs made headway in districts where there was either a history of social or political movement, or an autonomous group, which was rooted in the district—be it Tamil Nadu Science Forum or KSSP. In the other areas where the programme was totally controlled by the bureaucratic machinery, it could hardly be called a movement. The state-sponsored mobilization of people during the short environment-building phase cannot be equated with a movement. Evidently, the "movement" collapsed whenever a sensitive and enthusiastic district Collector was replaced.

Manisha Priyam, who travelled with the literacy *jatha* in four districts of Bihar—Jahanabad, Dhanbad, Gaya and Arrah in 1993—reported that the environment-building programme of literacy was a tremendous success in these districts as it rode piggyback on the other existing or earlier movements. She further reported, "J.P. movement may not have been a very cohesive force but its activists, the ex-Sangharsh Vahini people, played a crucial role in that phase. They were able to relate to the people through literacy songs, which they composed."[15]

Keeping these subtleties in mind, a few questions that arise are: What is the literacy movement after all? Can there be a movement without an agenda for transformation and struggle? Can there be a state-supported movement? What would such a movement stand for? If literacy is a movement, what kind of leadership has emerged? Who are the leaders?

Deconstructing "Community" and "Participation"

However much the progressive NGOs participating in the TLC would like to believe that their social and political stands remain uncompromised, in their efforts of celebrating the success of the agenda of community participation, they often start echoing the government sentiments. This could well be their strategy for retaining the space for larger political goals. However, those larger goals have remained elusive so far. Also, their articulation of stands from public forums sometimes brings them rather close to the government's stand. Two of this author's recent, revealing experiences regarding community participation are a case in point. One was with the BGVS national-level leaders in a national workshop on continuing education and the other was with a senior DPEP functionary speaking from an NGO forum on the importance of the community's role in universalization of primary education. On both the occasions, the two very different people were eulogizing the successes of community participation in their respective arenas, i.e., literacy and PE. On both the occasions the participants asked them remarkably similar questions: Community is not a homogeneous notion. It is either various communities unequally and differently placed within a society, or various groups in a community unequally placed. Can an education programme or movement overlook this reality? What is education for—maintaining the status quo in the name of peace and harmony or challenging it and opening avenues for transformation—at least in the minds and attitudes of the people? Can the struggle for equality, equity and dignity be divorced from education?

The responses were also remarkably similar. While there was no disagreement on the heterogeneity in the communities and conflict between various vested interests, there was a sense of satisfaction also. Literacy campaigns and DPEP work, they said, had been able to transgress the problems of inequality within the communities. In any case, "why discuss about these issues and create further cleavage", said the DPEP functionary. The community is divided and the divisions are deeply entrenched, a participant from Bihar insisted. Would the educationists at least try to understand its impact on the lives of people at the lowest level and train the volunteers to keep their eyes and ears open towards humiliating discriminations which exist, another one asked. The discussion on both the occasions reached a dead-end.

Never before in the history of education in India has there been a government education programme so widely covered by the media, which has generated so much curiosity and interest, and earned the goodwill of the people as TLCs. And also probably never before have so many actors of the civil society—NGOs, journalists, social scientists, teachers and independent philanthropists—been engaged as observers, evaluators, trainers or reporters as in the TLCs. On the one hand, this shows the power and outreach of the state and, on the other, the weak trends and powerlessness in the civil society. Thus, by participating in the literacy campaigns on the state's initiative, actors of the civil society helped the state in putting up a pro-people face, radicalizing it in a way. The "creation of liberal space" argument does not hold much water, as it has never been clearly spelt out how this would be utilized in building consciousness and awareness in the people independent of the state.

According to Neera Chandhoke:

Civil societies are defined by the practices of their inhabitants. These practices may lead to the sphere becoming a captive of the State. Equally, the sphere may realise its potential for mounting a powerful challenge to state-oriented practices. The presence of civil society is a crucial, but not an adequate precondition for ensuring State accountability. Whether the State can be made accountable depends upon the self-consciousness, the vibrancy, and the political visions of the civil society. An inactive civil society leads to unresponsive States; a politically self-conscious civil society imposes limits upon State power. And if the political practices of a self-conscious civil society transgress and transcend the boundaries of the State-sponsored political discourse, a crisis of legitimacy of the State results.[16]

The question is whether the boundaries of state-sponsored political discourse were transgressed or those laid down by the state were accepted in the literacy programme. The experience is that the boundaries were not crossed and hence the legitimacy of the state was not challenged. "For the legitimacy of the State lasts precisely as long as the 'political public', in the words of Habermas, accepts the boundaries prescribed by the State and the political activity is contained within these boundaries."

Mass education and mass literacy are important for any society and this need not be stated. However, the content, organization and political objectives need scrutiny. Claims of empowering potential have to be judged or assessed against the disempowerment of the powerful elite. Power to the underprivileged presupposes struggle for power-sharing, a concept obviously not entertained in any government-sponsored empowerment programme, be it literacy, women's empowerment or elementary education.

On the contrary, in the context of education, the notion of community participation envisages different social and economic groups under one hegemonic notion of a community. "Mobilizing the community", "involving the community", "going to the community" have become the ultimate catch phrases to silence any questions regarding the inefficacy of decentralization and democratization without power-sharing through struggle. Education per se probably cannot actively play a leading role in a political struggle. However, it certainly plays a role in making people underplay and overlook the domination of groups and individuals in a heterogeneous society.

Historically, the community development programme was one which was based on the notion of overlooking the division in the rural community. A.R. Desai writes in his famous book on rural sociology:

The word "community development" itself is a novel nomenclature in India. As the report of the Team for the Study of the Community projects and National Extension Services (popularly known as the Balwantrai Mehta Committee Report) states, "We have so far used such terms as rural development, constructive work, adult education and rural uplift to denote certain of its aspects. The word 'community' has, for the past many decades, denoted religious or caste groups or, in some instance, economic group not necessarily living in one locality. But with the inauguration of CDP in this country, it is intended to apply it to the concept of the village community as a whole, cutting across caste, religious and economic differences."[17]

Prof. Desai further writes, "The organizations for rural change are dominated by the upper sections of the rural population. As pointed out by the Programme Evaluation Report, 'When one considers the pattern of membership in village organizations, be they co-operative societies, *vikas mandals, gram panchayats* or *nyaya panchayats*, one clearly finds that the membership is confined to the large cultivators and that the smaller cultivators as well as landless agricultural labourers, have practically no stake in the organizations of the village'."[18]

An analysis of the experiences of CDP is not intended here. However, it will not be out of place to reproduce some portions of Prof. S.C. Dube's report, referred to by Prof. Desai, which is an excellent commentary on the experience of noble intentions of bringing the community together resulting in reinforcing the power structure of the village community. Inconsequential as it may be for the educationists, grim realities, which have become grimmer over the years, have to be stated nevertheless. As Prof. Dube pointed out:

The Community Development Project sought the co-operation of the existing village institutions such as the village panchayat and the *adalati* panchayat schools and co-operative societies. Persons holding offices in these bodies or otherwise prominent in the activities were regarded as "Village Leader", and the development officials made a special effort to work closely with them. Some others who had contacts with politicians and officials were also included in this category and, were consulted in matters connected with the project .... Thus a group of village people having contacts with the world of officials and politicians largely came to be viewed as the local agents of change .... The first mistake was in assuming that these people were the leaders .... Because of their association with the officials and the urban ways of life these leaders as a group had come to possess a special status within the community, but the average villager did not trust them without reservations. Some of the common stereotypes regarding government officials applied in a modified form to these village officials who were recognised as sharing a semi-government status .... Among others included in the category of "traditional leaders" were the important and influential people in the village .... Naturally most of them were from the dominant landowning group. In identifying power and status with leadership, an important and emerging aspect of group dynamics was ignored .... The undue emphasis in working with "traditional leaders" was construed by villagers as an effort on the part of the Government to maintain a status quo in the internal power relations within the village communities and indirectly as a step to support the domination of the landowning groups.[19]

Almost all the evaluators drew the same conclusions, Prof. Desai wrote. He also points out that Dube's observations on *shramdan* as a voluntary movement of village self-help deserves attention as well. Dube wrote in his report:

> The village elite, as well as the upper status groups have, on the whole, welcomed the *shramdan* drives, and through them the construction and repairs of roads. They gained from it in two ways. First, the repaired and newly built roads facilitated the transport of their sugarcane and grain. Secondly, in these drives they could assert their position of leadership and prestige in the village ... because of their status they assumed supervisory roles in this work, and left the hardest and less desirable part of the job to be done by the people of the lower status and lower income groups. They not only had to work hard, but they also lost the wages for the day, which they otherwise might have earned. This explains why many of them viewed this thing as a revival of *begar*, a practice under which influential landowners and government officials compelled the poorer people to work without wages or at nominal wages and which is now prohibited by law.[20]

Community Participation: What could it Mean?

In the context of TLCs, community mobilization primarily meant community participation during the environment-building phase. The response to this strategy has been uneven across districts, as has been reported in writings and press reports—from extreme enthusiasm to a damp squib. In many places even the environment-building phase was stage managed and bureaucratized. The enthusiastic response to mobilization in several districts, such as Pudukkottai, Nellore, Chittoor, Jahanabad, Gaya, Midnapore, Dumka and many others, is a reminder of the interest shown by some sections of the "community".

In the post-literacy campaigns, and now post-literacy and continuing education programmes, an even more active role is expected. As the education departments of a few states, especially Madhya Pradesh and Rajasthan, are talking in terms of decentralization and "handing over" the responsibilities of primary education to village education committees, a new power elite and new power alignments are likely to emerge. How much of this centrally controlled decentralization, without any strong political organization of the underprivileged people, is going to democratize the polity is still to be seen. There is no disagreement that the scenario is going to be quite action-filled and complex.

I would like to end this article with a grim reminder of atrocities on women, dalits, tribals and poor people, which are on the rise. This is basically to remind all of us how unfeasible a homogenous, harmonious and peaceful notion of a village or an urban community is, however noble the objectives may be. Unfeasible is probably an understatement as unequally placed different communities need nothing short of political power to overthrow the hegemonic structures of oppression. The state designs literacy programmes but it neither allows the realization of its functional goals nor the goals of empowerment. The functional goals may not even be achievable without structural changes. In any case, like the undifferentiated notion of community, the goals and purpose of education remain out of the agenda of such a discourse. Unanimity on this issue cannot be assumed. Education for empowerment presumes development of not just the functional skills, but ability to analyze the society and also to be able to change it.

One doesn't have to look for cases of caste oppression in the columns of academic journals or sit through academic discourses in universities. Information, if at all it is power, is littered all around us. P. Sainath has been regularly writing on this issue, covering discrimination children face in schools as well, in the columns of *The Hindu*. A visit to any of the schools, urban slum or rural school, is an eye opener. Even if "all is well", one may find a dalit student made to sweep the classroom, upper-caste children withdrawn because of the appointment of a dalit teacher or harijan children not able to attend school as they are not allowed to pass through the fields of upper-caste farmers. These incidents seem to be particularly less harmful when compared to many other where a slight challenge to the "norms" leads to violent oppression. Children in the village schools sit on floors or different *phattis*, and are addressed derogatorily by the teachers and fellow students. Silent acceptance of numerous forces of humiliation certainly leaves the environment peaceful and probably "harmonious" too. Certain other manifestations of such humiliation and indignity inflicted on the people could be non-violent but alarming when people "peacefully" either drop out or withdraw from educational institutions.

However, when people decide to assert their identities and exercise democratic rights elsewhere, things no more remain peaceful and harmonious. This does not happen only in the villages or schools. Higher educational institutions are as engulfed by this as primary rural schools. The recent incidents in a medical college of Shahdara, Delhi, are a case in point. Dalit students in this college are alloted a separate floor in the hostel and separate tables in the mess, and are addressed as *shaddus* by other students. This was going on peacefully and "harmoniously" for years until last year when some dalit students could take it no more. The result was a violent reprisal, uproar, some media coverage and denials by the college authorities, and a "peaceful settlement" for the dalit students who faced the possibility of losing a year and ruining their career.

Public memory is short. However, Chunni Kotal's story from West Bengal still haunts us. Her life and death is a chilling reminder of the fact that for dalits, tribals and poor people there are no short cuts to a life of dignity, and the struggle for equality is long-drawn. As Mahashweta Devi reminds us, Chunni Kotal was the first graduate from the Lodha-Savana and Keria-Savana tribe. She worked as an agricultural labourer and studied along with that. She was harassed all through her struggle for higher education by the upper-caste and upper-class people. When she tried to do a post-graduation in Anthropology, the harassment reached its peak and she committed suicide. Mahashweta Devi writes, "In West Bengal, even after so many years of Left Front rule, the first woman graduate from a very backward tribe was openly abused because of low caste and birth and nothing was done about it. No one was ashamed, no one cared."[21]

Susie Tharu, who has reviewed Mahashweta Devi's book, writes,

> This story of Indian education is only one of the many chilling accounts in the collection. Tribal people constitute about one tenth of the country's population, yet they account for over half of those actually displaced by dams and other large development projects .... Hunger is endemic in these areas and inevitably therefore also malnutrition and disease. Drinking water is scarce, the water table falling rapidly. There are few doctors. As a rule tribal children, like dalit children, do not make it to school. If they do, they are unlikely to survive.[22]

Community participation in the context of education entered the arena of policy documents at a time when the notion of community was also invoked by a number of social scientists who were critical of understanding the Indian social system through western categories, particularly the categories that give centrality to the so-called "rational individual." Analysing this trend, Jodhka writes in a recent article,

> For some, recognition and revival of community was important because it could become a medium through which one could counter the growing violence and alienation in our society and protect the native cultural traditions. For others, recognition of community differences was important for a genuine democratisation of the Indian society. It was only through such recognition, they argued, that the process of homogenisation that was first initiated by the colonial rulers but was being continued by the post-colonial State as well could be countered.[23]

Caste and gender discrimination is rampant in all educational institutions and so is class discrimination. The extent is so enormous that it is not deemed wise to touch these volatile issues. It is considered best to look the other way or, even better, to internalize this as the norm in the society.

Coming back to "community participation", one expresses a concern with a deep sense of anguish and sadness. TLCs, despite all their political underpinnings and agenda, were a massive social intervention and did catch the imagination of a large number of students and young and energetic people in some parts of the country. What creative awareness-building options or avenues did these interventions open for them? The agenda has always been top-heavy and internationally driven—from the initial total literacy campaign, to the post-literacy and now continuing education programmes, to the formation of self-help groups. There was no scope for documenting their experiences and for sharing the grim village-level realities they encountered without being burdened with target-oriented, top-heavy agendas. Did these hundreds and thousands of volunteers develop a deeper understanding of the social realities? Did they go back as socially more aware persons? Perhaps they did in some districts, but that was not because of literacy but rather in spite of it being their immediate agenda. And how many of them lingered on in the hope that this voluntary work may land them a *sarkari naukri*, only to be frustrated in their hopes!

Village education committees and power to the panchayats are indeed welcome changes. However, such actions loose their significance in a hierarchical rural society unless the political organizations of the powerless are strong enough to counter the attacks on dalit panchs, sarpanchs, ward members and dalit women, as has been documented by many. So far, it's only in Rajasthan that a forum fighting for dalit woman panchs and sarpanchs has been heard of.

Any attempt to involve people or to give them control over their lives in principle needs to be struggled for. In that context, all genuine attempts at community participation have to be welcomed. But the warning sounded by actual experience also needs to be taken seriously. Given the fractured state of our social polity on the lines of class, caste, religion, region, gender and ethnicity, presided over by an overtly bureaucratic state, "community participation" can very easily acquire dangerous and retrogressive forms. This only implies that we need to deconstruct and spell out our understanding in greater detail rather than oversimplify it. And this understanding can acquire strength only by analyzing previous experiences and encouraging more interventions in the field.

Notes and References

1. Jain, Shilpa (2000), "Rethinking Centralisation for Nurturing Learning Societies", *Vimukti Shiksha*, March.
2. See Mathew, A. (2000), *Indian Engagement with Adult Education and Literacy*, in EFA Assessment 2000, New Delhi: NIEPA and MHRD, p. 16.
3. Ibid., p. 37
4. Ibid., p. 36
5. Ibid., p. 40

6. See Athreya, Venkatesh B. and Sheela Rani Chunkath (1996), *Literacy and Empowerment*, New Delhi: Sage Publications.

7. See Chaudhary, Rajender (2000), "An Insider's Review of the TLC", *Mainstream*, vol. XXXVIII, no. 22.

8. Sundararaman, Sudha (1996), "Literacy Campaigns: Lessons for Women's Movement", *Economic and Political Weekly*, 18 May, vol. 31, no. 20, pp. 1193–97.

9. See Saxena (1992) "Myth of Total Literacy in Narsinghpur", *Economic and Political Weekly*, vol. 27, no. 45, pp. 2408–10.

10. Saxena, Sadhna (2000), *Shiksha Aur Janandolan*, New Delhi: Granthshilpi Publications, pp. 171–88.

11. MHRD (1986), *National Policy on Education 1986*, New Delhi: GOI, p. 9.

12. Mishra, Laxmidhar (1998), "National Literacy Mission: Retrospect and Prospect", *Economic and Political Weekly*, vol. XXXIII, no. 44, p. 2811.

13. Ibid., p. 2812.

14. See Saxena 2000, cited in note 10 above.

15. Priyam, Manisha (1994), "Field Report from Bihar", unpublished.

16. Chandhoke, Neera (1995), *State and Civil Society*, New Delhi: Sage Publications, p. 10.

17. Desai, A.R. (1987), *Rural Sociology in India*, Bombay: Popular Prakashan, p. 611.

18. Ibid.

19. Ibid., p. 619.

20. Ibid., p. 619–20.

21. Tharu, Susie (1998), "Chuni's Story", *Economic and Political Weekly*, vol. XXXIII, no. 46, p. 2916.

22. Ibid.

23. Jodhka, Surinder (1999), "Community and Identities: Interrogating Contemporary Discourses on India", *Economic and Political Weekly*, vol. XXXIV, no. 41, p. 2959.

5

The Community in Charge: Shades of Experience from Madhya Pradesh

Anjali Noronha

Ideally, education should be seen as a partnership between teachers, parents/community and students. This oft-mentioned statement tends to become rhetorical in the absence of any concrete manifestation of this partnership. Though the role of the teacher and the student are fairly clear, the roles of the parent and community are quite nebulous. In any reference to "community involvement in education", it is necessary to define (*a*) the meaning of community, (*b*) the nature of its involvement and (*c*) the aspects of education in which involvement is referred to. Community has been variously defined in the discourse on education as "parents", the "larger community" and "elected representatives" or members of such local structures as village education committees (VECs).

It is apparent here that "community" is not a homogeneous, monolithic entity, but one that lends itself to varying interpretation. It also has a local class-caste composition. If the term "community" is taken to mean parents, the background of the children determines the class-caste composition. If, on the other hand, "community" means the elected representatives, their class composition would influence the nature of involvement as well as the nature of conflicts arising from such involvement. The role(s) played by the community members also depend on their socio-economic and educational background and status.

Involvement is also of different kinds. There is a spontaneous or more generic kind of involvement that exists and evolves in society. There is also a more political involvement that arises either out of the actions of political pressure groups or out of mandates of political masters. The more spontaneous kind of involvement is seen to take the shape of: (*a*) parents being partners in their children's education by supporting them at home; or (*b*) parents and community leaders showing interest in schools by contributing time or resources to support school development, solve problems of space or facilities, or lend a helping hand in school matters. Political involvement often takes one of the following forms: (*a*) playing a watchdog role—supervising and keeping an eye on the teacher; (*b*) controlling the use of resources and their deployment; (*c*) raising issues for larger educational change; or (*d*) influencing the curriculum and the way it is implemented.

In the following section, it is argued that the more natural or generic forms of community involvement in education, which existed till the late 1960s, were first removed in order to build a more centralized, universal system of education. There is now an attempt to replace this with a more political involvement determined by a central mandate, and see it as a form of sharing of power and control rather than as a partnership. In later sections, this article will examine the facets of this new involvement in different sectors of school education, with a view to understanding its implications for sustainable quality improvement in education.

The last decade has seen a lot of attention focused on the dimension of community participation and involvement in the context of school effectiveness. A number of recent studies categorically show that positive involvement of parents and community members in education, particularly elementary education, has positive effects on students' achievements, irrespective of social class.

A Glimpse of History

A brief historical sketch would be helpful in understanding the forms of spontaneous community involvement at this juncture. If one looks at the school system in 19th-century Bengal and Bihar, before British influence extended to the interiors, we get instances of schools that are collaborative ventures between teacher and community from the Adam's Report edited by Joseph DiBona—*One Teacher One School.*[1] The community at that time made sparse arrangements for the study of the pupils in vernacular elementary schools. These schools were sometimes organized along religious lines, but often revealed an underlying harmony in which the two major religious groups—Hindus and Muslims—studied with and were taught by teachers of different backgrounds. The arrangements included caring for the teacher as well. The teacher was sustained by a combination of fees and contributions in cash and kind. There were differences in the well-being of such teachers, depending on the wealth of the community that supported such a school. One teacher taught five to 15 children of all ages (from six to 16 years of age) and also arranged for peers to learn from each other. This vernacular education was not exclusive, i.e., children of different castes were allowed to participate in education together. However, very few children received education. In fact, some castes were not allowed to educate their children at all and the absolute poor could not afford an education. There was usually no separate, exclusive space for the school, which was often used for other purposes when the school was not functioning. The community also contributed space and materials for the students. The content of education was not stipulated by any central authority, but loosely outlined by the teacher and the community together. Such education, though more or less totally supported by a section of the community, catered to a very small proportion of the populace. Universal elementary education was never an objective of the times.

In British India, local bodies like the panchayats and municipalities were set up and, apart from other functions, they had the responsibility of organizing school education too. The government stipulated the content of education, but the organization and administration of the school was left to the local bodies. Gram Panchayat and Nagar Palika schools were common throughout Madhya Pradesh till the 1960s. Many an old headmaster of repute was usually called up by a council member for the job of a teacher as soon as he finished high school—that's how he initially became a teacher. Many of the buildings, as well as stories of what happened in those times, bear testimony to the fact that the middle classes, particularly, were very involved in the educational development of their area. There are also anecdotes of the setting up of private schools and colleges by citizens, especially for girls, not so much for profit as for extending educational opportunities.

Much has been written about the involvement of local communities in education in the south and the east. The *Ezhavas* of Kerala are a case in point. Madhya Pradesh, unfortunately, does not bear testimony to such widespread initiatives. However, here too, sporadic attempts are found in every region where enlightened members of the middle class have furthered the cause of elementary education in their area. The girls high school in Harda (in the erstwhile Hoshangabad district) and the boys high school in Shahpur (Betul district) were both set up by such private initiatives and later taken over by the government.

Universal elementary education became one of the constitutional prerogatives of independent India. To fulfil this responsibility, major initiatives and resources were needed. From the late 1960s, the government effected a takeover of educational establishments as well as of the cadre of teachers. Teachers were now recruited from across the state, instead of locally. The large numbers of qualified teachers needed to universalize elementary education were not available locally—so the argument went. This marked the beginning of 'professionalization' on the one hand, and distrust of the teacher on the other. The teacher's post was made transferable. It became a policy not to post teachers in their hometown or village, and to transfer them every few years lest they developed vested interests. Thus, in place of a teacher who had been one of the most trusted members of the local community, here was a more qualified person, perhaps, but one who hardly knew her/his students or their community. Many teachers from other places, who were often more educated than the local community, looked down on them and did not consider themselves accountable to the local populace. Thus, a large inspectorate system came up to monitor the functioning of schools. Transfers, instead of being used to refresh teachers, were used rather as punishments. It only became evident later that "punishment postings" adversely affected teaching.

Another negative effect of this centralization of education was its alienation from the community. The notion began to proliferate that everything belonged to the government and not the community—therefore it was the government's responsibility to look after it. Buildings which were earlier maintained by the local bodies now began to fall into disrepair. Teachers, since they were now the employees of the government, were at its beck and call. They were required to do everything under the sun—from surveys to elections—taking precious time away from teaching. Centralization and professionalization, though born out of an intention to improve quality, failed to effect such a change.

The work of a teacher was looked upon more as a job than as the vocation it had been considered earlier. Rising unemployment made it one of the most coveted jobs for the middle classes. Writ petitions against recruitment procedures prevented the filling up of vacancies in the 1980s, leading to a huge shortage of teachers. To add to these, the mounting pressures of universalization led to unacceptable teacher-student ratios. A centralized cadre of teachers spending time on non-teaching tasks, and shortage of teachers with increasing enrollments led to plummeting standards of education.

Even in this bleak scenario, the community was coming forward in certain places, and in certain others headmasters were garnering support from the community to improve conditions in schools. I would like to cite just a few examples from my personal experiences in this regard.

The primary and middle school of Abgaon Kalan is a case in point. It had to accommodate eight classes while it had only one useable room in 1984. The teachers would commute from Harda—10 km. away—enter from the back and attend school barely from 12 p.m. to 3 p.m. If asked by the villagers, they would complain about lack of facilities. Abgaon is a well-to-do village and one faction of the farmers decided to collect donations for the school. They collected Rs 40,000. With this money they built three complete rooms and two verandahs on either side of these rooms. Each of the verandahs was divided into three classroom sitting spaces—these were like half-covered rooms—the dividing walls of the verandah providing space for the blackboard. Thus a new school was built for just Rs 40,000. They fenced the back of the school and even made a garden. They then told the teachers: "You didn't have space—we've made it for you. We've done our bit, now we expect you to do yours. We don't want to see children in the village between 10.30 a.m. and 4.30 p.m." The people would then sit at the platform (*chabutra*) in front of the school and see that the teachers entered from the front. If they saw a teacher coming late or leaving early, they would not forget to quiz him/her on the reasons. What more does one need as an example of community partnership?

Another example is that of taking community support to solve the problem of the shortage of teachers. There were a few primary schools which encouraged volunteer teachers to teach in the formal school free of cost. All that the volunteers asked for was a certificate for the time they taught. At a certain point, the government got wary of the fact that these youth would ask for jobs from the government. It therefore passed orders that no-one should be allowed to teach voluntarily—thereby also asserting that the school was not an institution for the community to own.

Panchayat Involvement in Primary Education

We have seen that in earlier times, there was a spontaneous positive collaboration of teacher and community. Usually, the node of such collaboration was a good teacher or a good headmaster. Even today, there are some cases where this is so. The community participation sought by the government of Madhya Pradesh through orders of decentralization of power, however, is more of a political sharing of power.

In the early 1990s, three major concerns marked thinking in primary education, namely, (a) concern for universalization, (b) concern for quality, and (c) concern about increasing financial burdens arising out of administering a centralized system. It was at this juncture that a move towards the sharing of state power came through the 73rd Amendment to the Constitution relating to Panchayati Raj. These concerns combined to give shape to the attempts at "community involvement" in education in the 1990s in Madhya Pradesh.

The 73rd Amendment of 1993 gave the thrust for decentralization of management of education and devolution of powers in the case of school education to the Panchayati Raj bodies. Madhya Pradesh has been one of the first states, post 1993, to actually implement this devolution of power. The school education department is, perhaps, the largest in terms of human resources. This department was one of the first to be handed over to the panchayats. The move to decentralize can be seen first and foremost as a motivation to reduce costs of administration, then as a motivation to give power over lakhs of schools, teachers and finances to local politicians in order to extend state patronage, and only subsequently as a motivation to effect school improvement.

The roles required of the Panchayati Raj bodies in the handing over of schools reflect these motivations to a large extent. These are:

1. To meet every month to monitor attendance of students and teachers.
2. To certify the attendance of teachers so that they might get their salary—the state government would continue to provide their salaries.
3. To supervise any construction and maintenance related to school buildings—money for which would be made available largely by the government.
4. To make purchases for school teaching–learning materials, etc., with finances made available from government.
5. To assess school/learner needs—making a school improvement plan.
6. To mobilise local funds where required.

While decentralizing control over schools, there was an obvious tension over aspects of such control. For example, the panchayats still do not have a say in the content of primary education—the what and the how of what happens in schools. Since the primary education system itself is not homogeneous, there are varying degrees of participation of and control by the community.

Two Types of Schools, Three Types of Teachers:

Within the primary education system in Madhya Pradesh, there are two types of schools and three types of teachers. This structure needs closer consideration. The different types of schools are (a) formal primary schools, and (b) Education Guarantee Scheme (EGS) schools.

Formal Primary Schools

There are over 80,000 formal primary schools in Madhya Pradesh, with over 200,000 full-fledged teachers. The supervision and running of these schools have been handed over to the Gram Panchayats through Village Education Committees (VECs) with the primary school headmaster as secretary. This means that school expenditures are to be borne through the

VEC which comprises mostly of panchs and nominees of other representatives (MLAs and MPs). It is mandatory to have only two parents on this committee.

The formal primary school in Madhya Pradesh, today, has two types of teachers: the formal school teacher—an employee of the government—and the shiksha karmi—a more local teacher working under the janpad panchayat.

The Education Guarantee Scheme (EGS) Schools

Apart from the formal primary schools, there are the Education Guarantee Scheme schools. Over 20,000 of them have come up on demand in the last 3–4 years. The demand has to be made by the parents who want their children to go to school. For example, parents of 25 children in tribal areas and 40 in non-tribal areas may demand a school. The government guarantees that the school would come up within three months of such a demand being placed in front of the Gram Panchayat. The community of parents also nominates the guruji who would be teaching their children and the sarpanch forwards the application. In actual practice, however, most of the time the sarpanch tells the people or the collector informs the sarpanch that there's a possibility of an EGS school being opened in his Panchayat because the population is scattered at a distance of more than a kilometre from the school. The sarpanch then motivates parents to get together and raise the demand. In such cases, even though the parents may not actually initiate the demand, their coming together to sign it perhaps makes them more conscious of the fact that the school has been opened for their children.

Both these types of schools are at present under the supervision of the village education committees. This structure of VECs is presently under review and change, making it into a Gram Shiksha Samiti (GSS)—a body elected directly by the community groups with more parents (50%) in it. There is more involvement of the larger community (i.e., parents) in the running of the EGS schools as (a) these are started on community demand and (b) the community contributes the space for setting up the school.

Alternative Schools

Though alternative schools (AS) no longer exist as a separate entity, it is important to mention them here, as many of the elements of community involvement that have been implemented though the EGS were taken from the experience of AS. The alternative school was a primary school with flexible timings, which was set up to provide access to education for drop-outs and people who had no access to the same. The space was provided by the community, the government provided the salary of two teachers—one male and one female—at the rate of Rs 1,000 per month. The emphasis was on a local teacher. The community made the initial selection, but the final selection took place only after rigorous training on the lines of the Shiksha Karmi scheme of Rajasthan. Even though qualifications were reduced even upto Class VIII for women—so that a local person could be taken as a teacher due to the rigorous training and screening—quality was maintained in the first 1,000 alternative schools. The teacher-student ratio was kept below 1:32. It was an ungraded school allowing for freedom of pace of learning. A School Management Committee (SMC) was set up to oversee the running of the alternative school. The SMC of the AS was informally nominated by a consensus within the community and had to have the local panch or the sarpanch as the chairperson. This was very different from the formal VEC of the formal school. In the first couple of years itself, the response of the community was very positive. Apart from providing space, many contributed by constructing schools; they would often be found in the schools, and monitored the attendance of the children too. Some of the positive factors of the AS have been incorporated in the scaled-up EGS scheme. Rigour of training, however, is much less in the EGS than it was in the AS.

The three types of teachers are:

1. The formal school teacher who is an employee of the education department, getting a full-fledged pay scale.
2. The shiksha karmis on probation in the formal school, recruited by the janpad panchayat on approximately half the pay of a formal school teacher, funds for which are provided by the government of MP. These teachers are employees of the janpad panchayat in the sense that they are recruited and posted by the janpad panchayat. They are more likely than the formal school teacher to be a local person.
3. The EGS gurujis, nominated by the village community and the sarpanch, and formally allowed by him to run the school for the

community. They get Rs 1,000 as stipend and are independent persons running a school that is managed by the village community. They do not have any permanence of tenure.

Academic Package in the Two Types of Schools

It is important to mention here the academic changes that have been taking place in these schools in the last few years under the District Primary Education Programme (DPEP). These changes have been made under the control and centralized aegis of the Madhya Pradesh State Council of Education Research and Training (MPSCERT) and the Rajiv Gandhi Prathmik Shiksha Mission (RGPSM), and not under any community pressure or control.

The formal school is organised in year-wise classes and has sets of textbooks that are part of the seekhna–sikhana package. This package includes a teacher training and cluster monitoring system which is the responsibility of the SCERT. When the EGS system initially came up, it followed the formal school seekhna–sikhana system, but since the EGS schools as well as the alternative school package were under the RGPSM, and the SCERT was at that time not particularly dynamic, the RGPSM decided to institute the AS non-graded system and package in the EGS schools. Thus the two systems not only have a difference in their structures and amount of community involvement, but also in the academic aspects and school organisation as well as the amount of attention being paid to them. Which of these factors account for what portion of the difference in quality cannot be ascertained easily.

Review of Community Involvement and its Effect on Primary Education

Having laid out the scenario of primary schooling in Madhya Pradesh, we will now review the community–school and community–teacher interaction in the different types of schools and with different types of teachers. We will see what effect, if any, this interaction has on the schooling of the children and their learning. The following sources have been used as the basis for the review:

1. The para teacher study done by Bodh for DPEP. The AS, EGS and Shiksha Karmi schemes of MP have been studied under this and the formal primary school teacher has been used as a backdrop.
2. Rashmi Sharma's comparative study of teachers and shiksha karmis in 10 schools of MP (EPW, June 1999).
3. Data based on the personal field observation of five EGS gurujis and two shiksha karmis as well as their related communities.

The Community and Formal Schools

Even after the devolution of powers over primary education to the Panchayati Raj institutions in Madhya Pradesh, panchayat involvement in most formal schools across the state remains limited to primarily the recruitment and control over shiksha karmis, and some involvement in the disbursement of funds for construction and mid-day meals.

Though signing on the salary slip of all the teachers—and through this, the monitoring of their attendance—is mandatory in the new devolution of powers, in most cases the slip is signed by the sarpanch only when the teachers themselves take the initiative. This too is done without actually monitoring the attendance of the teachers. Often one comes across cases where teachers who have been regularly absent have no problems getting their salary, due to their congenial relations with the sarpanch, while a fairly regular teacher may be harassed because he has dared to cross paths with him. The limitations of the involvement of Panchayati Raj bodies are obvious from such cases. Since the panchayat representatives may not have a direct stake in the betterment of the school (their own children may be studying elsewhere) but may have more of a direct stake in the well-being of the teacher, power given to them may, in fact, work to the detriment of the school.

Another argument for decentralizing power was that a large centralized structure could not supervise/monitor/control properly. Hence Gram Panchayats, by virtue of being closer to the schools, would be able to monitor better. Many of these measures rested on the lack of confidence on the teacher. And the teachers were indignant that they had to be supervised by illiterates. The result has been that where the teacher is of a higher caste or class than that of the sarpanch and the panchs, and chooses to be lax, the panchayat is unable to do anything. Most panchayats, even after five years, do not have much sense of ownership of the formal schools. VEC meetings are usually very irregular and ineffective.

In short, it is either where their involvement is mandatory, or there is money or jobs involved that most panchayats become active. It is difficult to find a formal school where VEC meetings take place regularly and attendance of children is monitored. The village education register, which was to be maintained in every primary school to monitor attendance of children, is conspicuous by its absence in almost every school.

However, there are examples of panchayats where formal participation of panchs and sarpanches has led to their involvement in controlling cheating, actual supervision of midday meals, collecting resources for the schools when needed and participating in school activities. These examples are usually found where the headmaster/senior teacher is active, thereby creating a sense of collaboration between community and school which leads to an effectively functioning school. The fact that the VEC meetings normally take place in the school has also made the school less daunting to the members.

On the positive side, too, in the eight formal schools surveyed in the para teachers' survey and the 10 schools surveyed by Ms. R. Sharma (EPW, June 1999), it was found that most panchayat members graced the occasion at functions like, Republic Day and Independence Day. Members of the eight schools gave prizes from their side as well as monetary support on such occasions. In most schools, they helped in construction and repair work by contributing money and labour. Teachers of all the schools surveyed in the para teachers' survey said that the VECs and community members do encourage parents to send their children to school.

In the two formal schools of Harda district—Boondda and Khama Pandwa surveyed by us, too, the representatives and parents encouraged children to go to school. Attendance was quite high in both villages at 75 to 90 per cent. When asked about the satisfaction with the facilities in these schools, most parents and representatives over all the 20 schools—eight of the para teachers' study, 10 of Rashmi Sharma's study and the two surveyed by us—showed satisfaction. They were also fairly unanimous in their preference though they had no complaints about the formal school teachers, they had a preference for the shiksha karmis.

Compared to these few examples of collaboration and well functioning schools, there are an equal number of cases of corrupt practices, while the majority of the panchayats still remain indifferent and uninvolved. The involvement of the larger community and parents is, however, rare.

Perceptions and opinions of panchayat members and parents on whether the formal school being under the panchayat is an advantage or disadvantage differed. While nine out of 17 panchayat representatives (approx. 50 per cent) felt that this was an advantage and only three felt that it was a disadvantage, a mere 10 out of 45 parents (approx. 20 per cent) felt this to be an advantage while a majority of them (26) were non-committal. Both parents and panchayat members are as yet unclear as to what kind of improvement is needed in primary schools. Only 25 per cent of both parents and panchayat members cited more and/or better teaching as being needed, while a majority declined to comment. Complaints against non-teaching tasks by the community are muted; however, concern over schools being closed and teachers not being available is being articulated.

It can be seen from the above that the panchayat and community's role in formal primary education is as yet limited and nebulous. It is, to some extent, not very different from what it used to be in the 1950s and 1960s. The largely alien formal school teacher recruited by the state education department may be one of the reasons for the community's distance from the school as well as for some of the tension between the two. However, the panchayats and village community seem to be more comfortable with the locally recruited shiksha karmis and gurujis as we shall see below.

The Community and Shiksha Karmis

Two characteristics of shiksha karmis seem to stand out in both the studies (R. Sharma and Bodh):

1. Shiksha karmis are more likely to be local to the place of posting than the older formal school teacher.
2. In spite of being more local, shiksha karmis are likely to be more qualified than the older formal school teacher.

The former aspect makes it more likely that they are conversant with the local language and culture and are therefore better able to build a rapport with the children. Parents and representatives are quite vocal in articulating that this makes them more conscientious teachers.

According to R. Sharma, even if the shiksha karmis are from a nearby village, they are more likely to stay in the place of posting, since it would most probably be non-transferable. In spite of the fact that the shiksha karmis are recruited through Panchayati Raj structures and are local, a majority of representatives and parents interviewed by Sharma were not aware of the difference between older teachers and shiksha karmis.

Compared to the earlier teachers, shiksha karmis have taken the super-vision and control of Panchayati Raj institutions more in their stride. Though the shiksha karmis in Sharma's study seemed less concerned about interference, about half of them mentioned misbehaviour by the sar-panches. The older teachers had a "very negative response to schools being placed under the panchayats—the reasons given were interference by panchayat in schemes like midday meals and lowering the dignity of the teacher. Some shiksha karmis also said that panchayat control made the school run better. The shiksha karmis appeared to experience the positive and negative control of panchayats more intensively in terms of actual behaviour but were less critical of it as a system.

The rapport between community and shiksha karmi is a little more than that with regular teachers. This is perhaps because in the case of regular teachers, a change is required from older norms—a culture change—whereas with shiksha karmis, it is a fresh beginning, they are growing up accepting this culture. Add to it the fact that the person is local and at least 60 per cent likely to be of a scheduled caste or tribe (SC/ST), or a woman, and the confidence of the villager in dealing with a young local educated person rather than a middle-class, middle-aged stranger is much more.

In summary, we can say that though the quality of interaction between school and community, and between teacher and community in the formal schools leaves much to be desired, an interaction has begun between the two across the board. Though at this point, the positive and collaborative relationship between the teacher and community that marked the spirit of interaction in the 1960s and 1970s, however limited, is being replaced by more of a watchdog role, it has not yet died down. The majority of the interaction is that of the representative body asserting control and accountability, but this relationship is not without its creative tensions, and therein lies the hope.

The Community and the EGS School

The EGS system was part of a programme to universalize primary education in Madhya Pradesh. A community campaign to survey the problems and bottlenecks in achieving the goal of universal primary education, called the *Lok Sampark Abhiyan*, revealed that primary schools were inaccessible to a fairly large number of habitations, particularly in tribal areas. It was to make primary education accessible to these deprived populations that the Education Guarantee Scheme was evolved. The EGS schools serve remote and backward areas. It is not surprising, therefore, that in almost all districts every EGS school has a larger percentage of SC/ST students and girls than the formal schools. These students either did not go to school at all earlier, or went to a slightly far-off government primary school. Thus as the Bodh study says, the EGS schools have given back their childhood to a large number of children, especially the girls.

The setting up of a separate system for such deprived people, particularly one on which the government spends much less money than the formal system, obviously raises the question as to whether equal opportunities are being provided to the children of these deprived castes and classes. In order to understand whether the benefits accrue only to the underprivileged classes from this system, we must also understand the composition of the teachers recruited in these schools. Though the composition of students studying in these schools is definitely skewed towards the scheduled castes and tribes, the same is not the case with the composition of teachers. If we look at the composition of gurujis in Shahpur block (a primarily tribal block) we find that though the children coming to the EGS centres are primarily tribal, 24 out of 45 gurujis are either from other backward castes (OBC), or are Yadavs, Brahmins or Chauhans. There is only one female guruji in the whole block. It is significant to note that there is no reservation in the recruitment of gurujis either for SC/STs or for women. Hence, in a block with more than 80 per cent tribal population, more than 50 per cent gurujis are from the economically and socially dominant castes.

In the para teacher study done by Bodh, one out of four was a Brahmin while the population served comprised of ST, OBC and SC in that order, with less than .01 per cent of other castes. All the four habitations had a literacy of less than 5 per cent. This may perhaps be the major reason for non-reserved categories harnessing the jobs even where the clientele is underprivileged. Also, because of the non-reserved nature of the job, privileged castes are acquiring a larger proportion of jobs even in the deprived areas. Since the government has initiated the scheme—even though the local panchayat runs it—people are seeing this as an opportunity for later permanent recruitment. On the basis of the above studies, it is clear that most EGS gurujis have taken up the job as a career. All the five gurujis interviewed by us were either SC or ST and had cleared Class X or XII. They wanted to study further and improve their career prospects.

The community and panchayats also see the EGS as a major opportunity to enhance the career prospects of their youth. Generally, the community, including parents and representatives, feel that the guruji's lot should improve. Most of them are satisfied and even positive about the guruji's commitment. Some want (like in Sangwani) that the school should grow into a government primary school. The sarpanch is also of the opinion that it would be difficult for the panchayat to manage the school for too long.

There has been a mixed response to the dual system of primary education by the community. As regards the effectiveness of the schools, out of a total of nine EGS schools (four of the para teacher study and five reviewed by us), the community was satisfied with the regularity and effectiveness of all of them. In one school (Malpaun) a parent preferred it to a nearby government school, while in all the others, the people were happy to equate it with the normal primary school. However, in the two villages of Harda district—Malpaun and Khama Pandwa—the people felt that the two streams should be kept separate. They felt that the EGS would function well only if it was kept separate from the government system. One person in Malpaun even felt that their EGS guruji worked well due to her being a local person and from a scheduled caste, enabling the people to keep her in check. One can see the interplay of conflicting views about the government in these responses. On the one hand, people are extremely cynical about the government due to the high politicization of the centralised government system. On the other, they feel that the government cannot shirk its responsibility towards the people.

As far as the cooperation of the community with the guruji is concerned, four out of the five gurujis interviewed by us said that they get ample cooperation. Only one was dissatisfied. However, all gurujis complained of three- to four-month delays in getting their payments. In the para teacher study, the gurujis mentioned that they would like to get an enhancement in their salaries.

The management of the EGS schools is under a school management committee with the local panch as chairperson and five parents/guardians nominated by the community as members. This was the pattern of the management committee of the AS, which had worked much better than the regular VECs. A proposal is presently on the cards to make this the pattern for the formal school VECs in Madhya Pradesh. It is been seen elsewhere that the committees which have a larger representation of parents and interested individuals function much better. It has been seen in some of the districts visited—Betul (Shahpur block) and Harda—that both panchayat members and parents have a greater sense of ownership of the EGS centres than of the primary school. Apart from their signing the demand to set it up, there may be other reasons for this—the fact that the school may close down if attendance of children is not appropriate may not be the least of them.

Children in Primary Schools and the EGS

The aim of all innovations and reforms in education, whether academic or structural, is to improve the education and learning taking place in schools. Observations of classrooms of the EGS schools, the shiksha karmis and the formal school teachers do not depict a pattern which indicates that one type of school and classroom is categorically better than the other. There are variations in all kinds of classrooms whether they be of EGS gurujis, shiksha karmis or of the formal school teachers. There are good and poorly functioning classrooms to be found in each system. By and large the guruji and shiksha karmi classrooms have been found more friendly, lively and regular, with less corporal punishment. There could be a number of reasons for this:

1. The younger age of the guruji and shisha karmi, and the fact that they have entered service in the present atmosphere of friendliness towards the student. They do not have a baggage to unlearn.
2. The shiksha karmi and guruji are more likely to be local and hence more familiar with the children's language and culture—hence they mix more easily with the children.

3. Both the shiksha karmi and guruji, since they are not employees of government, do not have the burden of other non-teaching work. They can thus devote more time to teaching.
4. The teacher-pupil ratio in EGS schools is likely to be more conducive.
5. There is more frequent and regular monitoring of the EGS schools as much more attention is being paid to this newly-born system, often to the neglect of the 80,000 formal schools.
6. The formal school teachers have undergone both pre-service and in-service training. The better teachers are made to teach Classes 4 and 5.

In spite of all this, as far as the learning taking place in schools goes, it is difficult to say at the moment that one system is better than the other. Informal discussions with children of different types of schools have shown very similar patterns of learning. However, conceptually focused teaching was found in the classroom of one of the formal school teachers.

It should be very clear at the outset that EGS school system is in many ways different from the (state) government-run primary school system. It is not possible to claim greater efficiency than the government school system or to debunk it totally, unless at least three or four whole blocks of the two systems are rigorously studied and compared. What is presented in this paper is a very rough sketch of a few very small sample studies that might at best give indications of the strengths and weaknesses of the two systems. Both the teachers and the students are often more regular in the EGS schools. The fact that the school may close down if the attendance dips below two thirds of the children enrolled encourages teachers to keep the attendance of children in their school from declining. In the Phophliya cluster of Shahpur block, attendance dropped alarmingly in most schools in November due to two reasons—extended Diwali celebrations in the village and the illness of a large number of children. The attendance in the EGS centre of Sangawani, however, was relatively better than that in nearby primary schools. The EGS guruji said that he goes to children's homes to collect them when they are absent, while the other teachers said they only mentioned it to the parents if they met them on the way. The difference, according to the academic co-ordinator, lay in the fact that the guruji was afraid that the centre might close down if attendance dipped below 15. It is clear that it is not only because of the involvement of the community, but also because of applying some elements of the proverbial "carrot and stick" that the EGS centres seem at present to be functioning better. It is a question worth asking as to why the government is not applying similar conditions on formal primary schools.

In Conclusion

Universalization of primary education has been an elusive goal for the country as a whole, but more so for the Hindi-speaking heartland. Pressures of globalization have not only turned the heat on universalization, but also put pressure on state governments to do this without increasing its financial liabilities regarding the educational infrastructure. The government of MP has done this ingeniously by increasing access in a time-bound manner, while at the same time not increasing its direct responsibility by expanding the educational structure. It is also cutting costs by giving only a Rs 1,000 grant for the guruji's honorarium. It has responded to the demand for jobs and the pull for power from below through the involvement of public local representatives in the EGS and Shiksha Karmi scheme. Increasing access to about 500,000 children through the EGS system with community participation is a first step in the right direction. Yet, at the moment community participation is more at a level of assertion of power by the panchayat representatives over the education system. In many cases Panchayati Raj Institutions (PRIs) get bogged down in their own conflicts and power struggles. (Sometimes, the appointment of a shiksha karmi may cause more concern than the learning of a child). Whether the struggle for power over the educational system and jobs will be transformed into real participation of the parents and common people in educational issues and in improving the quality of education, or whether this change can be sustained at all is still to be seen.

In both formal primary schools and EGS centres, it is clear that the involvement of Panchayati Raj institutions in education is lending a certain vibrancy to the system. More than anything else, a positive ambience towards education is being created, where villagers have begun showing an interest in their village school. However, direct participation of parents/ guardians and concerned citizens has shown more positive results as in the case of EGS committees. This has been suggested by various studies too. It is a welcome fact that the MP Government is increasing popular participation by bringing about a change in the VEC structure for all schools.

At the moment, people including panchayat members have come forward to set up EGS schools very much like they try to take advantage of any government scheme. What effect this involvement can or will have on the quality of teaching and learning in the schools is not obvious at present. Certain problem areas are already coming up. These are:

1. In spite of unanimous support for local teachers, the government of Madhya Pradesh was not able to resist the force of unemployment in centralizing the Shiksha Karmi scheme. Moving away from the absolutely local, which is logically defensible to the block, is extremely dangerous—it compromises on both time and quality. Methods to retain local teachers and develop them must be worked out.

2. Gurujis have started facing problems in teaching the upper primary classes. They would need a lot of academic support to overcome these problems. These will require both human and financial resources.

3. The better gurujis have started leaving for more lucrative jobs. Whether any quality will be retained in the system if the more efficient personnel are not retained is a grave question.

4. The gurujis have already formed unions and are demanding permanence. Can and will the government resist this pressure? If it does give in, will not the same ills of complacency which dog the formal school system plague the EGS?

These problems cannot be resolved unless the government is serious about resolving them and opens itself out to looking at solutions outside of itself—in academics and civil society.

Where do we go from here?

What is required is a two-pronged approach:

1. Strengthening people's capacities for educational development and management on the one hand.

2. Strengthening the teacher's (guruji's) professional capacities on the other.

The government must also facilitate a system where teachers can periodically meet and enrich themselves professionally. The development of the "cluster" would be ideal in this regard. The professional development of teachers is the development of the society itself. The disbursal of minimal grants and leaving it to the management committees will not develop good educational institutions. For this, the civil society fora must mobilize public opinion on education. And the government must increase the space for such public fora to proliferate these processes, instead of taking on all tasks itself or confining them to its own institutions. A creative relationship between the three—government, political bodies like the panchayats and public fora or civil society organisations—can best develop the capacities of the committees to develop quality education. Time, effort and money will have to be spent on this. The government must show a commitment to this quality by increasing funds and infrastructure to sustain the system while nurturing decentralized management through the broad-based school management committees. Quality development of the gurujis will require the development of quality institutions to support it. At present, the state academic institutions are ill-equipped for this. It will also require progressive increase of the guruji's salary, linked to her/his performance and development indicators. There has to be way to evaluate the development of their capabilities rather than just their qualifications.

If, however, under pressure of cost cutting the government just provides the present funds and leaves the rest to the community, chances are that some schools would develop into good schools, with more contributions from the community, while many would close down. However, the large majority would deteriorate into the small private-school-like exploitative setups now mushrooming even in villages. Here the schools may be more regular, and children may learn to read and write and parrot facts, but they would certainly not be getting a good education.

Only if proper professional development of the gurujis is planned for rigorously will it convert to good quality. Gurujis must get a living wage so that they can concentrate on teaching and learning. All this requires funds. Hence, the matter of generation of finances for these schools must assume great importance. Cost-effective alternatives are welcome, but low-cost alternatives cannot and will not sustain a quality system. A remuneration of Rs 1,000 for a primary school teacher just will not do. Good education is not and cannot be a low-cost affair.

Another matter of concern is that the idea of a common system of education and equal opportunities is getting eroded by inferiority financed schools like the EGS on the one hand and private schools on the other. It is inherent in the EGS scheme that even the backward communities must contribute space for the school. Ironically, it is not mandatory for the comparatively well-to-do rural middle class and urban poor population (even the urban poor are much better off than the schedule castes and tribes in the village) to contribute anything towards their children's education. These are the parents whose children go to formal government schools. It is even more inequitable that the amount of subsidy per child for the general category of students increases progressively for higher education. It is not that one is arguing the rural poor should not contribute space and labour; but in return for this contribution, progressively increasing funds should be made available by the government through their managing committees. These funds can be generated by making it mandatory for better-offs to contribute progressively for their children's higher education.

Not only the EGS, but the formal schools must also get attention for quality improvement. Political will to support decentralized management of the government school system must be garnered by the state. Otherwise, the centralized monolith will become the model for the nascent system, bringing down its dynamism. The role of the state must be to facilitate institution building for quality and management support. At the moment, a lot of attention is being paid to EGS to the neglect of 80,000 formal schools. This is also cause for concern.

Finally, it is not enough to get the local community interested and involved in education. The intelligentsia, civil society institutions and individuals need to be given a viable platform. At the moment, the politicians and bureaucracy determine everything. The question of how we can legitimize the role of civil society institutions is crucial today. Only if the best minds, wherever they are, and social commitment are put together will a truly effective school with the community and civil society working together be possible.

Note

1. The first edition of the Adam's Reports came out in 1835–38, at a time when English officials like T.B. Macaulay, aided by large landowners and local traders, dictated a

foreign educational policy that neglected the great majority of Indians. At such a time, Adam's meticulous and detailed reports demonstrated the vitality of a vibrant Indian rural vernacular education system supported by local communities, totally unaided by the government in Bengal and Bihar. The revival of these reports in 1982 by Dr Joseph Di Bona contributed significantly to the knowledge of indigenous vernacular education in 19th century India.

6

Dynamics of Community Mobilization in a Fragmented and Turbulent State

Vinay K. Kantha
Daisy Narain

Defining Bihar as an Entity

Broadly speaking there are three categories of descriptions one is likely to come across in the media and literature on the situation of contemporary Bihar. In the first category, one can place the bewildered or exasperated exclamations of the analysts calling it a riddle, an enigma—the prime reason behind that being the near inexplicable fact of massive poverty in the midst of plenty. Bihar is seen by many as a land of unrealized potential—a sleeping giant, perhaps. In this kind of a description, there is an implicit castigation of the policy planners and the managers of the system in the state, and yet there is a flicker of hope that it will progress sooner or later. Another array of descriptions can be placed in the second category which perhaps expresses a deeper despondency. Bihar represents the backwaters of modern India—the most backward state—economically and in respect of many other indices of development. Some observers, especially from the media, write relentlessly about the anarchy and lawlessness prevailing in the state. Massacres and scams hit the headlines of newspapers with sickening frequency and one cannot straight away blame the reporters for painting Bihar with a broad black brush.[1]

The above two descriptions no doubt capture a substantial part of the reality of contemporary Bihar and surely cannot be interpreted as prejudiced and exaggerated. However, there is a third kind of description which can be quite useful in comprehending the contemporary dilemmas about the state. Bihar is sometimes described as a microcosm of India. The basic structural feature implied in the description is the diversity within the state. Heterogeneity is a defining feature of Bihar. The existence of many languages and culture groups in different parts is only one aspect. Even locally, there are serious differences almost everywhere in terms of status, aspirations and identities, which sometimes result in fragmenting the society, and creating and recreating various communities. Until a convergence and channelization of their energies materializes, the resultant reality would always be an apparition of anarchy.

The aforesaid three descriptions of Bihar are significant and useful for analyzing any development in the state, including the progress or the lack of elementary education, or even the role of the community in this sphere. Yet the present context of the state cannot be grasped unless one takes a look at history, particularly the recent part of history. However, before that, let us have a detour to examine in what meaning the term "community" is to be taken in this article.

Understanding Community

In today's development discourse, community participation stands at the centre stage of all discussions. Most of the failures of the development projects were taken to be on account of the fact that the population concerned were kept out of all the processes related to design, formulation and implementation. The top-down method of devolution of development strategy came under serious review, and the inclusion of participation and participatory methods of integration has become an essential dimension of development.

However, when one talks of community, another important fact needs to be kept in mind, and that is the nature and meaning of the word community.[2] Let's say that any idea of a community is based on an idea of identity, which also implies a difference. The word community has a traditional connotation and quite often the understanding of the former is merged with the "other" form of community. Pre-modern communities or primary communities have set social forms, very intense, by which people are classified as similar or different. More importantly, these are communities which are not formed on account of the "convergence of interest" that underscores the identity of the other form of community. In contemporary discourse, the interest-bonded communities are those that are being structured and encouraged to participate in the development process. However, because the bonds are weak and uncertain, the picture of the primary community is sought to be evoked so as to draw on the strengths of the traditional community. Because of the newness of its form, the pretension involves taking the contemporary, interest-bonded communities to be immemorial, ancient ones. The earlier communities do not have a territorial identity—these are, for example, religious or caste communities. Larger collectives are now being constructed by creating linkages of common interest—from health to education. In this, the concept of the village as a community is fixed with a territorial identity and at the same time is created above the traditional identities of communities existing in villages that transcend territorial boundaries (for example, linkages with castes or religious groups residing in other villages). Somewhere along the line, intrinsic to the concept behind the formation of the interest-based community is the idea of community advantage, both participatory and of the individual. So long as this advantage is apparent, the cohesiveness remains, but has to be continuously perceived.

The words "participation" and "participatory" appeared in the development discourse around 1950. Even development establishments recognized that development projects floundered because people had been left out. However, "participation" which is also an intervention has to be taken in all its seriousness, so that it does not become a tool for manipulation. The notion of empowerment is integral to the concept of participatory development. One begins with the presumption that one does not have the right kind of power, but also that somebody else has the secret of power to which one has to be initiated. But people are not powerless, they have the power to resist. Later on in this article, it has been pointed out that in Bihar there was a strong resistance to colonial education. This shows a similar expression of power, constituted by the thousands of centres and the informal networks of resistance which people set up.

Therefore, in the context of extending education through community participation, what has apparently happened is the projection of the utilitarian principle of maximum good for the largest number that builds up a common interest, which, in turn, can bind the village into a community. At the same time, by using the word community, identification is sought to be established with the traditional community.

In the course of establishing such communities, the earlier relationships in the village are not taken into account, and this results in the problem of non-participation by some sections of the villagers, the monopolizing of schemes by others and the gradual waning of interest in general. This point could be further explained by citing the evidence of Joint Forest Management. The forest communities perceive an advantage in community organization, which has succeeded in securing for the members either grazing or collecting rights, or protection of their forests from encroachment. This has led to the evolution of close-knit community structures. In the context of education, the question that looms large over the horizon is whether the community perceives that education is important for them.

Historical Context: Education and Community

One of the significant features of the educational scenario in modern India, and Bihar in particular, has been the gradual but sure ouster of the community. The agenda of education for the policy makers who were responsible for effecting comprehensive changes in the system of education was anything but communitarian. The axis of educational planning shifted from community to state—a phenomenon which began in the colonial times—and afterwards, even if there was a change in direction, it was by no means a reversal. Perhaps one more platform which is emerging in the meanwhile is the market. Education is sometimes viewed as a commodity which can be bought in the market—private schools have mushroomed with differential fee structures catering to the demands of various strata of the society, both in the urban and rural areas. Let us have a quick look at the broad contours of change.

Colonial Times: It is not without extraordinary significance that in the discourse on education one of the most commonly used phrases is "modern education"—a phrase which was consciously distinguished from "traditional" or "Sanskrit", "indigenous", or "Persian/Arabic" education by

British officials and "educated" Indians alike. Persons like Charles Grant or Lord Macaulay, with an apparent claim of superiority of their knowledge system and culture and a supercilious contempt for traditional knowledge, stood for the imposition of a new system of education. The much talked about debate between the Anglicists and the Orientalists after the Charter Act of 1813 predictably concluded in favour of the former. The Indian share of support for it was not inconsiderable. To quote Raja Ram Mohan Roy,

> *The Sanskrit systems of education would be the best calculated to keep this country in darkness....* But as the improvement of the native population is the object of the government, it will consequently promote a more liberal and enlightened system of instruction, embracing mathematics, natural philosophy, chemistry and anatomy, with other useful sciences which may be accomplished with the sum proposed by employing a few gentlemen of talents and learning educated in Europe, and providing a college furnished with the necessary books, instruments and other apparatus... [italics added].[3]

As Hetukar Jha points out, the popular opinion was, however, against the Anglicists. James Prinsep recorded in his diary that some 30,000 people signed against the abolition of madarasas and Sanskrit colleges in Calcutta. In Buchanan's accounts, and subsequently in the famous educational survey of William Adam carried out in 1823–24, it has been brought out that in Bihar and Bengal an extensive system of indigenous education existed even in the interiors. In fact, Adam went as far as suggesting that the Government should initiate measures to support mass education, which alone according to him could solve the problem of education and morals. While appreciating the report as "valuable and intelligent", Auckland decreed that an elitist system of education starting with the upper and middle classes was all that the government was prepared to support.[4] In 1840, S. Macintosh, who was the headmaster of Patna High School, tried to take up the cause of vernacular education. He realized that for any vernacular education to succeed in this province it must be "closely connected with the habits of the people", but for want of funds he had to close 11 schools that he had started in the neighbourhood of Patna.[5]

Meanwhile, zila schools were coming up in Bihar in various districts. The Patna zila school started in 1835, Ara in 1836, Bhagalpur in 1837 and Chapra in 1839. An almost parallel trend was the arrival of Christian missionaries. Roman Catholics were the first to come to Bihar. Fr. Joseph Mary, who cured the Rani of Bettiah, arrived in Patna in 1739 and started a church there. Sisters of the Institute of the Blessed Virgin Mary opened St. Joseph's Convent in 1853. The Gossner Evangelical Mission came to Ranchi in 1845 and started a school in 1846. Clearly, neither of these two initiatives were at the community level. To sum up, it can be readily concluded that the introduction of modern education led to an exclusion of the community. At best, there was a sprinkling of Indian support at the higher levels of society.

As a matter of fact the exclusion of community was at several levels. The erstwhile system of community support and involvement or some kind of community control was gradually disappearing. An interesting example related to the holding of examinations and the conferment of status of a scholar can be cited from Mithila. There were two systems of examination. According to Dr. Ganganath Jha, there was a system of public examination that continued to be held till about 150 to 200 years ago called *Saryantra*. Even after its disappearance, the *dhoti* examination conducted by the rulers of Mithila remained popular. Though Adam's report has not mentioned it, Buchanan has described at least the royal examination system.[6]

One of the crucial implications of the ouster of the community from control was the replacement and complete supersession of the indigenous system of knowledge by a new knowledge system that was by no means related to the lives and needs of the people at large. Education got removed from the community at the level of language as well. There is one more point which needs to be highlighted and taken note of. It has been widely reported by historians that the popular feeling was positively hostile to the new institutions. A number of schools had to be closed soon after they began, and most of them failed to attract students. There was a conscious boycott at least in the beginning, and even later the lure of education remained restricted to the middle class.

On another plane, a similar debate regarding the rights of community versus the role of the colonial government in the management of forests has been reported by Ramachandra Guha.[7] Dietrich Orandis, the first Inspector General of Forests who was a German botanist by training, strongly favoured a decisive say for the community. Given the imperial psychology of the post-revolt era, the Forest Act of 1865 clearly conceded that the law should not abridge or affect any existing rights of individuals or communities to forest lands. But those who favoured the appropriation of more authority by the colonial state like Baden-Powell indeed had the last say. The Forest Act of 1878 limited the right to private property and vested the forest service with greater powers to oversee forest use, while emphasizing commercial forest management. Guha rightly remarks that there was a continuous ouster of rural communities during the British times—a mentality which lingered on during the post-independence phase when community forest users were perceived as the driving force behind deforestation. Village rights were at best seen as generous "concessions or privileges". The story of land settlements is too well known to be recounted. Some historians have already examined the manner in which there was a colonial intervention in the health sector as well.

In a nutshell, it can be averred without doubt that during the British times there was an appropriation of power and authority by the colonial state over resources as well as activities to establish a domination and hegemonic control over Indian society. This design necessarily entailed dilution or even extinction of the role of the community, which hitherto enjoyed a privileged position. Given the iniquitous distribution of power within the community and the limitations of the traditional knowledge system, there were undoubtedly problems every where in the pre-colonial times as well, though of a different kind and order. Rather than attempting corrections or improvement, the end result of the supersession of the whole concept of community involvement led to severe distortions of a new variety.

Anti-colonial Struggle: Bihar was not among the enclaves of early modernization in the British times, yet it remained in the vanguard of the struggle against colonialism. Anti-British sentiments were strong and pronounced among sections of the people right from the early period of British rule. South Bihar was the site of strong tribal revolts, breaking out one after the other throughout the 19th century. Soon after the Ho revolt, the Kol insurrection reached its peak in 1831–32. The Santhal hool (rebellion) of 1855 was the bloodiest tribal revolt of the British era. Even after the beginning of the national movement under the banner of the Indian National

Congress, Birsa Munda rose in revolt in the Ranchi area between 1895 and 1900. Many tribals, including the Tana Bhagats, were subsequently recruited to the mainstream national movement.

If tribals constituted one traditional group bound by primordial loyalties rising intermittently against the British, the Wahabis represented another form of traditional resistance to modernization. It is no sheer accident of history that the revolt of 1857 and the Khilafat movement were both strong in Bihar, while the currents of modern nationalist ideology had to wait for several decades before making an impact. No less important is the fact that Bihar moved to the forefront of the national movement in the era of mass movements. Elite politics was presumably of much lesser strength and appeal, while the subaltern represented the real strength and character of the society in Bihar. Gandhi combined the appeal to traditional values with reliance on the masses, and that explains his enormous appeal and following in the state of Bihar from the days of the Champaran satyagraha onwards.

Sometimes it is pointed out by social scientists that despite being an area of early colonization and not lacking in intellectual resources or social energy, the Bengal type of renaissance was not witnessed in Bihar. It can perhaps be interpreted as a cultural resistance to the process of modernization that was inaugurated by the colonial regime.

Years after Independence: From the point of view of development or education or even community participation, it would be meaningful to divide the post-independence history of Bihar into three phases. The two dividing lines could be placed in the years 1967 and 1988. The period of three annual plans between 1966 and 1969, euphemistically described as the plan holiday, is a watershed in the history of Indian polity and economy. Likewise it marks a transition in the recent history of Bihar. Around 1988, several new initiatives are noticeable and the framework of economy also got comprehensively restructured by the year 1991. This was another period of major transition in the history of India and so was it for the state of Bihar. The similarity between the national scenario and the situation of Bihar nearly ends there because the outcome of the transitions on both occasions was not exactly a replication of the aggregative national scenario. The third phase of history brings us to the contemporary situation.

Postponing a discussion on that, a brief description of the earlier two phases is attempted below.

The ideological consciousness of the articulate section of the Bihar society got intertwined with the national agenda ever since the advent of Gandhi in Champaran in 1917. Bihar contributed a few memorable leaves to the saga of the struggle for independence and went on to accept the national agenda of development in the post-independence period. During the 1950s, Bihar witnessed land reforms, a modicum of economic progress, a fair growth of educational opportunity and finally, a little community participation in many spheres. In fact, the first glimpse of such an agenda as well as initiative can be traced back to the Congress ministry of 1937–39, when an adult education programme was taken up with a lot of enthusiasm. This was resumed in the years after independence supplemented by a fairly widespread library movement. The community development programme may have been relying excessively on the bureaucracy and panchayats may not have been permitted much say in matters of development, yet there was enthusiasm which would not die out quickly. The promise of community–state synergy for accomplishing the major task of smoothly planned development died a slow death, albeit not without some progress. No new definition of community could be built up around the ideology of development sponsored by the state during that phase. Unfortunately, the two wars at the time of the third five-year plan, coupled with severe drought hitting the state in the mid 1960s, led to a kind of economic crisis which shattered the dream of planned development of the first phase. The Congress party was thrown out of power and naxalism arose at the other end of the society. Nurtured on the promises of the Indian Constitution and electoral politics, aspirations had soared and a sense of frustration was setting in, leading to a phase of political fluidity and the fluctuating fortunes of political parties and combinations.

Community Participation and Educational Intervention in Bihar

An overview of some of the significant educational interventions is given below before attempting an aggregative appraisal. The interventions examined include: (*a*) Total literacy campaign (TLC)—a brief study of TLC in

Bhojpur in the context of community participation and empowerment, (b) Bihar Education Project and State Programme for Elementary Education Development, and (c) *Lokshala* programme.

The total literacy campaign in Bihar was initiated in 1992 and today there are 40 literacy districts. Of these, in 16 districts the TLC phase has been completed, and the post-literacy phase has begun in 14 districts. Dumka, which has produced outstanding results, has moved into the phase of continuing education (CE). When the literacy programme began in 1992, Madhubani and Madhepura produced such exciting results that these began to be cited as model examples in Bihar. Yet the enthusiasm generated soon declined and the second stage of the campaign could not take off in these districts. Different patterns have emerged in Bihar with regard to these campaigns. While the much publicized Dumka literacy campaign was spearheaded by the collector himself, in Bhojpur the local network of activists and volunteers took the lead while the collector and the governmental machinery maintained a distance. The Jehanabad campaign has progressed in a seesaw fashion and in the second stage of revival, as the earlier workers were ignored, participation remained at a low ebb. In some thickly forested areas of Hazaribagh that have come under the grip of left extremist groups, the literacy programmes have made reasonable progress. The area of Katkam Sandhi, a forested area which had never responded favourably to any government-sponsored scheme also came under the influence of the literacy campaign. The collector's initiative allayed suspicions and the extremist groups have welcomed the literacy campaign. Among the extremist groups, TLC is taken to be an example of the increasing intervention of the West and they consider the World Bank–supported TLC to be an American initiative for deeper intervention. Kaimur, bordering Buxar, is a hilly area notorious for the activities of the local dacoits. Despite the continuous dread of the dacoits, initiatives taken by the local *mukhiya* and the collaboration of the district magistrate has helped to extend the literacy programme in this region.[8]

The Bhojpur Experience

Separated by the river Son, Bhojpur lies adjacent to Patna. Bhojpur, a region of high agricultural activity, is known as the rice-bowl of Bihar and is a cauldron of political activity. The literacy campaign in Bhojpur, known as *Bhor*, was initiated in 1992 (although the National Literacy Mission sanctioned the programme after considerable delay in August 1993). Community mobilization reached a high water mark in the period between June 1992 and August 1993, and very soon *tola* committees constituted with a "bottom-up" approach began to mushroom. However, elders of the community were not involved despite realizing the importance of doing so; neither was there any involvement of the government officials.[9]

The delay in the sanctioning of the project *Bhor* deflated the level of enthusiasm raised. A misplaced anticipation that the community participation aroused would be matched by the participatory zeal of the government led to the formation of committees and *kalajathas*, even before the sanction of the project. The delay led to a substantial drop in the level of enthusiasm. In programmes where the community is expected to be a participant and where a community bondage is sought to be created on "commonality of interest", gaps such as these not only dampen the zeal, but also disintegrate the "bonds" that bind the community. *Drishti*, the total literacy campaign run by the East & West Educational Society in four panchayats in the Fatwah block, completely on a voluntary basis with no involvement of governmental officials, faced an even more difficult situation when the demands raised in the field could not be met due to the delayed sanction of the project.

Bhojpur's mobilization was primarily the work of a group of committed followers of Jay Prakash Narayan. However, they lacked the requisite strong organizational structure, and wide reach and rapport with the people. There was a romanticization of the belief in the commitment and mission leadership to be provided by them. This led to the belief that the involvement of the collector was not essential. This, in turn, was matched by the lack of involvement of the collectors themselves who took it as just another government programme. As a result, the entire network of government staff remained detached from the campaign, and provided little support even at the crucial stage of teaching and learning. Even the committees from the tola upwards to the block level had very little space for government officials.[10]

Even after the sanction came through, there was another period of inactivity in which the involvement of the society was again affected. Rumours soon spread about the money being taken for voluntary activity, which caused further alienation. However, over a period of time, strong efforts were made to overcome this obstacle.

From community participation to empowerment, the *Bhor* programme does come across as some kind of a success story. Even the important step towards women's empowerment did not lag behind. *Sakhiyaro* groups came up, but not before the end of 1995. A *dukh sukh* sharing platform was created. However, there were no representatives from the *sakhiyaros* in the core team. The tola committees that had been constituted had nearly 60 per cent representation from the scheduled castes.

In the villages of Bihar, the caste/class dynamics does become an important point of consideration. Interestingly, in the context of TLC in Bhojpur, it is the upper-caste leadership from the Rajputs, Bhumihars, Brahamans, etc., that has taken the initiative. However, it is significant that the Yadavas, a dominant caste in Bihar politics, have been found to be disinterested.

Various related issues which cropped up in the course of the campaign were taken up for action, e.g., forcible closure of liquor shops and construction of a 5 km-long rural road. The recent spate of massacres had violently disturbed the region, with caste tensions running high. Yet at present there is a relative calm. Among the various factors, the impact of the *Sanjeevani* campaign by the literacy volunteers has been widely appreciated. The members of this group have succeeded in bringing together the antagonistic sections and initiating a dialogue. After nearly 11 years, the land in Sahar, the birth place of naxalism in Bihar, is now being cultivated. Even more significant was the widows' meet after the massacres. Women from different caste groups experienced a bondage in their common suffering and decided to fight against caste tensions.

A little deviation at this point may not be very out of place, if we shift from Bhojpur to the tribal district of Dumka—one of the most backward districts in the state. Dumka is an example where, despite the lack of any vibrant social movement, a social capital could be built up. The intense involvement of the collector's institution helped transform the literacy campaign into one of mass mobilization and the negative role of the bureaucracy was converted into a positive role effecting a state–society synergy.

The participation of women is probably the most distinctive feature of *Akilbatti*, where the movement was virtually taken over by women and literacy rode piggyback on other developmental programmes. While in the earlier phase the intensity of the literacy campaign relegated primary education to the background, the enthusiasm roused prepared the necessary ground for the improvement of primary education in the next stage. Primary school teachers were asked to go back to the schools and the "Jago Bahana" groups took up the vigilance of the primary schools. Once again, the state–society synergy was very effective. Also of significance was the formation of the two committees, the *mata* committee and the *hopan gatha* friends of the little children—committee, comprising of one male and one female volunteer from each village to motivate and assemble the children and take them to school.

Bihar Education Project

The Bihar Education Project (BEP) covers all components of elementary education and has been expanded in a phased manner in 27 districts. Taking the block as a unit for its programmes and activities, participatory planning and implementation are important characteristics of the project. Among the major components of the programme are the organization of Village Education Committees (VECs). From 1995 to 1996, BEP made a concerted effort towards the reorganization of the VECs and the training of VEC functionaries.

A study conducted by NIEPA as a part of the second all-India survey of educational administration, titled "Educational Administration in Bihar,"[11] studied the role and functions of VECs. The studies are focused on the VECs in the villages Itachildri, situated in Bero block in Ranchi, and Jonha, situated in the Angara Block of Ranchi. While Jonha is almost a tribal village, Itachildri has an equal proportion of tribals and other castes.

The VEC formed according to the earlier notification of 1988 by the state government suffered from the basic problem of the members being nominated by the Block Education Officer (BEO) and of the *mukhiya* being the president. During 1991 to 1992, BEP restructured the character of the VECs. The president is now directly elected by the Gram Sabha and the *mukhiya* is not necessarily the president. Instead of village-level committees, school-wise VECs have been constituted and Rs 2,000 is provided to the VEC, with a 5-day training to the members. It is important to note that at Jonha a *sthaniya samiti* existed since 1958, which concerned itself with educational matters and continued to function till 1972.

The study notes that despite the restructuring, problems still exist. Village-level dynamics plays its role, influential persons want their own representatives in the VEC and as the number is restricted to 15, not every caste can be represented. In spite of the fact that VECs claim to have carried out their functions, it was found that 35 per cent of the people surveyed at Jonha did not know that there was a VEC; in this respect, the Itachildri VEC appears to have greater popularity. At both places, the general opinion was that VECs have contributed towards improving the enrolment of children, but very few could say anything about their initiative for the improvement of school buildings.

The teachers who were surveyed, however, gave a different response. All the teachers reported that VECs do not prepare education plans. They were of the opinion that VECs should not be equipped with any administrative or financial power and that they should be made accountable to the BEO. However, as far as their role in mobilizing children and decreasing drop-out rates was concerned, the teachers responded favourably.

Coming to the government machinery, the assessment of the VECs is extremely poor. The resolutions of the VECs are not sent to the block- or district-level education officials. Demands concerning the construction of schools and for teachers were sent to the district magistrate or deputy collector, but this is generally unreported. The VEC members reported that their decisions were hardly ever attended to by the BEP or the government officials.

The impact of the formation of VECs is perceptible. The NIEPA report mentions a tremendous increase in enrolment, especially after the restructuring in 1993. It states that in Itachildri, as a result of the VEC effort, enrolment increased to 92.2 per cent and 100 per cent in the 6–11 and 11–14 age groups respectively. The report draws the following conclusions:

1. Influential persons in the village secure a place for themselves or their favourites.
2. Where there are experienced, retired persons and elders involved, the performance is better. VECs are not reconstituted according to the provision after two years.

3. The lack of response from either the government officials or those in the BEP leads to frustration and ebbs their voluntary spirit.
4. While meetings should be held once a month, the frequency of the meetings gradually decline after the initial period.
5. Meetings of the VECs should be held in different tolas so that the entire village can participate. The advantage of this arrangement was noticed in the Jonha block.
6. The training is quite ineffective. In Jonha none of the members could recall what they had learnt in training, and they felt that the training was not relevant in conducting VEC activities in local situations. Members of *anganwadis* and Primary health centres are not aware as to why they have been given representation.
7. The main difficulties are financial and administrative. As nothing can be charged in areas where half the population is living below the poverty line, the prospect of mobilization of donations is very weak.
8. There are administrative lapses. Even on the request of the VEC, irregular teachers are not transferred (this is because of the association that teachers have with BEOs), while good teachers are transferred without consulting them.[12]

Based on these conclusions, the report has the following suggestions to offer:

1. There should be a restructuring of the composition of the VEC to make it more representative.
2. More powers should be allocated to the VEC.
3. There should be a system of continuance of training for all members of the VECs.

Another Study on BEP [13]

Recently, a concurrent appraisal of community mobilization under DPEP (III) was done as part of an aggregated research at the national level sponsored by the technical support group of Ed. CIL (Education Consultants Limited). As this study points out in its report, the following three types of strategies were formulated under the process-based new approach of VEC formation worked out after two successive workshops in September and December 1997:

1. BEP worker/teacher–based campaign.
2. Campaign based on *utprerak dals* (mobilizers).
3. Campaign based on *abhiprerak dals* (micro-planning/facilitator groups).

In fact, three kinds of activity roles were defined in the said workshop to undertake specific responsibilities in VEC formation or micro-planning exercises. These roles were to be performed by activity elements/groups named *utprerak, abhiprerak* and *prerak. Utprerak* would assume the role of mobilizer; *abhiprerak* would be a facilitator with a full understanding of the conceptual framework and process of micro-planning; *prerak* would be the village-based conductor who actually implements the plan of VEC formation and micro-planning.

The teacher-based campaign approach envisaged a campaign by the school system itself. An *utprerak*-based campaign relied upon the involvement of sensitive people from outside the system. *Abhiprerak*-based campaigns were more intricate and envisaged more intensive involvement of villagers in the entire process. In the appraisal it has been noted that the involvement of people was the least in the teacher-based VEC formation. Even *utprerak*-based campaigns were often hurriedly done. The micro-planning-based exercise which involved longer training and higher-level interaction has been suggested as the most useful among the three strategies.

Most of the VECs formed in BEP districts have been *utprerak*-based. According to the report, till 31 August 1999, as many as 31,718 VECs were formed, while micro-planning was completed in only 914 VECs. In another part of the report it has been noted that out of the 20 VECs covered by the study, head teachers were "enthusiastic and willingly cooperative" in only three while they were found to be "indifferent/noncooperative" in as many as 11. Teachers were also generally not found to be enthusiastic about the VECs, taking them to be a parallel system of supervision and control.

In relation to the social composition of the VECs, there is a clear dilemma which is reflected in the conclusion and recommendation of the report. The report approvingly notes the higher representation given to the weaker sections as primary stakeholders in the reconstitution of VECs. It says that the biggest representation on VECs was clearly of scheduled castes in the plains and of tribals in the plateaus. Both these categories have in fact been given substantially higher representation in their respective regions—proportionately more than their size in the state population. This may be construed as a positive bias, considering the goal of universalizing primary education.

On the other hand, regarding the performance of VECs, the study found only two out of 20 VECs "functional and active" and four more "active on their own". The rest were either "functional only when prompted" or "dormant". It is further noted that VECs in the semi-urban set-up or VECs whose members came from non-agrarian occupations and were themselves educated seemed to do well while those having the chairman or a majority of its members as landless wage labourers, having no exposure to education, lacked self-esteem—particularly when head teachers also showed their calculated indifference.

This dilemma brings into focus a few basic questions: Which community are we talking about? Who will represent the community the best? How do we structure interest-bonded communities, and whose interest are we securing anyway? In the case of the fragmented and turbulent society of Bihar, these issues assume acute significance. Caste identities are strong and lately quite aggressive, making it difficult to work out commonalities of interest around which VECs could be structured. Further, in every village there are a few identifiable aggressive individuals or groups and if they smell power and influence anywhere they are bound to step in and assume a dominant role for themselves.

State Programme for Elementary Education Development (SPEED)

SPEED is a more recent experiment in primary education launched in Bihar in January 1998 which, because of its late start, had the advantage of learning from earlier experiences. Empowering the community to take up the cause of strengthening primary education is an important agenda of SPEED. The programme has spread to eight blocks in five districts—three in Nalanda, two in Deoghar, two in Giridih, one in Sahebganj—and to some panchayats in Garhwa. School-based Village Education Committees were formed and as of now there are 800 VECs. Probably taking lessons from BEP, SPEED has made modifications in the process of constitution of the committees and the training of its members. While the BEP has a four-day programme of organization and training, SPEED has extended this period to 20 days in a given panchayat. If there are NGOs active in the area, they are contacted initially, and in the course of organizing a meeting of the Gram Sabha two animators are selected and motivated to work for the programme. Micro-planning and VEC formation go hand in hand. The village education plans are also being drawn up.

Even during its short existence, the level of community participation and mobilization achieved by SPEED is noteworthy. There are examples of people sitting together and solving problems arising on account of religious differences. Women have on various occasions taken the lead and if male squabbles delayed the selection of the *adhyaksha*, they solved the impasse by selecting a woman as the *adhyaksha*. Financial mobilization is another remarkable example of community involvement. In Noorsarai block in Nalanda district where there are 88 VECs, the public contribution was over one lakh rupees.

The VECs have succeeded in mobilizing the teachers and with some exceptions teachers have remained involved in the programme. In the course of the teachers' strike in Noorsarai, people volunteered to carry on teaching in the schools. There is evidence of community mobilization in areas other than education. In the Sarwan block in Deoghar, VECs staged dharnas for the improvement of water supply and solving of problems related to land.

As such, though SPEED has made some headway within a short span of time, the problem that looms large in the future is the question of sustaining interest in the programme at the grassroots level.

Joint Forest Management

While speaking about community mobilization and primary education, it would not be altogether irrelevant to consider community participation in forest management, which is sought to be secured through Joint Forest Management (JFM). What is important to understand is that most Indian communities carry with them a long legacy of resource rights and tradition, some of which date back to centuries. In this context, policies and legislations more supportive of community resource rights began to be formulated around 1988, reflecting the concern for community participation. In 1988, the national forest policy proposed the creation of a people's movement to protect forest resources.[14] Even here, doubts still persist as to whether the decision marked a historic swing towards greater decentralization or an attempt by the government to control the acquisition of public forest by local communities. The institutional arrangements, with its corresponding rights, vary from one state to another. While in Orissa it is the panchayat, Bihar has VDC. There are pitfalls here as well—where the government has moved in to establish JFM, it has undermined the growth of independent local initiatives. The development of micro-plans with participating communities has been quite discouraging, as there is a lack of co-ordination and plans are not subject to community input. Among the community types in Bihar, the community forest management groups have grown rapidly. These have emerged out of local initiative in response to the hardship experienced by the people due to the degradation of forests. These are examples of very encouraging roles of community mobilization.

Lokshala

The *Lokshala* programme in the Karpi block of Jehanabad district is part of a national initiative which was planned before the workshop in Nauni, Himachal Pradesh, in 1995. The workshop was jointly organized by Bharat Jan Vigyan Jatha (BJVJ) and Maulana Azad Centre for Elementary and Social Education, University of Delhi, with the support of Indian National Trust for Art and Cultural Heritage. According to the Nauni declaration "schools need to be transformed into community-managed social institutions [rather than being viewed as state-controlled prescriptions] where children first understand the world they live in, then participate in it and eventually intervene to redefine it".[15] The programme is running in 21 panchayats and there is an organizing committee for each panchayat. Unlike BEP and SPEED, the composition of the committee is flexible and left to the choice of the village community.

However, the factor of external stimuli is as unmistakable as in other programmes. The main organizer, Akshay Kumar, is from the area itself but does not permanently reside there. He has a background of left politics and substantial external contacts. In terms of ideas, inspiration and part of the financial requirement, there is clear support from outside. Further, even for enthusing the local youth volunteers a ploy used was the lure of the pride of working in collaboration with the teachers of Delhi University.

In the process of mobilization, however, considerable local involvement and resource support could be secured. The Nauni declaration promises "to explore and establish a decentralised, disaggregated and location-specific approach to planning and management in education". Local youth were involved in teams of two each for the survey of government schools of six villages and for writing the history of four villages. In October 1997, a *loksansad* was held in Nagwan panchayat, which was culmination of the first phase of mobilization. The *sansad* witnessed a heated debate on various problems of schools by the local villagers. It is true, however, that but for another *mahila sansad* and a somewhat delayed *loksansad*, this kind of activity has almost ceased.

The school in Jhunathi village had no building; the three lady teachers belonged to the locally dominant caste group and they would seldom come to the school. With monetary contribution and *shramadan* by the villagers, a roof was erected and now classes are being held regularly in the school. Another interesting programme was a people's audit of the rights of children.[16]

However, there is another side of the picture which should not be ignored. One of the most common questions put to the investigators in the beginning was as to what their personal gains were. Expectations are bound to be generated but their fulfilment is often in doubt. With the main organizer staying away for a few months due to medical reasons, there was clear sagging of interest and mobilization. There is a need and expectation of financial support from outside, which has got delayed, resulting in slackening of efforts.

It is generally seen that any one-time activity or phase of enthusiasm is fairly common and not too difficult. The bigger need as well as task is that of sustaining the project. Can the community take the entire charge of support and supervision on its own even if the basic cost of running the school is borne by the government? Though this remains uncertain, there have been short-term interventions that have effected worthwhile changes. *Lokshala* ideologues speak about the empowered school where "the community has to be empowered not only to participate in the educational process and its planning, but also to control it". But the manner in which to bring it about, especially outside the framework of panchayats, is yet to be worked out.

Loci of Initiative

The stimuli for the current phenomenon of community mobilization in Bihar, as perhaps elsewhere in the country too, come from outside. Independent local initiative, particularly in the field of primary education, is extremely rare—even local resources are just not enough. Whether it is finance or ideology, there is an external input which provides the first seed for mobilization. In most cases, it is under a project which has been conceived and designed outside the community, possibly outside India. In many cases there is an external funding involved. Ironically, a global thrust for local participation is the theme of the World Development Report, 1999.[17] A section of social scientists and activists are uneasy about this phenomenon and their concern may not be altogether unfounded. On the other hand, rejection of the initiatives for that reason alone may not do justice to the people because after the initial thrust a local dynamics is likely to emerge at local levels, which form a variegated pattern.

Interestingly, however, if there are reservations about the source and use of money at the highest academic level, somewhat differently, reservations are noticeable at the sites of the programme. At one level it is the fear of manipulation, at the other it is more generally the issue of misuse of money. Caution is needed on both counts.

External ideological input and a top-down approach may result in a situation where the felt needs of the community are obfuscated and an "echo effect" is created when some articulate persons from the community start mouthing the phrases smuggled from outside. At times, responses to the new opportunity will be autonomous. After all they are not inert masses, especially in the politically conscious countryside of Bihar, and they may push an agenda of their own.

An important question is posed by a Cambridge researcher, Indu Bharati, regarding the relationship between market and mobilization. Contrasting the Tikapatti (a block in Purnea district) mode of mobilization, based on a liberal ideology, with the naxalism-dominated political mobilization of central Bihar, she points out that the former is found suitable for the markets. Her study is focused on rural women, but it has substantial relevance to the rural poor and illiterates as a group. Bharati raises another fundamental point whether the whole issue of mobilization or empowerment is merely "outsiding" them, i.e., putting these sections of the population in touch with the outside world in terms of ideology and market forces. An accompanying dilemma emanates from the internal constraints of the community, which is particularly pronounced in the case of women. At a different level, a similar problem has been posed by the noted educationist Krishna Kumar, in one of his articles appearing in the EPW, suspecting a connection between the literacy campaigns and the liberalization of economy to serve the interest of external forces in the market.

Indu Bharati, while contrasting the Tikapatti model with the Jehanabad/ Bhojpur situation, points out the alienation of the upper middle-class women as a consequence of the mobilization of the lower classes in the latter case. In the above scenario, there are two contrasting problematics which need deeper analysis. On one side, it is the alleged hegemonic agenda of the market in Tikapatti and on the other, it is the question of rupture of cohesion in the traditional community. In the philosophy of Gandhi and Tagore, both the dilemmas are resolved, but in the contemporary development paradigm both persist. Dreze and Sen raise the question of market-excluding and market-complementary interventions, and express their considered preference for the latter.[18] The whole debate is of immense relevance and has varied ramifications in the context of community mobilization for primary education.

Another conceptual/theoretical problem arises due to the near-universal presence of the state in these mobilizations—of course, their role varies from project to project and from place to place. Civil society on its own fails to provide the impulse, even though it has to play an important role at some stage. Synergization of the two is a complicated process that throws up many kinds of dilemmas and difficulties. For Indians, the government is generally an external institution, different and removed from the community—especially as it was implanted from outside during the British times. During the era of freedom struggle, there was a relation of antagonism which developed between the state and the community. Ironically, once again this relationship is characterized by an essential ambivalence—

antagonism on the one hand, combined with an enormous sense of dependency on the other. The planners as well as the mobilizers will do well to keep these factors in mind.

For any successful mobilization of the community, the clout and the credibility of the initiators is of great importance. Involvement of government machinery does help substantially, as do linkages from outside, even though it gives rise to expectancy and a demanding attitude which needs to be curbed and discouraged. The presence, support or active involvement of the collectors has provided strength to the total literacy campaigns in many districts. Ultimately, however, reliance has to be placed on the non-government functionaries—NGOs or individuals. The government can help in setting them up initially, provide resources and infrastructural support, and finally, oversee and support the institutional arrangement that evolves in the process.

NGOs have a definite advantage over the government functionaries on several counts. They are usually closer to the community and the people's expectations from them are not that direct and great. They have greater operational freedom. Individuals have a big role in these mobilizations. Removal or inaction of key individuals may cause a setback to the programme—something which was experienced again and again in the total literacy campaigns, especially at places where the collector was the prime mover rather than an activist. Dumka is one such example, which can be juxtaposed with Bhojpur. Of course, activists, if not already widely known, have to work hard and long to establish their credentials. Even afterwards they have to be cautious, lest they land up in controversies relating to financial irregularities or partisan attitudes. In Bihar, cases have been registered against the secretaries of the *zila saksharata samiti* in a number of districts. It is difficult to say in how many cases they have really indulged in corruption and whether it results from the mere lack of capacity in financial management. Regarding the programmes in this light, is a delicate responsibility which devolves upon the administration, and in a lot many cases they and virtually smothering the programmes. Due to the delay in the release of funds, the tempo of the work is found to be completely broken, and restarting it takes extra time, energy and money—and sometimes this simply does not materialize.

In community-related initiatives, it is of utmost importance that the interest of the volunteers and the potential beneficiaries is sustained by ensuring clarity of programmes and availability of resources. In Jehanabad, and elsewhere in India, the *Lokshala* programme took off with great fanfare. There was a considerable amount of spade work and mobilization, but the scheme was not cleared by the ministry of HRD. Dozens of district-level literacy programmes have suffered a similar fate due to delays.

Teachers' Role

Teachers constitute a community unto themselves, which has not been effectively mobilized even though their role remains critical, especially in the programmes relating to primary education. Teachers' bodies are almost unconcerned with regard to these matters. At best, there has been some individual involvement. Teachers are capable of taking up a dual responsibility. They can help in community mobilization and more importantly, they can play a direct role in improving the schools and teaching. In TLCs, *Lokshala* programmes, etc., there are reports of the participation of individual teachers, but the number is small and the community as such is not involved. As a matter of fact, teachers as a group are considered a problem by the organizers as well as the community—they are regarded as an obstacle or an ill-functioning part of a giant system which is in need of repair or replacement. Training is one input contemplated by the organizers to motivate and reorient them, but a complete attitudinal change as a group is a distant goal. One of the indices of the success of community mobilization has been its capacity to put pressure on the teachers to come to the school and teach. The community might succeed in the first objective, but no unwilling non-co-operative teacher can be forced to teach well.

Process of Mobilization

There are different types of models of mobilization. TLCs rely almost entirely on environment building through *kala jathas*, etc. In watershed management, NGO-initiated awareness programmes are attempted. For the primary education–related programmes, both BEP and SPEED have relied on the NGOs to organize VECs that would undertake microplanning. In Independent programmes like *Lokshala* or *Drishti*, the process is less clearly defined, with advantages and disadvantages of their own. One thing which emerges very clearly is that instruction and opposition are best tackled or the least troublesome when the process of mobilization is collective and transparent—for example, in the constitution of the committees in open general meetings. The use of cultural activities is now being incorporated with good effect in the programmes in a substantial way, even in the programmes on primary education. In fact, techniques evolved for the early phase of mobilization are showing good results. However, problems do occur afterwards. The question that soon comes up is what the incentives for the volunteers are. Apparently monetary incentive does not go very far, particularly when the activities are to be made continuous and extensive. The feeling of importance when an ordinary worker starts interacting with ease with the officials is of considerable value. This psychological concept combines with a place acquired by workers in a new power structure that starts emerging in the villages. This has its own strengths and weaknesses.

It is widely noticed that the members of VECs or similarly constituted groups in other programmes acquire a sense of new-found importance. A new power structure is introduced in the village, which may either remain broadly in line with the one that existed before or modify it somewhat. Usually the more articulate persons of the community are likely to gain in influence. In a limited sense there is the empowerment of the community, but it remains debatable if it does mean empowerment of the community as an integral unit. On the other hand, given the apparent reluctance of the state and its functionaries to transfer real control and authority to the hands of VECs, it is at best a pressure group or a weak control mechanism. Perhaps the community emerges as a rival site of authority and the state authorities, rather than working in tandem, resort to a strategy of ignoring and sidelining them.

At many places the fragmentation of society along the lines of caste, ideology or other interests comes not only in the way of mobilization, but also affects the relationship between the NGOs and the government functionaries. Especially when there is a transfer of key government officials, the new persons may be prejudiced by the rival groups, leading to a loss of trust. Such a problem was widely reported in the TLC programme. VECs are on a different footing and there is not much of resource flow involved.

Therefore, this problem is less likely to occur and yet the coordination-related problems are severe in their case. Actual power still being vested in the government officials and the involvement of the district-level or development officials being meagre or absent, the expectations of the community are unlikely to be fulfilled, resulting in a waning of enthusiasm.

Coming back to material incentives and rewards, for the target group or the community at large the benefits are neither tangible nor direct in respect of primary education as those are obtained only in development-related or income-generating programmes. The scheme of joint forest management, for example, creates a material interest—there is an economic benefit that is going to accrue to the community and hence a vested interest is created in the community. Howsoever beneficial education may be in the long run, given its inability to add to the immediate earning capacity of the learner, and occasional apprehensions of various kinds among the illiterate parents, their interest is quite uncertain. It is indeed encouraging to see that despite the gains of education not being so visible, a large number of poor families show interest in education and get dissuaded only because of the unsatisfactory state of affairs in the schools due to a variety of reasons. Education may not be sufficient, but at the same it is a necessary condition for vertical mobility. This is clearly recognized by poor and illiterate families, and that explains the increasing tendency among them to send their children even to private schools after paying fees. The recent PROBE report and many other studies reveal beyond doubt the growth in demand for education among the poorer sections of society.[19]

Dual Expectation

Community in the context of mobilization can be visualized in two principal roles—that of provider and consumer. There is a parallelism between advertisement campaigns and these mobilizations with a primary focus on demands and rights. In a state like Bihar, the level of political consciousness even in the countryside is fairly high. The criss-cross of political and project-based mobilization can generate various patterns depending upon the nature, of effectiveness and strength of either. The role of the state, as represented by its functionaries becomes ambivalent, more so in the context of the generally arrogant and unresponsive mindset of the functionaries. Further, even if the demand for education is augmented and a demand for better education is created, the outstanding issue remains the management of the supply. In this scenario, both state and community can play the role of providers or contributors. On certain occasions, which are few and far between, the community is seen to come forward to supply men and material for building or repair. In a much larger number of cases, the community asks for it and the state fails to respond. As for demand and aspirations, the deprived segments are as a rule more enthused, and hence involved, but as providers the expectation shifts to another class in the village. How far they collaborate will depend on the local situation. In a nutshell, as a result of this kind of mobilization, a new dynamics is likely to be introduced in the local context. For want of an institutional arrangement like PRI (Panchayati Raj Institution), what shape it will take, how influential it will become, or what impact it will create are highly uncertain. One thing, however, remains fairly certain: wherever VECs are active and strong, teachers' attendance and the enrollment position of children will improve, at least to begin with. The task before the project managers is daunting in many ways at every stage, both in the process of mobilization and afterwards.

As the programme progresses, it is faced with many dangers—one of the first dangers is that of disenchantment, of routinization and loss of enthusiasm. This is noticeable in most of the places where the programme is old enough, for example, in the Ranchi BEP programme. Often the most important factor is the non-redemption of early promises—for example, VECs would make recommendations while the officials of the education department would not pay any heed to them. Internal conflicts and competitions, and rivalries within the mobilizing groups can pose another problem after the initial enthusiasm has died down. From some areas, there are reports of the mobilized groups slipping into an agitated mould, something which is quite common otherwise in the state. In the Sarwan block of Deoghar, VEC members staged a dharna on issues not related to education.

Bihar is known as a graveyard of schemes and projects. Hence, caution is very much called for, and the need is to move ahead of rhetoric and mobilization. The society in Bihar is not lacking in energy and enthusiasm. As long as supply and management issues are tackled well, the involvement of the community is likely to yield results. After all, history confirms that community has played a role in the management of education in the past. Today it is not a question of simple revival, rather it is a question of creating a new arrangement in a far more complex and fluid situation.

Notes and References

1. Bihar remains in the news with disturbing frequency, usually for the wrong reasons. There is a considerable body of literature on different aspects of the contemporary state of affairs in the state. Among the general overviews, one can refer to Das, Arvind N. (1992), *The Republic of Bihar*, New Delhi: Penguin; Gupta, Shaibal & Alakh N. Sharma (eds) (1987), *Bihar—Stagnation or Growth*, Spectrum Publishing House; Kantha, Vinay K. (ed.) (1992), *Bihar Economy—A Reconnaissance*, Print-Aid Publications; Prasad, R. C. (1992), *Bihar*, Second Edition, India: National Book Trust.

2. For a conceptual discussion on "community", see Kaviraj Sudipto (1992), "The Imaginary Institution of India, in *Subaltern Studies IV*, New Delhi: Oxford University Press.

3. Sharp, H. (ed.) (1920), *Selections from Educational Records*, Part I, Government Printing Press, Calcutta, pp. 3–4.

4. See Jha, Hetukar (1985) *Colonial Aspect of Higher Education*, New Delhi: Usha.

5. See Datta, K. K. (ed.)(1983), *Comprehensive History of Bihar*, Vol 2, Part I, Patna: K.P. Jayswal Research Institute.

6. See Jha, Hetukar, cited in note 4 above.

7. For further information on Joint Forest Management, see Guha, Ramachandra (1996), "Dietrich Brandis and Indian Forestry: A Vision Revisited and Reaffirmed", in Mark Poffenberger & Betsy McGean (ed.), *Village Voices, Forest Choices*, Oxford University Press.

8. As reported by visitors to the area from ADRI, State Resource Centre for Literacy, Patna.

9. See Srivastava, Manoj (1998), "Promoting Adult Literacy in India Through State-Society Synergy: A Comparative Study of Mass Literacy Campaigns in Kerala and Bihar", Mimeographed version of paper presented at the Graduate School, Cornell University.

10. See Srivastava, Manoj, cited in note 9 above.

11. See Sinha, A., R. S. Tyagi, U. P. Singh and D. N. Chaudhary (1999), *Educational Administration in Bihar*, New Delhi: NIEPA.

12. See Sinha, A *et. al.*, cited in note 11 above.

13. See Bhushan, Shashi (1999), "Re-induction of Community towards Owning and Empowerment of Village Schools in Bihar", Mimeograph, Renaissance Centre, Bihar.

14. For further information on Joint Forest Management, see Guha, Ramachandra, cited in note 7 above.

15. Nauni Declaration, 31 May 1995.

16. See BJVJ (1995), "Lokshala Project for Universalisation of Elementary Education", Bharat Jan Vigyan Jatha Documentation, March.

17. See World Bank (2000), *Entering the 21st Century: World Development Report 1999/2000*, New York: Oxford University Press.
18. See Dreze, J. and Amartya Sen (1995), *India, Economic Development and Social Opportunity*, New Delhi: Oxord University Press.
19. See *Public Report on Basic Education in India*, New Delhi: Oxford University Press.

7

Community Participation in Primary Education: The Karnataka Experience[†]

N. Shantha Mohan
M.D. Gayathri Devi Dutt
Piush Antony

The National Policy on Education of 1986 and the subsequent revisions made in 1990 have envisaged a greater role for community in the field of education. While the provision of equal access to education and universalization of elementary education are obligations to be met by the government, developments during the last 50 years have not demonstrated success through the efforts of the government alone. It is in this context that during the past two decades, issues related to "relevance", "appropriateness" and demand-based education have come up for consideration in education policy and practice. It has been found in many studies such as PROBE that more than half of the drop-outs gave "irrelevance of education to the life situations in which they are in" as the main cause for dropping out from school.

National governments as well as international development agencies have realized the role that community can play in the realm of education, and have strongly advocated community participation as a critical element

[†] The authors wish to acknowledge the co-operation extended by organizations and communities during the fieldwork.

in the strategy for reaching the goal of education for all. Community participation is taken to mean active participation of the clientele (especially parents) in the affairs of education, including planning, finance and management.

This article brings out the experiences of community participation from the state of Karnataka, which stands as an average state with respect to the whole of India as far as education development is concerned. Karnataka has been involved in implementing externally-funded education programmes, like the District Primary Education Programme (DPEP), and has seen several innovations at the school level, spearheaded by non-governmental organizations. Lessons learned from such experiences would help further the role of community participation within the education sector. This article draws heavily on the field work conducted and the secondary literature available on the agencies and programmes that are taken as case studies.

While there are various trends in the extent and quality of community participation that has been achieved, this article tries to focus on a few successful initiatives by the community to achieve universalization of elementary education (UEE). These cases are taken up for discussing the experiences at different levels and the modes of participation, and for representing various streams of organizations, interventions and processes. The selection of case studies is not exhaustive but illustrative of significant initiatives and modes of participation. The case studies include the DPEP representing the government initiative, two NGOs (Vikasana and Samuha) with varying agendas for primary education and strategies for community participation, one externally aided development project (TIPP-II), and an initiative planned and carried out entirely by the community. A critique of various efforts will be made in order to identify factors that promote participation of the community and to evolve strategies to strengthen and adapt existing community structures to ensure enhanced participation.

The following section presents an exposition on the concept of community participation as understood by various stakeholders, especially the government, and the policy directives issued in this connection. After that, this article takes stock of the education progress in the state of Karnataka, to contextualize the space for, and role of, community participation and the various projects/programmes for augmenting education in the state.

The next section provides experiences of community participation achieved in the case studies. The last section brings out lessons learnt from the experiences and recommendations for future strategies.

Space for Community Participation

The term "community participation and empowerment in primary education" is a comprehensive one and encompasses two important principles. On the one hand, it can be construed as the total participation of the community in the system to facilitate the achievement of the goals of UEE. On the other hand, complete community participation could be considered as a tool for self-development and empowerment of the community. These two aspects are interlinked, and the demarcation is subtle. Therefore, one of the indicators for measuring community participation is the proportion of the child population in schools. The more the number, greater is the community participation. If all the children of a specific age group in a village are attending school and learning regularly, community participation is total. This type of participation also ensures community development because it fulfils the most important requirement of development (i.e., literacy) which, in turn, enhances the individual's economic mobility and range of choices. Another aspect related to this is the manner in which the communities create conditions for greater participation of children in education and the obligations of the communities vis-à-vis education. Does their role end with the participation of children, or is there something beyond this? Are there any specific roles and responsibilities of the community that would enhance effectiveness of the education system? What are the implications of such participation on the specific roles of the government, educational bureaucracy and other stakeholders? These issues are particularly important in the Indian context, as a significant proportion of the enrolled children are first-generation learners and the stakes are high in the country for investing in education.

Community Participation in Education— Genesis

Historically, education was under the purview of communities, though only a few privileged ones. In colonial India, the privileges enjoyed by these communities began to be extended to other sections of the population, through efforts from within the community. However, the movement to enhance community participation has travelled a long way from a state of informal initiative to a formalized policy intervention, in recent years. The transformation of participation may be summarized through the following stages:

1. The first stage consists of creating awareness among the parents about the importance of sending their children to schools regularly. This assumes that persuasion, rather than enforcement or compulsion, is the means of ensuring universal participation of children in primary education. This is evident from the legislative measures indicative of a shift from compulsion (as specified in the Compulsory Primary Education Act, 1961) to persuasion, combined with incentives to promote universal primary education as elaborated in various policy documents on UEE and EFA.

2. The second stage is characterized by increased awareness which, in turn, creates more demand for education. The government not being totally prepared to meet this increased demand, communities are invited to provide the schooling facilities in unserved areas. This intervention fulfils the twin objectives of providing facilities to promote UEE and mobilizing community resources for education.

3. In the third stage, community support is sought and ensured while framing the provisions for establishing and managing new schools. This ensures not only participation, but also a sense of ownership as communities often provide the required space and other infrastructural facilities to run the school.

4. Sustainability of community participation is then to be ensured through the setting up of school betterment committees, which include members of the locality. These committees are primarily responsible for reviewing, organizing and mobilizing human, physical and financial support to better the functioning of schools.

5. Thus, community support, which begins as merely supplementary to the functioning of the school, shifts the emphasis to ownership of schools by the community. Community participation thus gets integrated into the action plan for the goal of UEE. The constitution of Village Education Committees (VECs) and vesting authority in them

to oversee the functioning of the primary school is one such example. Such committees have been constituted in both project and non-project areas, delegating certain powers and functions in the governance of primary education.

6. Community participation is further enhanced through the implementation of legislative measures proposed under the 73rd and 74th amendments to the Constitution. Through these legislations, the elected members shoulder the responsibility of delivering services both in the social and development sectors. Decentralized governance entitles the community to be active partners in the process of planning, designing, implementing, monitoring and evaluating the school activities through the VECs. Further, this ensures the effectiveness of their representatives in monitoring the functioning of schools through the mechanism of Gram Sabhas (village gatherings).

The move to empower communities is influenced to a great extent by the programmes and interventions of other agencies. The total literacy campaigns have created a conducive environment for active participation of the community in promoting awareness of the role of education in the development of individuals as well as of the community. Evidence indicates that there has been a consistent increase in the enrollment rates of both boys and girls in the post-literacy-campaign period. NGOs working for the empowerment of women, children and disadvantaged groups—through their programmes covering sectors like health, child labour, self help groups, etc.—have also created a ripple effect and have been promoting an integrated approach to human resource development, including basic education.

Primary Education in Karnataka: An Overview

Policy Interventions in Education

Participation of communities in promoting enrollment and improving the quality of education in primary schools has to be understood against the state's obligations and initiatives since independence. The directive principles of the Constitution of India as specified in Article 45 urge that "the State shall endeavour to provide within a period of ten years from the commencement of the Constitution free and compulsory education for all children upto the age of fourteen years". Following this, Karnataka introduced the Karnataka Compulsory Primary Education Act of 1961, which has provided for the enforcement of compulsion at the lower primary stage. This Act envisaged partnership in implementation only from parents as it catered to those who voluntarily participated by sending their children to school.

Prior to this intervention of 1961, "community participation" was visible only to the extent of providing the schooling facility for formal or non-formal or informal structures of education (the facilities in terms of space and building for starting primary schools and other education centres.) In order to support the implementation of the CPE Act of 1961, the government was obliged to provide for schooling in the underserved areas. This provided the local communities an opportunity to open new schools. Though community schools were in an encouraging number at the secondary level, it was not the same at the primary level. The norms for starting schools in an underserved habitation were a population of 300 and the readiness of the community to provide a temporary/permanent venue. Through these means, hundreds of schools were started annually between 1961 and 1980. In addition to providing formal schools, the non-formal stream of education was also advocated under the *Akshara Sena* programme in 1984. It envisaged a target of opening 3,200 non-formal education (NFE) centres. This target remained unrealistic to serve the needy regions as NGOs were found to be concentrated in urban areas, and the rural areas which needed NFE the most remained unattended both by the government and NGOs. However, the grant-in-aid system enabled many local communities to start schools, though not in a uniform manner across the state. While the local communities in the districts of Bombay-Karnataka (which formed part of the erstwhile Bombay state), old Madras province and Kodagu expanded primary education utilizing grants from the government, the districts of Hyderabad-Karnataka region (part of the earlier state of Hyderabad) did not make much progress towards this due to various historical reasons of backwardness.

Taking cognizance of the role played by the community, and in order to inspire them to be a part of the governance of schools, the government introduced the scheme of establishing school betterment committees. These committees took keen interest in improving infrastructural facilities by mobilizing community resources. Also, school children were given incentives from the public for meritorious performance and regularity of attendance.

The Karnataka Education Act of 1983, which was enacted only ten years later in 1993, insisted the state government direct primary education to be compulsory in any area after ensuring adequate number of schools and teachers. While it reiterates the duty of parents to send children to schools, it also allows for "compelling" circumstances that prevent children from attending the school. Though this Act casts a duty on parents to send children to school, judicially it is clear that "compulsion" must first rest on the state to provide the necessary facilities for imparting free and compulsory elementary education. Not only was the state unable to fulfil this obligation, but it also diluted the legislation from compulsion to persuasion along with the Prohibition of Child Labour Act to Regulation.

The 73rd and 74th amendment to the Constitution is an important move in recognizing the inevitability of community participation in development and in all social sectors. VECs that have come up as a sequel to the amendment carry an element of official legitimacy. Despite the tussle that exists between the earlier school betterment committees and the VECs, the latter are gradually taking root, mainly due to the statutory powers vested in them. The constitution of these committees has been made mandatory by the promulgation of an executive order issued in 1995. These VECs comprise seven to 15 members, one third of the total membership being women. They also have representatives from SC/ST/minorities/parents/teachers/*anganwadi* workers and other persons interested in education. Creating public awareness, involving the public in the affairs of primary and secondary education, ensuring total enrollment and retention in primary schools, and promoting adult literacy are the functions of the village panchayats, under the Panchayat Act, 1993. In the light of these facts, the following functions and powers are assigned to the VECs:

Functions: Supervision over adult education, early childcare and non-formal and formal primary education, generation and sustenance of awareness in the village community, and ensuring the participation of all segments of the population are important functions. In addition to this,

VECs also promote enrollment drives and persuade enrollment, reduce drop-out rates, assist in the smooth functioning of the schools, mobilize resources for school improvement, prepare plans to attain UEE, and coordinate with other sectors for supporting primary education.

Powers: The VEC members visit schools to check attendance and other registers, report to the authorities on the regularity of students, teachers, school functioning, deficiencies and requirements of the school. It also undertakes repair and construction work, recommend annual budget and frame the school calendar.

Training is imparted to the members of the VECs in order to enable them to perform in accordance with the tasks assigned to them and to ensure their empowerment.

Education as a Fundamental Right

Though yet to be realised, another significant successful effort has been making education a fundamental right. In the landmark judgement of the Supreme Court in 1994, (J.P. Unnikrishnan and others *vs.* the State of Andhra Pradesh), the court categorically pronounced that the child has a fundamental right to free education up to the age of 14 years. This judgement thus converted the obligation created by the Article into an "enforceable right". In Karnataka, a recent High Court judgement brought into focus the duty of the state to provide free and compulsory education to children upto the age of 14. The court has held the view that "the State shall reimburse the educational expenditure of children up to the age of 14 studying in private schools to fulfill the constitutional obligation under Article 45 of the Constitution either to the parent directly if claimed by them or to the schools directly, in which event the concerned schools shall reimburse the amount to the parents". However, this judgement has subsequently been stayed.

The above discussion clearly reveals that while on the one hand there has been an increasing pressure built on the state to fulfil its obligation to provide elementary education to all children below 14 years of age, on the other hand, there has been the realization that the devolution of powers to the community is the only way to achieve the goals of UEE. The establishment of school betterment committees and VECs are, in this sense, the recognition by the state that participation of communities has to be integral to any programme aimed at UEE. Therefore, these committees are to be taken as efforts to invoke the much needed participation of communities.

Initiatives to Promote UEE

Several steps have been initiated by the state towards achieving universalization of elementary education. They comprise:

1. Community involvement in enrolling children in the 6–9 age group in school.
2. Opening schools in schoolless habitats with a population of 200 persons (as against the government of India norm of 300 persons).
3. Upgrading lower primary to upper primary schools and construction of classrooms.
4. Recruitment and training of teachers to provide for a conducive learning environment for children.
5. Holding teacher–community meetings to facilitate the participation of the community in collectively seeking solutions to problems faced by teachers with regard to pupil participation and achievement in primary schools.

Despite these efforts, several studies have reflected the absence and invisibility of the community in the education system. And the gap that exists between the noble plans and poor effectiveness in implementation is attributed to the absence of communities as proactive partners in the process. Though the concept of community participation in education has been recognized for quite some time and built into the system by various government initiatives, it is for ever evolving and manifesting itself in different ways. The very process has been highly dynamic, constantly changing the mode of participation.

Profile of Primary Education in Karnataka

An overview of relevant statistics about the state and primary education is presented in table 7.1.

The demand for education in the state is on the increase as indicated by the rise in enrollment and the corresponding increase in the number of

Table 7.1 Karnataka at a glance

Population	4,49,77,201	
No. of districts	27	
No. of taluks	175	
No. of villages	27,066	
Literacy rate	56%	
Districts with lowest literacy rate (less than 40 for female and 63 for male)	Raichur, Gulbarga, Bidar, Bellary, Mandya, Mysore, Kolar and Bangalore rural	
No. of primary schools	46,000	91% population covered; 96% of them within 1 km
A primary school for	Every 200 population	
Upper primary schools	18,283	60% population covered within their habitation; 85% covered within 3 km
No. of teachers	45,00,000 (1996–97)	
Teacher–student ratio (60,000 teachers appointed in 1997–99)	Total 1:43 Rural areas 1:60 Urban areas 1:17	Chikmagalur 1:28 Raichur 1:49 Bijapur 1:52
Government schools	80%	*Source:* 6th All India Education Survey
Aided schools	10%	
Unaided schools	10%	
Total child population	16.2 million	
Child population (6–14 years)	9.4 million	
Enrollment in:	Government schools	Private schools
Urban areas	50%	55%
Rural areas	50%	10%
Children in primary schools (enrolled)	822.5 million (1997)	Girls in schools 48%
% of children attending school	Rural 65.3%	Urban 82.4%
Children out of schools	Boys Girls Total	
Number (in million)	10.73 15.31 26.05	
Per cent	22.7 32.8 27.7	
State budget	Rs 17,81,863.00 lakh	
Education outlay	Rs 2,95,519.03 lakh	16.58% of state budget
Expenditure per child	Rs 1,350.00	90% for salaries
Elementary edn.	54.5%	Rs 2,200 crore
Secondary edn.	32.7%	
Higher edn.	12.0%	

Source: Human Development in Karnataka, 1999, and other GoK publications.

schools. Efforts towards UEE in the state has been envisaged through the triple measures of:

1. Universal access wherein a primary school will be available within walking distance for all children,
2. Universal participation—all children who enroll will continue and participate until the completion of the course, and
3. Universal achievement—all children who enroll and participate will have achieved the prescribed levels of learning.

While universal access has been achieved by providing schooling facility within the habitation for about 96 per cent population, universal participation and universal achievement do not match the extent to which access has been provided. About 2.7 million children in the age group of six to 14 are still outside school. Among the children in the school, the difference in the gross and net enrollment ratios indicates that only around 80 per cent of the school-going children actually end up in schools. Out of this 80 per cent, nearly 42 per cent of the children drop out of the school at different stages. These ratios have regional, caste/class and gender disparities, which continue to exist in spite of several efforts and interventions made by the government, NGOs and other agencies.

Tables 2 and 3 show regional and gender disparities with respect to GDI, HDI and literacy and primary education across different districts of the State.

Table 7.2 Comparative rankings of Human Development Index (HDI) and Gender Development Index (GDI)

District	HDI rank	GDI rank
Kodagu	1	1
Bangalore Urban	2	3
Dakshina Kannada	3	2
Uttara Kannada	4	4
Chikmagalur	5	5
Shimoga	6	6
Hassan	7	7
Bangalore Rural	8	8
Belgaum	9	10
Chitradurg	10	9

Table 7.2 continued

Table 7.2 continued

District	HDI rank	GDI rank
Dharwad	11	11
Tumkur	12	12
Mandya	13	15
Bijapur	14	13
Kolar	15	14
Mysore	16	16
Bellary	17	17
Bidar	18	18
Gulbarga	19	19
Raichur	20	20
STATE	7	5

Source: Karnataka Human Development Report, 1999.

Table 7.3 Disparities in education

Districts	% below poverty line	% of SC	% of ST	Gaps in literacy ratio	% of drop-outs Boys	% of drop-outs Girls
Bangalore Urban	31.42	14.7	1.1	14.13	27.43	39.72
Bangalore Rural	38.17	19.5	2.9	23.36	37.33	38.36
Belgaum (10)	29.86	11.4	2.3	27.96	54.78	48.48
Bellary (17)	44.50	18.8	8.9	26.74	42.64	55.52
Bidar (18)	56.06	20.7	8.3	28.44	66.53	67.96
Bijapur (13)	28.98	17.3	1.35	29.63	46.93	64.50
Chikmagalur (5)	15.61	19.3	2.6	19.25	54.50	60.14
Chitradurg	39.00	17.5	3.25	23.52	33.69	44.75
Dakshina Kannada	8.91	6.4	3.9	16.44	09.30	6.07
Dharwad (11)	49.75	11.5	2.05	26.17	42.11	49.76
Gulbarga (19)	45.54	23.6	4.1	27.59	58.40	61.62
Hassan (7)	14.44	17.4	1.1	23.67	40.60	49.64
Kodagu	20.73	12.1	8.3	14.13	11.80	15.66
Kolar (14)	45.45	25.7	6.9	24.94	34.51	41.00
Mandya (15)	30.16	13.8	0.7	22.48	39.10	43.32
Mysore (16)	28.94	20.3	3.6	18.28	46.04	50.97
Raichur (20)	25.11	11.5	7.55	27.38	51.09	72.70
Shimoga (6)	25.56	16.3	2.3	19.82	47.60	44.03
Tumkur (12)	40.64	17.7	7.3	24.56	30.37	43.06
Uttara Kannada (4)	24.97	7.5	0.8	19.62	55.71	52.57
STATE	33.16	16.4	4.3	22.92	41.34	46.28

Source: Karnataka Human Development Report, 1999.
Notes: 1. Figures in the parenthesis in first column indicate GDI/HDI rankings for 1991.
2. Drop-out rates are for the year 1997–98.
3. Highlighted figures in the columns demonstrate disparitites across different indicators.

Table 3 clearly depicts the nexus between poverty, backwardness, gender disparity and education disparity within and across districts. In the case of Karnataka, HDI and GDI rankings of districts are almost the same, which is not a common pattern for many other states. It can be discerned that disparities in education vis-à-vis gender and class are linked to the overall development of the district. The higher figures under each indicator in the above table are highlighted to develop relationships across the indicators. This demonstrates that districts having lower GDI/HDI show higher gaps in literacy rates. However, districts that have better GDI/HDI do not exhibit better performance with respect to indicators like drop-out rates. For example, Chikmagalur district, with a GDI/HDI of 6, has a high drop-out rate of 60.14 for girl children—very close to the 61.62 of Gulbarga district, which has a GDI/HDI rank of 19! Such contradictions exhibited by the districts compel us to question the criticality of indicators that determine the development processes. However, the point remains indisputable that certain sections of the community are not able to catch up with the overall development of the districts. The education of girl children is of particular importance when looked at in the light of these statistics.

This highlights the fact that especially due to the non-participation or low participation of certain sections of the community, greater efforts are necessary to involve the community in the education process. It can be seen that caste and financial status have clear, direct links with low participation in education. Efforts to develop demand systems among these sections, and create conditions for their participation, become hallmarks of strategies envisaged in many education projects. The case studies presented in the following section demonstrate the experiences and strategies of community participation.

Case Studies

District Primary Education Programme (DPEP)

Launched in 1994–95 across four districts, DPEP now covers 11 districts in the state. These districts were initially identified for their lower literacy rates. DPEP aims at augmenting the state government's efforts at achieving universal primary education in these districts by providing access for all children to formal or non-formal education systems. It also aims at ensuring universal participation by children in the education system and improving the quality of teaching–learning transactions at the primary level. It focuses on improving access, participation and achievement of children from marginalized groups, particularly girls.

The project has envisaged community participation from a development perspective. This involves redefinition of the term "beneficiaries", commonly used in the development sector, and of the relationship that exists between a "giver" and "receiver". The giver is all-powerful and has the freedom of choice, whereas the receiver is powerless and receives without a choice. This redefinition has enabled the communities to articulate their demands. The first step towards this was to create awareness about their potential to create demand. For this, a five-part mass communication strategy was employed using print and non-print media—conducting of *kala jathas* (cultural processions) and enrollment drives, organization of *chinarra melas* (children fairs), preparation of films in a participatory mode encompassing the entire arena of primary education, formation of VECs and their training, and conducting of micro-planning exercises.

Kala jathas spell out the importance of universalization of elementary education with special focus on that of the girl child. The *kala jatha* teams formed at the district level perform in the targeted villages so that communities are enthused towards sending their girl children to schools.

The initial focus on girl child enrollment gradually attained the dimension of universal retention and universal achievement, with a reinforcing tone on access and enrollment. Parallel to this initiative, the regular "enrollment drive" programmes were launched. This also helped in campaigning against child labour.

Malka is a social film that establishes the importance of the girl's education and highlights the mother's empowered role in determining the prospects of the girl child. The film was selectively screened during campaigns and training programmes of teachers.

Chinnara mela is a child-centred campaign programme built into the project implementation with the active association of an NGO called BGVS. This programme is planned keeping in mind two objectives: to break the caste and gender barrier among the students, teachers and the community members at large, and to practice joyful learning and communicate this pedagogic philosophy to the community. In this programme, two villages are identified and 50 children from each village are picked. One village plays host and the other is the guest. Each host child's house accommodates one guest child, without taking into consideration the caste, class or sex of either of the children. Staged in a common place in the villages, groups of children numbering four to five are formed. Games are carried out by them during which they visit various corners of the stage—namely, corners for language, mathematics, environmental science, etc.

The open classrooms employed in this case effectively convey to the community a joyful way of learning and a participatory approach to the teaching process. What is more interesting in this experiment is that the entire village becomes the classroom for children to learn. Through this, the community is made aware of the pedagogical issues and their participation is strengthened and sustained.

The "Nalikali" Experience: H.D. Kote is one of the blocks of the DPEP districts in Mysore which experimented with a novel methodology in teaching. It has been successfully carried out since then in the whole of Mysore district. It is referred to popularly in the area as the *Nalikali* programme.

The *Nalikali* programme is a multi-pronged approach to UEE, for it empowers the teacher, makes the curriculum relevant by making it locally specific and promotes learning. The whole strategy is "child centred". In the process, the teacher reviews the curriculum and prepares the activity cards for both teacher and student. Even the alphabets are not taught in a sequential manner. Five letters—*ra, ga, sa, da, ta*—are given foremost priority in view of their extensive usage in the day-to-day life of the community. Similarily, in mathematics, computations are taught upto number five and only later are the higher numerals taught. The children learn in groups and join different groups every day according to their learning levels. While teaching environmental sciences, children are taken out on a household survey in order to learn the concepts by observation and interaction with the community members. For example, the information on domestic animals, their food habits, etc., are obtained from the heads of the households.

Initially, the community was hesitant and skeptical about learning in the absence of textbooks. But the improvement in the performance and behaviour of the children, both at school and at home in terms of their confidence and life skills, has encouraged the community to participate actively.

The teachers also feel empowered, as they create and impart their own curriculum, which, in turn, motivates themselves. Since teachers draw content and material from within the community, it enhances their interaction with the community and thereby, the relationship with the community members is strengthened. This continuous interaction with the community ensures the participation of the community in UEE.

Village Education Committees: The enactment of the 73rd and 74th amendment to the Constitution provides scope for the active participation of the community, both in the development and social sectors. Village education committees were formed as a sequel to this strategy. As discussed earlier, the constitution of these committees has been made mandatory by the promulgation of an executive order issued in 1995. The VECs comprise seven to 15 members, one third of them being women. They also have member representatives from SC/ST, minorities, parents, teachers, *anganwadi* workers and other persons interested in education. Since creating public awareness, involving them in the affairs of primary and secondary education, ensuring total enrollment and retention in primary schools and promoting adult literacy are the functions of the village panchayats, these have been assigned to the VECs.

Village education committees are formed in all the targeted villages of DPEP. Though the formation of the committees falls into the pattern followed in the rest of the state, great care has been taken during the training of members to communicate the supportive role of the community. All the training centres in the state follow the training module developed jointly by the Directorate of State Educational Research and Training (DSERT) and DPEP.

After the completion of training, a few positive interventions are made by the VECs. These interventions range from improving the facilities, preventing children from child labour, enrolling the drop-out children, facilitating innovative teaching practices, etc. However, even though VECs with their entrusted powers ensure community participation, the positive integration of the community's larger concerns into the system is yet to be taken up.

Micro-planning Exercises: The micro-planning exercises practised by NGOs in development sectors like watershed management and agricultural development have been adapted to the education sector. As for other developmental issues, the micro-planning exercise for primary education adopts a child-wise education plan prepared employing the five-component activities at the village level: (*a*) social mapping exercise, (*b*) seasonal chart, (*c*) resource mapping, (*d*) children's survey, and (*e*) children's workshop.

The micro-planning exercise is not universally covered, but has still succeeded in helping people understand their situation in a proper perspective. Several success stories have been reported. This practice has helped the department in evolving/adapting the exercise to assess the training needs of teachers. There can be a household survey focused on the study facilities available, support for study, suitability of the language learning imposed, material available for transaction, etc. Though the coverage is fairly satisfactory, the expectations in terms of village-specific plans for education are not coming forth.

Joint GOI/UN System's Community-based Primary Education Programme: To further complement the state government's measures to promote primary education, and to supplement the decentralized management of elementary education (by entrusting it to elected bodies from the village to district levels), it was felt that the capacities of communities have to be enhanced to participate effectively in the management of schools. The project, recently implemented in the 10 backward blocks with low female literacy, has designed the interventions to specifically enable this participation.

The community-based mechanisms initiated by the project to transform the existing schools into community schools are: (*a*) establishment and empowerment of VECs, (*b*) media and communication, (*c*) micro-planning, and (*d*) *chinnera melas*. This intervention is strengthened by the empowerment of VEC members through a specially designed training programme. The programme has just taken off and hence data on the performance is not readily available. However, stray reports of enhancements

in enrollment and participation in mobilization programmes indicate positive trends.

Vikasana

Vikasana is an NGO working in the district of Chikmagalur—a prosperous
district in Karnataka that has witnessed a high drop-out rate of girl children. Amidst proliferating prosperity, quite often, disturbing strands of
deprivation can easily be found. This is true of many capitalist endeavours,
and is exemplified by manifestations of inequity prevailing in industrialized
cities, high-productivity agriculture zones and plantations. Though the
question of equity in distribution and growth in market economies
remains unaddressed, the human misery in these areas carpeted under the
overall per-capita growth is being pulled out in recent years. Chikmagalur
district, which stands fifth in the HDI/GDI in the state, is a case in point.
Its forest cover and rainfall make it conducive for many commercial crops.
Coffee and arecanut plantations, the major commercial crops of this area,
absorb a lot of migrants from the nearby plains. These migrants, over gen-
erations, bereft of any significant improvement in their social or economic
status, form the majority of the local poor. Eight hours of work in plantations and in agricultural fields by couples—that too, mostly on all seven
days—for wages much below those prescribed by the minimum wages Act,
contribute to the persisting underdevelopment. It is a common sight to see
the older children given the responsibility of caring for the younger ones,
and children not attending school being absorbed as child workers and
sometimes as bonded labourers.

Vikasana—formed by a group of young, committed social workers in
1989—began its work towards development alternatives for the poor
households in the Amruthpura *mandal* through education and socio-
economic development. It identified child labour as the major problem of
the area. A special household survey was carried out in the area, which
identified about 300 child labourers in 10 villages. These children were
involved in the agricultural sector, coffee plantations, bamboo industry,
cattle grazing, etc. Vikasana decided upon education programmes as an
entry-point activity. This comprises of non-formal education (NFE) for
school drop-outs and child workers, and functional literacy classes for
adults. The organization has also started two crèches for the children of

working mothers. Along with these, it started an intensive awareness campaign involving children and the community members. Child workers were motivated to attend the NFE centres and subsequently enroll in formal schools. Children who were unable to reach the expected standards of performance were provided with skill training for vocational occupations. Meanwhile Vikasana got involved in the state-level campaign against child labour.

While these efforts were progressing, one of the major hurdles was the existence of bonded child labourers. After motivating the parents and children, the lack of an enabling environment defeated the purpose and relapses were commonly found. The timing of the school, distance to the school, lack of transport facilities and parents' work schedules were the main factors that impeded sustainability of the efforts to retain children in the school. A residential school emerged as the solution. Vikasana mobilized the community members to work towards the fulfilment of this. They identified a place on top of a hillock, belonging to the forest department, for the school. The community provided labour and construction materials. Teachers were also selected from the neighbouring areas. Residential coaching for child labourers was commenced in the month of June 1998. As of now, there are 24 children in the school. These children, all below 12 years of age, were working for more than two years as cowherds and domestic helpers. One cook-cum-ayah and two teachers stay in the school. Along with alphabets and numbers, children are taught songs, street plays, dance, painting and stories. Trained personnel from Vikasana design the curriculum so that children find it more interesting. "Learn while playing" is a motto followed for all the subjects. These children are trained to join formal schools in one year. According to their age and potential to cope with the formal school curriculum, they are prepared for particular standards.

In 1998–99, Vikasana could enroll 27 children back to formal schools from the NFE centres. To monitor their performance, the staff of Vikasana has made an arrangement with these schools. Every Thursday, the Vikasana staff take up two hours of extracurricular learning for all the children in these schools. They also run tuition classes for children they have put back to upper primary classes.

The participation of the community in the day-to-day running of the residential school is worth mentioning. They donate grains, millet, cereals and vegetables. They have also taken charge of the maintenance of the school building. More importantly, half the salaries of the teachers are borne by the community.

However, the success of this programme in gaining the participation of the community has to be understood against the backdrop of the community development work Vikasana has been doing since 1989. Child labour having roots in the social, economic and cultural history of a community, Vikasana's approach has been to deal with it in a holistic manner, which addresses the underdevelopment of the community. In 1993, it started the watershed project. In the following years, it initiated self-help groups (SHGs) for both men and women. These diverse engagements with the community benefited them in tackling many of the causes that perpetuate child labour, and the reasons commonly put forward to prove the inevitability of child labour and its links to low economic status. As the project director pointed out, when lack of money prevents the parent from redeeming the child from bonded labour, Vikasana provides them loans through SHGs. If children are given the responsibility of younger sittings, the younger ones are taken into crèches and the older ones made members of NFE centres. Parents are motivated for this through the meetings of adult literacy programmes and SHGs. Formal school teachers are also made a part of the campaign against child labour, so that they keep a watch on absenteeism. If books and other paraphernalia are pointed out as road-blocks for sending children to school, the organization promises them free books from the government. When children are forced to get back to work, most often to compensate for the money their fathers have borrowed, they are trained to give befitting replies to the landlords. If children are dissuaded by labelling them as "uninterested in studies" or for the years already spent without schooling, NFE centres are suggested for motivation and re-learning.

Samuha

Samuha is an NGO working to "improve the quality of life of vulnerable sections". Since 1986, in partnership with donors like ActionAid and PLAN International, it has been working in 51 villages of Deodurg taluk of Raichur district. It has recently expanded its work to another 22 villages in Irkalghada of Koppal district. The project began with the agenda of integrated rural development, identifying education and health of children as important concerns. The education project has two main programmes— *Balakendra* (BK) and *Suvidya*. BKs are "early childhood stimulation centres" and *Suvidya* is for "improving the quality of primary education" in terms of classroom interactions.

The *Balakendra* programme is being run in 51 villages with 52 centres. These centres are run by the women in the villages, who are mostly illiterate. This programme caters to 3,043 children of upto six years of age. *Gramasanstha* or village institution is set up in each of the villages to monitor the centres. *Gramasanstha* meetings are held once in a month and a representative from BK attends the meeting to share the progress. Samuha provides training to BK volunteers in batches of 5–15 members from time to time. The organization also provides nutritious food to the children attending these centres. The programme has also created employment opportunities for over 613 local women as BK teachers. Seventeen BKs have been merged with *anganwadi* centres in the villages and 12 are in the process of being merged.

Suvidya is an educational resource group of Samuha which works with 42 government schools from 51 villages (9 villages do not have schools). *Suvidya* trains teachers from these schools in activity-based teaching to create an experiential learning atmosphere for children studying in these schools. Training is held on a quarterly basis for teachers, in which lesson plans and activities are designed and discussed.

Suvidya also works as a resource group for DPEP in the area of mathematics teaching for primary classes. The 42 schools supported by Samuha are DPEP schools. Teachers outside the project area also attend the training programmes given by Samuha and use these materials in their schools. *Suvidya* caters to 4,489 children from the I to V standards in these 42 schools. Small teams of *Suvidya* resource persons visit schools regularly and provide technical support to teachers. Mathematics, science and language labs are established in each of these schools, and are upgraded periodically. This team works in tandem with VECs and monitors the programme and shares the progress with the *gramasanstha* on a monthly basis.

Suvidya also undertakes programmes like sports days, summer camps, scholarship assistance for girl children, child rights awareness, etc., in these villages. It also runs programmes like educational resource centres for teachers and works intensively with a small group of teachers (core group) to create an independent resource group in the project area. This core group includes resource persons from DPEP training centres like BRC (Block Resource Centre) and CRC (Cluster Resource Centre).

Samuha has enabled community participation in multiple ways. The communities have contributed 5,000 sq. ft. of land for each *balakendra* and contributed their labour in the construction of the building. The community also took charge of the maintenance of BKs. The *gramasanstha*, which monitors the programmes and maintains records, is formed almost entirely of community members. The resource group works with VEC members, thus facilitating participation of more community members in the design of the programmes. The community organizes food for the children during sports day and arranges other cultural activities. Elder members of the community, especially the BK teachers, have been instrumental in documenting local stories, folk songs, which forms the basis for the alternate teaching curriculum developed by the core group.

Community Initiative from within—Case of a Tribal Hamlet

If the above cases illustrate how communities are mobilized by interventions of government organisations and WGOs, a Lambani *thanda* in the district of Chitradurg elucidates a case wherein the community itself has taken up the responsibility of heralding development through providing education for the younger generation. This *thanda* or hamlet of Lambanis, a nomadic tribe in the northern part of Karnataka, has around 65 households and a population of 500. Lalitha Bai, aged 85, and popularly known as the great grandmother of the *thanda*, takes active interest in improving the living conditions of the community members. Almost all the adults of these households work as agricultural labourers, construction workers and quarry workers. Since all the adult members of the community—men and women—engage in longer working hours, and their families are large in size, childcare was entirely managed by the elder children of the families. This age-old practice has seldom provided these children the right to dream of a school-going childhood. Lalitha Bai, being aware of her only engagement during the day and of other elder people—sitting idly in front of their houses—initiated a childcare facility. She mobilized the community members to organize the older women and men who were out of the workforce to take charge of childcare during the working hours. She formed groups of older people (4–5 in number) for this purpose. This arrangement proved agreeable for the community and has enabled the older children to attend schools regularly.

Along with the provision of childcare, this group was also able to document and teach children their oral histories, stories and folk songs. The children, freed from taking care of their younger siblings, were initially taught by a few educated youth of the community. The venue for this teaching was Lalita Bai's house. Eventually, youth groups were formed in the hamlet and they took interest in teaching. They demanded a school in the locality from the government. Started in 1989, this initiative was able to provide a high school, electricity and water supply for the hamlet within four years.

The *mahila mandal*, which was formed later, took up the issue of alcoholism in the area. With the help of other groups in the community, they banned alcohol in the premises of the *thanda*. Today, the *thanda* remains alcohol-free, with strict sanctions against those who consume alcohol. And in this hamlet of a nomadic tribe, one witnesses a culture of literacy that has set in, resulting in 100 per cent enrollment of eligible children in the school.

Tungabhadra Irrigation Pilot Project (TIPP)—Phase II

TIPP-II is a bilateral Indo-Dutch project to improve the standard of living of male and female farmers in the command area of the Tungabhadra project on a sustainable basis, by optimizing the use of scarce water under the best mix of technically possible, economically feasible and socially acceptable conditions. One of its objectives is to formulate gender policies that broaden the scope of opportunities from improved irrigation management and develop institutional structures that facilitate the participation of communities in interventions for redressing their problems in a participatory manner.

Uppal village of Sindanur taluk is a case in point which demonstrates community initiative in development. It is a remote village in the most backward district of Karnataka, viz., Raichur. The village has no access road and is located six kms away from the nearest bus stand. As such, barely any development efforts have reached this village, including the visits of the health worker or the teachers to the school. The representatives of the Gram Panchayat, belonging to the SC community, could hardly attend the meetings and negotiate their demands in the panchayat. A link road establishing communication, health and education were the priorities of the women apart from access to water for irrigation. Realizing the power-lessness of the panchayat representatives and the absence of collectives (women and other groups), the irrigation project initiated a process of developing an institution to provide the framework to address gender issues. The society thus formed is based on the principles of both a development and a co-operative society. The introduction of this society changed the negotiating capabilities of the community. Through the society, the community has been able to construct the access road through *shramadhan* and with the support of the Command Area Development Authority (CADA).

The only school in the area consists of four rooms with a strength of around 200 students. A single teacher attended to it, though the plan was for a strength of four teachers. The main reason for this was the inaccessibility of the village. The teachers posted to this school were perpetually on leave or visited the school infrequently. The development co-operative society took up this issue. They could exert pressure on the panchayat to enforce regular attendance of teachers in the school. The society now monitors the school functioning and attendance of the children, and mobilizes resources for the maintenance and necessities of the school. It has also initiated a process of voluntary service by the village youth (men and women) to interact with the children in the absence of teachers, organize functions and involve children in community work during health campaigns, eye checkups, etc. Figure 7.1 presents the kind of linkages that the co-operative society has with the formal institutions and the accountability sought from them. The society as it exists today functions as a pressure group in articulating and realizing the development concerns of the village.

Figure 7.1: Link between society and formal institutions

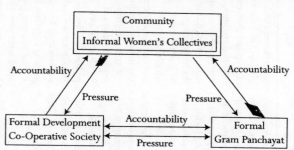

Community Participation—Potential and Limitations

An analysis of community participation from the case studies necessitates identifying certain parameters that facilitate/constitute it. The factors that contribute towards participatory intervention by the community are:

1. Identifying problems significant to the community.
2. Articulating and creating a demand for redressal.
3. Working together with people in planning intervention and implementation.
4. Working towards increased awareness of the community's strengths and weaknesses.
5. Creating opportunities for local people to get involved in decision-making.
6. Building the community's capacity to find appropriate solutions to their needs.
7. Identifying the hidden potential of community members in mobilizing resources and in strategizing practical actions.
8. Creating learning opportunities for every age group and, finally, a sense of ownership to ensure sustainability.

This involves representation of community members in decision-making bodies, in resource mobilization, and in access and utilization of resources. In addition, the sustainability of the intervention needs to be built into the community by making the imbibe a sense of ownership.

Table 7.4 Community participation in case studies

Organisation	Nature	Main area	Thrust area	Programmes	Technique	Process	Result
Vikasana	NGO	Development of the poor	Child labour	NFE and residential schools.	Community mobilization	Diversity of development programmes and interlinkages between them, recruitment of local people to decision-making bodies, resource mobilization from the community for the schools.	Reduction in child labour, re-enrollment of drop-out children, increased retention rates in schools, community participation in the functioning of NFE centres and schools.
Samuha	NGO	Development of the poor	Quality of education	BKs and Suvidya.	Working with the government, establishment of village committees, community mobilization, development of materials, creating resource persons locally	Support to government programmes by providing training to teachers, developing alternate material, need-based action to address diverse issues with the help of village committees.	Increased enrollment and reduction in drop-out rates, effective implementation of DPEP in the area, pedagogical innovations in science and mathematics, low-cost learning materials, formation of a core group of resource persons from the community.

Table 7.4 continued

Table 7.4 continued

DPEP	Bilateral government, programme	Primary education	Achieving UEE among the disadvantage groups	Quality improvement in curricula, capacity building for the existing education system.	Review of curriculum, street plays, films, establishment of new structures, campaigns and trainings, dissemination of materials.	Participatory preparation of modules and training for teachers, formation of VECs and training department for officials and public staff, providing equipment and materials.	Enhanced enrollment of children, reduced drop-out rates, innovations in pedagogy, community participation in the functioning of primary education.
Lambani Hamlet	Individual effort for community development	Community development	Girl-child education	Childcare and informal learning.	Older people taking care of the pre-school children, relieving the elder girls to attend school.	Conscientizing the community to take responsibility for underdevelopment and final solutions	Increased awareness about education, banning of alcoholism in the hamlet, overall improvement in quality of life.
TIPP-II	Bilateral development programme	Irrigation	Water management	Water user's association, institutional lies pressure groups, public co-operative and Socio-economic development.	Community mobilization through development co-operatives to influence panchayats.	A triangular nexus between community, development co-operatives and the panchayat to initiate and facilitate community development.	Community participation in the development programmes.

In line with this understanding on community participation, case studies have been analyzed for their diversity in community mobilization and participation in promoting primary education. Whether viewed from the perspective of the community or from the organization/programmes, two critical elements emerge as the most important determinants of effective community participation—first, involvement of community in decision-making, resource mobilization and implementation, and second, sustainability mechanisms located within the community. These two factors are used to critique the various approaches adopted to involve communities in improving primary education.

The case studies selected for evaluation consist of two NGOs—one collaborating with government and the other complementing the government's efforts—one government programme, one community initiative without any outside intervention and, finally, one development programme.

The common feature that exists in the two case studies of NGOs (Vikasana and Samuha) is a holistic approach. Their effort attempts to address all the developmental concerns impacting on the lives of the community. However, the evolution of the integrated process differs in both cases. Vikasana began its work addressing the issue of child labour. It started with non-formal education centres for child workers to re-enroll them into formal education. In trying to mobilize the community and enable their participation, they had to initiate several other developmental programmes which were of equal concern to the community—adult literacy programmes, self-help groups, health programmes, watershed project, etc. This holistic approach towards addressing the issue of low enrollment along with other developmental issues is considered to have effected the programme positively.

Samuha commenced as a developmental organization and eventually took up primary education, focusing on the pedagogical issues. In their efforts to improve the quality of primary education, they are complementing the governmental intervention (i.e. DPEP) by enabling the participation of communities. Both the NGOs, as a strategy to develop a sense of ownership among the community of the programme interventions and thereby build sustainability, resort to resource mobilization from the community. In other externally funded programmes, the communities were not entrusted with the sole responsibility and hence the resource mobilized formed only a meagre portion of the total financial resources required for the programme.

However, community participation being entirely facilitated by the interventions of NGOs, and their status as externally funded agencies, raise certain questions pertaining to the sustainability of community participation.

1. If the external resources are withdrawn, along with other programmes, will the community sustain the education programmes?
2. If the intervention ceases (NGOs physically withdraw), irrespective of other programmes becoming self-sustained or not, will the responsibility for running the residential schools, NFE centres and resource groups be taken up by the community?

Applying the same criterion for other case studies, similar issues emerge as concerns with respect to participation of communities in the programmes.

In the DPEP, with the fact of its being an externally funded government programme, what determines the sustainability of participation is the extent to which the communities are empowered. However, this empowerment process, being supply driven, is susceptible to any change in the policy or bureaucratic rearrangements and priorities. Quite often, such changes can undo the gains achieved.

The community intervention in the Lambani hamlet is quite unique and an ideal situation wherein the community, without any external intervention, takes the responsibility of identifying issues of concern and finding solutions from within the community. This initiative also has the potential for demanding fulfilment of their needs. Though initiated by an individual, sustainability of efforts lie within the community. This is enabled through the formalization of collectives (of various age groups). The possibility of creating newer groups through a few committed ones within the community exists as proof of sustainability for this kind of intervention.

TIPP-II, though started specifically as an irrigation project, developed institutional structures in the form of development co-operative societies, to mediate between the panchayat and the community. This society comprising of community members, due to its status of being a formal institution and at the same time a people's society, has been able to access government programmes as resources, mobilize the community, demand accountability from other formal institutions and, finally, act as an interventionist agency. Since it consists of community members, and being monitored by the community itself and motivated by the larger interests of the community as a whole—as in the case of Lambani community— sustainability is inherent in this intervention too.

Conclusion

Pioneered in the early 1980s, participatory methods and approaches provided a threatening response to the dominant development paradigm. The broad aim of participatory development has been to increase the involvement of socially and economically marginalized people in decision-making over their own lives, especially in the context of decentralized governance. Accessing primary education being intrinsically linked to the socio-economic and political development of communities and the choices people make about their lives, participation of communities has found a place in primary education programmes much before the movement of community participation itself, which took off in full swing in the latter half of the 1980s. Despite the stated intentions of social inclusion of various government programmes for promoting primary education, it has become clear that many initiatives overlooked the complexity of community differences and disparities in economic status, religion, caste, ethnicity and, in particular, gender. However, the present decade has witnessed serious attempts to rectify these shortcomings and has enabled community participation at various levels of programmes promoting primary education. Government efforts and selected non-governmental initiatives are critically analyzed to provide a comparative picture of various levels and modes of community participation.

What emerges as the single-most important finding in this analysis of the community participation experience is the fact that it has become crucial to all initiatives aiming to improve primary education. This centre stage that communities have come to occupy is one of the positive factors contributing to the increasing demand for primary education. Consequently, various innovative models are being practised to facilitate community participation and novel methods evolved employing techniques of management, communication, group dynamics, etc.

Another issue that needs further exploration is related to scaling up of successful community participation initiatives. Similarly, the quality and effectiveness of participatory processes adopted by NGOs in their programmes need to be disseminated through innovative strategies for replication. However, what is perturbing is the issue of sustainability of community participation in these efforts. As evident in the discussion above, whether it is a governmental, non-governmental or community initiative, unless mechanisms of sustainability are consciously built into the interventions, participation can be as short-lived as the intervention itself.

8

Making Sense of Community Participation: Comparing School Education and Watershed Development

Vinod Raina

The conflict between the state and society in India is perhaps most visible in the control and management of natural resources, as is evident from numerous people's movements centred on issues like forests, land and water. Whereas the nature of the state–society interface in education has some commonalities with that of watershed development, it also has major divergences, though in both these areas recent policy formulations seem to lay a greater emphasis on community participation. An uncritical attitude is very often unable to distinguish the difference in the use of the same term in these two vital areas of the country's development, as is evident from, say, the official and journalistic outpourings of recent policy and programme initiatives in these sectors in a state like Madhya Pradesh. The attempt of this paper is to explore such commonalities and divergences in order to establish that the term "community participation" denotes a much more complex and problematic process and set of issues than is usually understood, and to hopefully demonstrate that rational and sensible policy formulations require a serious understanding of such complexities.

Community in Education

Seeking community involvement in elementary education in post-independent India is a relatively recent phenomenon. The abortive community development programme, started in 1952, concentrated more on economic development, though even there it failed to take off because of the resistance of the bureaucracy to surrender its powers to community institutions.[1] The three-tier Panchayati Raj system suggested by the Balwant Rai Mehta committee in 1957 remained similarly stillborn, since regular elections to these bodies were not made mandatory. As far as education is concerned, the Constitutional directive that the state "shall endeavour to provide free and compulsory education till the age of fourteen in ten years" remained the hallmark of national policy. The inability of the state to do so in the 10-year period that ended in 1960 forced it to set up the Kothari Commission in 1966 to recommend what ought to be done. Among a host of recommendations, the Kothari Commission reiterated the responsibility of the state towards providing basic education by asking the government to provide at least 6 per cent of the GDP of the country for education—something the state has continued to disregard till date.

Though there are examples of religious bodies and other sections of society taking initiatives in providing school education, the reasons may sometimes be dubious. It has mostly been understood that the responsibility to bring in universalization of elementary education lies with the state. These examples include the work of Christian missionaries, the Arya Samaj through its DAV schools network, Muslim madrasas, and the schools of the RSS. Public schools—purely commercial, profit-making schools catering mostly to the rich—have of course proliferated in recent times in the era of privatization, and have sometimes in hilarious and ludicrous forms reached even the villages to cater to the needs of the growing rural elite. But in spite of all such non-state initiatives, more than 90 per cent of the nearly two hundred million children in the age group of 6–14 in the country are still dependent on the state school system.

Even before the passage of the 73rd and 74th amendments of the Constitution in 1994 that made the elected three-tier Panchayati Raj Institutions (PRIs) mandatory, the government had begun to concede that its delivery mechanisms were not adequate to meet the needs and aspirations of the majority population living in far-flung and remote areas. Independent of the state processes, the phenomenon of voluntary groups—mostly referred to as NGOs now—spreading to remote areas for work amongst needy communities gained momentum in the early 1970s, and by the mid 1980s, they had proliferated throughout the country. Accepting that the state delivery system was inadequate or insufficient to "take" development to the people, the sixth five-year plan document for the first time outlined the need to involve the community in developmental efforts, and identified the voluntary groups as the medium for such involvement and made budgetary provisions for their use. Such involvement was greatly sought during the poverty alleviation "*garibi hatao*" days and a separate body, the Council for People's Advancement and Rural Technology (CAPART) was carved out under the Ministry of Rural Development to exclusively cater to voluntary agency funding for rural development.

In the area of education, except for the sole and fortuous example of the Hoshangabad Science Teaching Programme—which was initiated in the formal middle schools of the MP Government by two voluntary agencies in 1972 and carried forward to primary education by *Eklavya* in the 1980s—curricular interventions in the formal schools have never been open for community groups or NGOs. But their involvement was sought in running the non-formal education scheme of the government of India, now nearly defunct, catering to out-of-school children. In a majority of such voluntary-agency-based non-formal education initiatives, the agency mostly arranged for the children to come together at a centre, and only a handful have engaged in working out innovative and local specific pedagogic methods and curriculum, the majority relying on the existing teaching–learning materials of official agencies. So except for one case in formal school education and a few instances in non-formal education, NGO and community-based initiatives have mainly been confined to management roles, to extend access.

It is in the beginning of the decade of the 1990s, also the Education For All (EFA) decade, that a greater stress can be discerned on ostensibly involving the community in school education and literacy. In school education, it has been linked mainly to externally funded special programmes. Rather than directly pass on these external funds to the concerned state education departments, a new mechanism has been invoked whereby state governments have created supposedly autonomous registered societies, in the manner of NGOs, and have run the programmes from such societies through a combination of education department officials and community organisations.[2] The Shiksha Karmi project and its associated resource support agency, Sandhan, the Bihar Education project, the Lok Jumbish project of Rajasthan, the Rajiv Gandhi Shiksha Mission of MP, and DPEP societies in various states are examples of such new institutionalization. A deeper examination of the functioning of these bodies, however, reveals the somewhat mythical nature of their purported autonomy and community involvement, the recent experience of the Lok Jumbish project providing glaring evidence to underscore the point. Apart from a token representation of a few non-governmental persons on the various committees in these bodies, community participation has been invoked through the formation of Village Education Committees (VECs). However, the nature of specific responsibilities of the VECs vis-à-vis the official machinery has been a recurring question, rendering the VEC process mostly nonfunctional, something that exists mostly on paper.

Around the time when such new institutionalization was being effected, elected PRIs were also being formed in many states as a consequence of the 73rd and 74th amendments of the Constitution. As is well known, one of the major tasks of the PRIs is in the area of school education, and a VEC structure is also envisaged in the PRI Act.

All of a sudden, therefore, from a situation where the running of school education was the exclusive domain of the officialdom, a situation has arisen where many other official institutions have got created, each with its own concept of community participation. Not to be left behind, a joint UN programme based on community participation has also been launched. Seeking community participation has therefore become the buzzword in school education, though it is very unclear for what purpose. The only issue everyone seems to agree upon is that the community must pressurize the hapless and generally overburdened teachers to perform and check their absenteeism, as if that is the major issue in school education, which implies a supervisory role for the local committee. Beyond that, except perhaps in Madhya Pradesh and in the earlier form of Lok Jumbish, very little is understood in terms of modalities and institutionalization of community participation in school education. With no resource support agencies outside the government-controlled DIETs in place, most of whom are of pathetic quality, how the capacity of the communities can be built up to handle tasks that may be assigned to them is totally unclear. The Shiksha Karmi project had the foresight to create its own innovative institution, Sandhan, and the Lok Jumbish project was successful in eliciting support from a variety of agencies, even from outside the state. But except for these examples, the support for most other initiatives still comes from the same old state-controlled structures—the SCERT and its allied institutions.

The case of Madhya Pradesh needs some elaboration. The government has attempted a vigorous decentralization of school education to the PRIs in the state, including even transferring the physical assets like school buildings to them. Teacher appointments and transfers have also been handed over to the PRIs. All this has been done through a flurry of government notifications.[3] One of the major initiatives concerns harnessing demand for children's education by allowing panchayats to open a centre under the Education Guarantee Scheme (EGS) if a requisite number of parents make such a demand. Government press notes claim the opening of thousands of such centres in the past few years, making EGS a major success story in the media. Such initiatives have not, however, left the regular school system untouched. The perennial shortage of trained teachers has been eliminated in a single stroke by allowing panchayats to recruit from their areas "lesser" teachers, shiksha karmis (SKs), for the job. They are different from regular teachers in terms of relaxation of minimum qualifications and do not require to have gone through any pre-service training. Consequently, their salaries are much less than that of regular teachers. With the recruitment of about 70,000 such SKs in one go, the state government has in fact abolished the post of a regular teacher and decreed that henceforth any teacher vacancy shall be filled only through the locally appointed SK.

The formation of EGS centre and the scheme of recruitment of SKs, both done locally, are seen as major initiatives in decentralizing education and seeking community participation in its implementation. That such initiatives are a departure from the past is readily apparent. But whether they strengthen or weaken the only diluted quality of school education is the question. It is well known that school achievement levels throughout the country, including Kerala and Himachal Pradesh, are abysmally low. Recognizing that as a fact, the central government was in fact forced to start the Operation Blackboard scheme a few years ago to strengthen the quality of school education in a variety of ways—infrastructure, teacher strength and quality, educational materials, etc. It has also been established in recent years that the lack of quality of schools is the single biggest factor in children's disinterest in schools and the consequent high drop-out rates from the school system. The logical conclusion, therefore, is that increasing access without improving quality would eventually lead to higher wastage of precious resources because of non-achievement, or worse, drop-outs. In such a scenario, enter EGS centres and the recruitment of SKs, ostensibly to meet the demand for access. With no policy to convert an EGS centre into a regular school in a given time frame, and a highly inadequate system of DIETs to cater to even the training of regular school teachers, not to speak of thousands of untrained SKs, the likely effect of the two together on the achievement of children in coming years is a frightening prospect. The nature of seeking community participation, which is not through a pressure from below, but through government notifications from above, raises important questions regarding the processes of decentralization. Some of these questions may be summarized as follows:

1. Is community participation from above, through notifications, a desirable process for school education, or any area of work, particularly when no viable safeguards and institutional mechanisms are designed to ensure that the quality of work does not further deteriorate? Or, as might happen in other cases like watershed, are the benefits of the outcomes likely to lack equity, widening the gap between the rich and the marginalized?

2. When we proclaim "decentralize education," or for that matter "decentralize X", is the term decentralize sufficient to ensure the improvement of education or X, irrespective of the particular set of internal parameters, structures, relationships and needs that education or X has?

3. Can community participation and decentralization be uncritically accepted as magical prefixes which, when attached to any activity, render the activity automatically desirable? Would, for example,

community participation or decentralization of corruption render corruption desirable? Is community participation a "neutral", "feel good", techno-managerial activity that can accomplish its goals without corresponding institutional, social and political changes?

It must not be misunderstood that the motivation for raising such questions is to debunk the notion of community participation altogether, and thereby endorse the prevalent non-participatory functioning of the government and its bureaucracy. On the contrary, these questions are being flagged in order to underline that the apolitical notion of participation is deeply flawed, and efforts have to be made to rectify it. But before attempting a general analysis on the concept of participation, it would be worthwhile to examine how it operates in the area of watershed development.

Watershed Development

Managing watersheds for rural development is a relatively new concept in India. The original concept of water management focused on large river valleys, in ways that would prevent rapid run-offs, soil erosion—limiting the incidence of potentially damaging flash floods—and the method usually employed to accomplish this was to build medium and large dams. A watershed is an identifiable drainage system, such as a stream or a river, containing a number of biophysical resources like soil and water, vegetation in the form of trees, grasses and crops, and providing sustenance for a number of enterprises such as pisciculture and livestock production. Watershed development is not merely concerned with stabilizing soil, water and vegetation, but with enhancing the productivity of resources in ways that are ecologically and institutionally sustainable.[4]

The natural terrain of watershed development is therefore local, around the drainage area, unlike large river valley projects that require more centralized approaches. The local nature of the task is, however, accompanied by a complex set of resource structures and their social control. Much of the land within watersheds is not under private control. Some may be under the forest department, some under the revenue department and some under communal, village-based ownership arrangements. In watershed development, therefore, one must contend with a multiplicity of resource controls, in addition to private ownership of land. This implies dealing with government departments in order to ensure that their resource-management strategies and practices are compatible with watershed approaches. With both government- and village-controlled common resources, institutionally sustainable rehabilitation and management are possible only where rural people act jointly to manage the resource. Community participation is therefore a natural choice in watershed development, and this may happen spontaneously or with outside support.

In watersheds where some resources are not privately owned, a contentious issue concerns the interaction between common property resources and private ownership. For instance, constructing bunds, terraces or check-dams on the upper slopes, generally on non-private land, can, under many geological conditions, recharge groundwater and increase the productivity of crops grown almost always on private land. The major issue, however, concerns the poor, landless and women, who rely mostly on the common property resources for fodder, fuel and other forest products. Watershed rehabilitation is essentially a resource-based approach to livelihood enhancement. Unless adequate safeguards can be built in, the danger is that as the commons become more productive, better-off farmers are tempted to take control of them, and the customary access rights of the poor are denied. The question of equity is therefore vital in watershed development.

This should illustrate that whereas community action appears a natural choice in watershed development, because of the varied nature of resource controls and their complex interactions, it would be nothing short of silly to assume the community to be homogenous in terms of benefiting equally through mere participation. Participation would have to go hand in hand with safeguards for the poor and marginalized, which most often is a political task requiring the active and sustained intervention of the state.

One may trace two broad reasons for the Indian state to adopt watershed development as a national policy. The social and environmental consequences of large river valley development—in particular, involuntary displacement of a large number of people—have resulted in the mushrooming of a variety of people's movements in many parts of the country, questioning such a path to water management. In any case, the continuous problem of floods and droughts, in spite of such large-scale projects, is a cause of misery to millions throughout the country. Parallel to these movements, sustained and successful experiments in participatory localized approaches to water management have also taken place in India through the voluntary sector, which have demonstrated the efficacy of such approaches. These include well-known examples from places like Sukhomajri, Ralegaon Sidhi, Baliraja and Palamau, as also organizations like the Pani Panchayat, Bharatiya Agro-Industries Foundation (BAIF), Mysore Relief and Development Agency (MYRADA) and the People's Science Institute to name just a few.

The government of India was finally compelled to take a policy decision and the publication in 1994 of the Guidelines for Watershed Development by the Ministry of Rural Areas and Employment marked a significant step in approaches that involve community participation with a high degree of decentralized decision-making and allocation of funds. Since this guideline document marks a watershed in the government's efforts to involve the community, at least on paper, some of its features are reproduced below:

1. "The breakdown of traditional institutions for managing common property resources and the failure of new institutions to fill the vacuum has also been responsible for the denudation of natural resources. The traditional community-based institutions have given place so far to individualised or market-driven exploitation of natural resources without any regard for adverse externalities of such actions, and to numerous official programmes for the development of land and water resources which are dependent almost entirely on the top-down bureaucracy with very little participation from the village communities.

2. "There are outstanding examples of success at Ralegaon Sidhi and Adgaon in Maharashtra, Kabbulnala and Mittemari in Karnataka, and Jhabua in MP.... Experience and knowledge available to us through these success stories have all gone into the preparation of these guidelines.

3. "Scientists have developed appropriate technologies to find solutions to most problems relating to watershed treatment. They range from simple check-dams to large percolation/irrigation tanks, from vegetative barriers to contour bunds. However, experience has shown that in a large percentage of cases, the farmers/villagers do not show

much enthusiasm for adopting these on account of several factors such as high initial investments, high operational/maintenance costs, or high technical input requirements. Further, in many cases, while the technology is quite suitable and simple, it is still unacceptable to the villagers on account of the socio-economic realities at the ground level which hinder its adoption. On the other hand, the farmers and the village community have evolved their own technologies based on local knowledge and materials, which are cost-effective, simple and easy to operate and maintain. While these may be practical innovations, they may not be the best technological options for the whole of the watershed taken as an integrated system.

"During the recent past several attempts have been made by ICAR/ SAU scientists, and many VAs [Voluntary Agencies] working on watershed projects, to investigate the scientific basis of local technical innovations. This has led the scientists to either give validation to the farmer's practices or improve upon their technical content without losing their comparative advantage of cost-effectiveness and simple and easy usefulness. These guidelines aim at encouraging this trend amongst the Project Implementation Agencies and ... ensuring upgradation and adoption of low-cost local technologies and materials for sustainable watershed development.

4. "Experience has shown that watershed development projects under different programmes often failed to achieve their physical and financial targets on account of inappropriate administrative arrangements or inadequate management skills of the project staff. Even in cases where progress has been satisfactory, development has not been sustainable in terms of operation and maintenance of assets created and common property resources because of inadequate participation by the village communities and User Groups. While the programme guidelines do emphasise the importance of people's participation in the developmental programmes, most successful experiments, largely of VAs and a few from governmental agencies, indicate that success is achieved through Government's/VA's participation in the people's programmes, rather than the other way around.

5. "The planning and implementation of watershed development projects involve the project staff of the implementation agency, whether governmental or non-governmental, and the village community that

is directly or indirectly dependent on the natural resources in the watershed area. Sufficient care needs to be bestowed on their orientation, skills' upgradation and motivation. The project staff needs training in technical content as well as the skill to recognise and improve upon indigenous technical knowledge. They also need to be trained in the tools and techniques of project management, Participatory Rural Appraisal [PRA] methods, community organization and other administrative and accounting procedures.

6. "The villagers need training and exposure to modern, scientific and technical methods, entrepreneurial skills to identify and exploit opportunities, community organization and team building to work in user groups. These guidelines provide for institutional arrangement and funding for community organization and training components.

Organization

- "80 per cent of watershed activities shall be carried out through self-help groups.
- "Around 50 per cent of the watershed community, that is those villagers who are directly or indirectly dependent on the watershed, are enrolled as members of at least one self-help group.
- "Separate self-help groups are organized for women, scheduled castes/tribes, agricultural labour, shepherds.
- "Around eighty per cent of the SHGs meet regularly at least once in a month and take all their decisions by common consensus.

Institutional Structure

1. Zilla Parishad/DRDA.
2. Watershed Development Advisory Committee.
3. PIA [Project Implementation Agency]: VAs, Universities, Corporation, Agricultural Research & Training Institutions, Cooperative Banks, PRI, Government Departments, Public & Private Commercial Organizations.

"PIAs will, with GP's involvement, pass relevant resolutions to make public contributions, conduct PRA, create community organizations & provide training for village communities. If VA etc. not present, ZP/DRDA may act as PIA.

"WDT: Each PIA (whether VA, PRI or GO) will institute a Watershed Development Team. Each WDT may handle 10–12 watershed development projects and may have at least four members—one each from the disciplines of plant sciences, animal sciences, civil/agricultural engineering & social sciences. Minimum Qualification: Professional degree in Agriculture Engineering or post-graduation in Botany, Economics/Sociology/Social Work. Relaxable in case of persons with field experience.

Located at PIA/Block level or other small town whichever is the nearest.

Watershed Association

"Where a watershed is coterminous with a village Panchayat or is confined within a GP, the Gram Sabha of the Panchayat concerned will be designated as the Watershed Association. At other places, the people directly concerned will be organized into a WA, which shall be registered. The WA shall receive seventy five per cent of the total funds for the WD [Watershed Development] project and only twenty five per cent shall go to the supporting PIA."

The reasons for reproducing some of these elements from the guidelines should be obvious; they incorporate major perspective and implementation details one rarely comes across in government documents. One could however ask the question, how effective has the programme been in the past six years since it was formulated? Though this paper is not meant to review the success or otherwise of watershed projects since the publication of these guidelines, the author has some first hand knowledge to assert that what gets written on paper and how it gets implemented often have very little in common with each other. As a practitioner working in association with the post-literacy country-wide watershed development projects of the Bharat Gyan Vigyan Samiti (BGVS), and as a member of the Executive Committee of CAPART which is the nodal agency for watershed programmes involving VAs, the major comment one can make is that neither of the funding agencies—the DRDAs or CAPART—have assimilated the spirit of community participation and control as visualized in the guidelines into their functioning. Because of this it has been a continuous struggle for PIAs, resource support agencies and field activists. In particular, the need to provide sufficient time and support for social organization has been overridden by the bureaucratic need to make expenditure within a financial year, so that financial targets are reflected as work done. Consequently, there has been tremendous pressure to get into actual civil work before the community organizations have been properly formed and trained, so that visible assets give an indication of project progress to questionable project monitors and evaluators. But that should not detract from the fact that some agencies have utilized the enabling guidelines to accomplish pioneering work.

Comparing Community Participation in Education and Watershed Development

Even though comparing education with watershed might sound like comparing apples with potatoes, the focus of comparison is on policy initiatives in community participation in each case, just as one may, with some validity, compare the agricultural practices in growing apples and potatoes. We may summarize the comparison as follows:

1. There is recognition of the traditional systems of managing common property resources in the Watershed Development Guidelines (WDG) and an acceptance of the fact that new institutions have not been able to fill in the vacuum created by the destruction of the traditional systems. In comparison, one rarely encounters even a mention of traditional systems in education, which is likely to elicit sniggers in official circles. Not only did a community-based traditional system flourish in school education prior to the organization of the formal school system by the British, but as chronicled by people like Dharampal, it operates even today covering a very large population, and was at the heart of Gandhi's notion of basic education (nai talim). Apprenticeship or the guru-shishya parampara does not operate only in the field of music, dance and arts in the country, but covers larger numbers in the productive and service sectors, like artisanal production, agricultural practices, repair of motor vehicles and other mechanical devices—the list is long. A large number

of children of the country in fact find productive vocations through such education, which is completely community based, operating in households or at the work place. But in educational policy, instead of recognizing and learning from it, it is completely ignored as if doesn't exist at all. Or the definition of education is so exclusively confined to that as operates in state-controlled formal schools that everything else must necessarily be excluded, which automatically eliminates a large chunk of educational activity operating at the community level.

2. The WDG openly acknowledges the effects of independent efforts in watershed work, be that at Ralegaon Sidhi, Adgaon or Jhabua, and declares that these experiences have gone into shaping the guidelines. Groups like Eklavya, Diganter, M.V. Foundation, to name a few, have done pioneering work in the area of school education, but it has never been utilized in formulating educational policies. The most recent example is the discussion document brought out by the NCERT for formulating a new school curriculum for the entire country. There was no attempt to base the document on experiences from innovative and pioneering efforts made in the country, or to involve them in preparing the document, as was done in preparing the WDG. At the state level, for example in MP, there was no desire to discuss and involve long-serving agencies in formulating the EGS scheme, the decision to do away with regular teachers in preference to SKs, etc. After formulating all these policies, the community was asked to participate!

3. There is a clear emphasis in the WDG on the comparative merit of knowledge generated at laboratories and the empirical knowledge that resides with communities through years of practice. The guidelines very clearly state that scientific and technical knowledge generated in faraway labs might find little social and cultural acceptance in real conditions, as compared to existing knowledge at local levels. Therefore it demands that the PIAs must recognise empirical knowledge and work out methods for the upgradation of such knowledge. Such an understanding and sensitivity to local knowledge is completely absent in the domain of school education. The paradigm that prevails here is one of arrogance about the 'fact' that subject experts have all the knowledge, which must be the basis for preparing teaching–learning materials and teacher orientation. Local knowledge systems, be that in languages,

literature, culture, production systems, materials, medicine and so on are completely ignored, in a sense treating such knowledge as backward. But it is from the same knowledge pool that the WDG exhorts the implementation agencies to draw upon! We also now have the spectacle of leading multinationals using local knowledge pools as the basis for legally stealing such knowledge from the people who are its repositories through the monopoly-patenting regime. But for the formal school system, a centralized authority must prescribe what is "modern", state of the art and frontier knowledge for all the children in the country. The community participation efforts in education have therefore remained confined to decentralizing management and administrative responsibilities, with the clear understanding that the teaching–learning process would remain centrally controlled and closed for any kind of participation, even from professional NGOs.

4. Another major highlight of the WDG is the nature of organization envisaged. The primacy of the community is clearly underlined by the fact that the bulk of the funding–75 per cent–would go to the community group, the watershed assembly, and not to a line department or even to the supporting PIA—which would receive only 25 per cent of the money. While recognizing such a primacy, the guidelines very realistically take cognizance of the need for field-based human resource support that should help the community group to undertake its tasks—hence the provision for the PIA, and in particular, the Watershed Development Team (WDT). So for every watershed project, a PIA that can be non-governmental and a WDT of qualified persons would be the support structure for the community group to fulfil its tasks. The lack of such an organizational perspective is a major lacuna in the case of education, where it is assumed that the line department would fulfil all the academic and management tasks, with a VEC overseeing only the monitoring aspects. And for all this, there would be no additional resource support structure except for what exists in the existing bureaucracy—the SCERT, DIETs or their lower tiers. That community participation requires drawing in a vast network of support structures at the local levels, particularly those that exist within the civil society and not in government structures, has yet to penetrate the thinking in education. It is naively assumed, as in Madhya Pradesh, that government

notifications defining the administrative (not academic) powers and delegating them to the PRIs is the end-all of educational decentralization and community participation. Academic decentralization that draws in the knowledge of the communities in the teaching–learning process, and a locally organized resource support structure to help the community organize to do so should have been the corresponding corollary from the WDG with regard to education, but it simply isn't. The need to promote and train local-level resource institutions has also been a major effort in the watershed development programme. For this job too, experienced and professional civil society institutions have been supported to continuously train other groups and individuals who could then perform the tasks of a PIA or WDT member. Consequently, institutions like the People's Science Institute in Dehra Dun, the one at Ralegaon Sidhi, Samaj Parivartan Sahyog in Dewas district of Madhya Pradesh, Bharat Gyan Vigyan Samiti[5] and many more have been performing the task of increasing the resource pool.

It is apparent, therefore, that in terms of vision, perspective, organizational details and sensitivity, the WDG could act as a blueprint for education and other sectors too, of course with suitable adoptions to suit the requirements and internal needs of the respective sectors.

What finally is Community Participation?

The discussion till now has been moulded more from the notion of community participation as expressed in policy formulations emanating from the state. Is that sufficient for analyzing such a wide-ranging notion? The answer has to be no, since community participation is not merely a set of guidelines or organizational procedures; it is above all a concept full of political meanings.

At one end we have the Marxian viewpoint from which community participation would appear as a retreat from the essential task of capturing state power through class struggle. Instead of leading the poor and marginalized into a political change, community participation could in fact, from this perspective, appear to provide legitimacy to the existing state by providing it with a smokescreen, as to how accommodating and sensitive the state is to the needs of the people. Its widespread use today prompted one commentator to describe it as: "the aerosol word of the 70s because of the hopeful way it is sprayed over deteriorating institutions,"[6] which sounds very apt for the institutions of India of the 1990s! A counterview might be that particular forms of community participation might actually lead people to fight for their legitimate rights, and need not therefore be inimical to the assertion of their political rights.

This necessitates a closer examination of the concept of community participation. In general, a participatory approach implies a major, but not exclusive role for local populations in allocating rights and responsibilities. The substance of participation is, however, ill defined and obscure—who is participating, how and in what; who has decision-making and regulatory powers, and who has access to resources and funds. Taken together, these constitute a set of political issues. We may outline a typology of participation in the following manner:[7]

Passive Participation: People participate by being told what is going to happen or has already happened. Decentralization of administration is often held out as a modality that increases participation. However, when the decentralization is no more than extending the reach of the administration to lower levels by adding tiers from the district to block to Gram Panchayat levels, the participation may at best be passive in that a local official is handy to inform people about the decisions of the government.

Participation in Information Giving: People participate by giving answers to questions posed by extractive researchers and project managers. A lot of participatory research ends here, since the analysis, policy formulations and implementation strategies are formulated by the project holders.

Participation by Consultation: People participate by being consulted and external agencies listen to their views. External agencies define both the problems and solutions. In this category, the interaction with the people may be more human than formal and the nature of consultations may be sensitive to the language, customs and priorities of the people.

Participation for Material Resources: People participate by providing resources—for example, labour—in return for cash or food. Many rural development schemes require such an assurance from project holders, and the quantum of participation is judged by the amount of non-cash contributions from the community. In fact many schemes already prescribe such participation in percentage terms as a norm!

Functional Participation: People participate by forming groups to meet predetermined objectives relating to the project, which can involve the development or promotion of externally initiated social organization and goals. One might cite the watershed development programme and the mass literacy campaigns as approximate examples of such participation.

Legislated Participation: People are endowed with constitutional rights to create local forms of governance. The 73rd and 74th amendments of the Constitution are examples. However, the functionality of such bodies is critically dependent on the actions of the state to devolve powers, resources and institutions to such bodies, and to equip them in every sense to perform their obligations.

Interactive Participation: People participate in joint analysis, which leads to joint action-plans and formation of new groups or strengthening of old ones. The People's Planning Process of Kerala, where every panchayat has made its five-year plan which has been incorporated in the overall ninth plan of the Kerala state, with assured funding for each of the local plans, could be an illustration for this category of participation.

Self-mobilization: People participate by taking initiatives independent of external change systems or agents. With some variation, many people's movements would fall in this category.

It needs to be emphasized that the above typology is neither exhaustive nor sacrosanct and it would normally be very difficult to fit real examples neatly into a particular category, since they would have overlap with more than one category. The categories are at best indicative of the differentiation in the term "participation".

If such differentiation can be traced to the term participation, the term community must also be complex, which it surely is. We find an increasing stress on the ideal of a culturally and politically homogeneous, participatory local social system in developmental literature. The focus of much participatory work on "community meetings" as the forum for decision-making, representing perceptions in the form of "community map" as if only one view exists, and striving for a single "community action plan" or a village plan that will somehow meet the needs of the entire community are signs of this ongoing simplification. Inequalities, oppressive social hierarchies and discrimination are often overlooked, and instead, enthusiasm is generated for the co-operative and harmonious ideal promised by the imagery of "community."[8]

Such romanticization is sometimes carried forward in the belief that "the people" can do no wrong, communities are inherently good, and community action is sufficient for the practice of alternatives and political action is to be avoided. The belief often extends to characterizing the state as the problem or part of the problem, and stating that alternative development must as much as possible proceed outside and perhaps even against the state. Thus, the state is defined as the enemy—bureaucratic, corrupt and unsympathetic to the needs of the poor. The emphasis, therefore, is to bypass the state and to concentrate instead on local communities, which are considered moral and autonomous. For many, the voice of the people cannot be in conflict with itself; it speaks truly. And since the state is regarded as venal, politics is best avoided; it would only contaminate the purity of face-to-face encounters in the neighbourhood and village which, in turn, would negate an authentic, people-centred participation. Such a reading of the community, akin to that of an all-but-anarchist programme along the lines of Kropotkin's writings, or even Gandhi at times, is a visible influence amongst many practicing groups.[9]

It should, however, be contended that though participation must begin at the local level with communities, a project cannot end there. Whether we like it or not, the state continues to be a major player, and we want it to be a major player if education is to be universalized or sustained livelihoods for the vast majority of the poor have to be ensured. Local empowering action perhaps requires a strong state, particularly in times when the dominant market mechanisms can marginalize the poor further without state-mediated safeguards.[10] Communities themselves have class, caste, gender, religious and ethnic fault lines. In particular, the universally subordinate role of women requires us to identify yet another source of social tension and conflict that cuts across all of the others, and operates not only in the community but at a much local scale, the household. Each of the several social groups within a territorial community is likely to see its situation from its own perspective and contend over the same and always limited resources—something most visible in the share of assets created under watershed programmes. Territorial communities are thus necessarily also political communities, rife with the potential for conflict. And these conflicts are unlikely to be contained locally. They are likely to spill over into regional and national political arenas. A politics of claiming is inherent in development, be that in the economic or the social sector, which is always about the use of common resources or entitlements (usually controlled by the state) and the removal of those structural constraints that ensure that the poor stay poor.

If community participation is to advocate the social empowerment of the poor, it must also, therefore, advocate their political empowerment. The case being made here is not to deny the principle of community participation in the pursuit of social and economic development, no matter how fractured the community may be. The point being emphasized is that it needs to be judged in each instance as to how much political empowerment it brings to the participants. A techno-managerial and apolitical approach to community participation may appear to give some short-term gains, but it contains the danger of increased political disempowerment of the poor, the women and the marginalized, which in the final analysis cannot be in their interest.

Notes and References

1. For a descriptive account of attempts towards educational decentralization in India, see, for example, T.N. Dhar (1997), "Decentralized Management of Elementary Education: The Indian Experience", in R. Govinda (ed.) *Decentralisation of Educational Management: Experiences from South Asia*, Paris: International Institute of Educational Planning.
2. See Raina, Vinod (1998) "External Funds, Internal Conflicts", *Seminar*, April.
3. See Govinda, R., "Dynamics of Decentralized Management in Primary Education: Policy and Practice in Rajasthan and Madhya Pradesh", article in this volume.
4. For a detailed and varied analysis of watershed development efforts in India, see, for example, John Farrington, Cathryn Turton and A.J. James (eds) (1999), *Participatory Watershed Development—Challenges for the Twenty-First Century*, New Delhi: Oxford University Press.
5. See Paranjape, Suhas, K.J. Joy, Terry Machado, Ajaykumar Varma and S. Swaminathan (eds) (1998), *Watershed Based Development—A Source Book*, New Delhi: Bharat Gyan Vigyan Samiti.

6. M.A. Jones (1977), *Organisation and Social Planning in Australian Local Government*, London: Heinemann, quoted in Irene Guijt and Meera Kaul Shah (eds) (1998), *Myth of Community—Gender Issues in Participatory Development*, London: Intermediate Technology Publications.

7. Adapted from M. Pimbert and J. Pretty (1997), "Diversity and Sustainability in Community Based Conservation", paper presented at UNESCO/IIPA Regional Workshop on Community-Based Conservation, New Delhi, February 1997.

8. For a thoroughgoing analysis of the fissures running through a community, particularly in gender terms, see Irene Guijt and Meera Kaul Shah, cited in note 6 above.

9. An analysis of the empowered community and its relation with the state can be found in Friedman, John (1992), *Empowerment—The Politics of Alternative Development*, Cambridge, MA: Blackwell. Case studies for the same can be found in Raina, Vinod, Aditi Choudhury and Sumit Choudhury (eds) (1999), *The Dispossessed—Victims of Development in Asia*, 2nd edition, Hong Kong: ARENA Press, distributed in India by Manohar Publications, New Delhi.

10. The tension between the state, market and community, and its operation in education can be found in Raina, Vinod (2000), "Decentralisation of Education", *Education for All 2000 Assessment*, New Delhi: NIEPA and MHRD.

9

Dynamics of Decentralized Management in Primary Education: Policy and Practice in Rajasthan and Madhya Pradesh

R. Govinda

There is a general consensus among all in India that decentralization of educational management and empowerment of the community in planning and management of primary education programmes are basic strategies critical for achieving the goals of universal primary education. However, these are operationalized in different ways across the country. This article attempts to capture and compare the approach adopted in two educationally backward states, namely, Rajasthan and Madhya Pradesh. Both the states have major programmes for achieving the goals of primary education for all, and have recorded considerable progress in the recent years with respect to enhanced participation of the community. Nevertheless, the models of decentralization adopted by the two states are quite different. Madhya Pradesh has followed a top-down approach of changing the legal provisions and transferring responsibilities to locally elected bodies. In Rajasthan, following the principle of building from below, informal group formation and capacity building among community members at the grassroots level in self-management has been given precedence over legal provisions.

Decentralization of educational planning and management is not a new subject of discussion in India. The need for decentralizing the educational management system in the country has been highlighted in several policy documents at national as well as state levels. In particular, the National Policy on Education, 1986, recommended extensive structural reforms to bring about decentralization in educational planning and management processes.[1] Following this, one could witness a new enthusiasm emerging on the Indian scene to change the existing management framework and to ensure greater involvement of the community in management of primary education. This is quite evident from the developments taking place in different states through the establishment of village education committees as well as the thrust created for local level planning under different programmes of "Education for All". The new Panchayati Raj Act has also added greater fillip to this move towards decentralization in the management of primary education.

While the country has continued its commitment to a policy of decentralization in education, the nature of the discourse has undergone sharp changes. In the early stages after independence, the decentralization rhetoric was always projected on the basis of ideological considerations.[2] As a country newly liberated from political domination by colonial masters, "power to the people" and "grassroots level democracy" were basic credos to be valued and implemented in their own right. The legitimacy of such propositions never came for critical examination. In contrast to this, the rationale put forth in the recent policy pronouncements are replete with more pragmatic considerations of efficiency and quality. For instance, the report of the committee set up by the Central Advisory Board of Education (CABE) on decentralization in India argues, quoting international trends: "It is increasingly becoming evident that the bureaucratic systems are not able to manage the challenges in the field of educational development and people's participation is seen the world over as an essential pre-requisite for achieving the goal of education for all. It is in this context that the committee perceives the entrustment of educational programmes to institutions of local self-government as a step in the right direction."[3]

Irrespective of the proclaimed rationale for initiating decentralized management, all such measures involve far-reaching decisions on power sharing and inevitably carry political overtones. Any operation aimed at achieving some form of decentralization is not merely a technical and

administrative undertaking—the nature and "degree" of power transferred within such a reform process are dependent upon political will and
the power struggles that underlie all efforts to achieve decentralization.[4] It
is, therefore, natural that implementation of decentralization has taken
varying routes and acquired different contours in different parts of India,
influenced by a number of background factors characterizing the state. In
fact, "[I]n the Indian federal set-up, most structural reforms fall in the
state sector. The centre can only offer incentives and guidelines. Even
where the central government has specific roles to play, implementation is
by-and-large left to state governments."[5]

It is within this context that this article attempts to capture and compare the approach adopted in two educationally backward states of India,
namely, Rajasthan and Madhya Pradesh. Both states have major programmes for achieving the goals of primary education for all and have
recorded considerable progress in the recent years. However, the models
of decentralization adopted by the two states are quite different. Madhya
Pradesh has followed a top-down approach of changing the legal provisions
and transferring responsibilities to locally elected bodies for primary education management. The progress made in this regard is substantial and
unique in its impact on the primary education scene in the state. In contrast, Rajasthan, under its major project of primary education known as
Lok Jumbish, has apparently followed the principle of building from below.
Informal group formation and capacity building among community members at the grassroots level in self-management has been given precedence
over legal provisions. This does not mean that there has been no attempt in
the former to promote community participation. But, the process is
couched in a system of change from above. Similarly, in Rajasthan, the
grassroots-level action for community empowerment has the tacit approval of the state government. However, the state government has not
promulgated any legislative measure to formalize the role and functions of
the community with respect to primary education.

This article explores the differing dynamics involved in operationalizing
the two contrasting approaches for decentralization of primary education
management, and empirically examines the relationship between these
measures and the change in the primary education situation in the two
states. It also discusses the various issues arising out of the two approaches,
such as: How broad-based is the level of community empowerment? Is

there a special emphasis on involvement of women and other weaker sections of the community? To what extent is the participation of the community in primary education management spontaneous, or is it only externally engineered? What are the changed roles and functions of the educational bureaucracy under the two approaches? Finally, what are the implications for the long-term sustainability of the measures initiated?

Collection of empirical information from the field was done at three levels in both the states—district, block and village. The Rajasthan study covered 16 villages from four different districts; in Madhya Pradesh, the field study included visits to 7 villages in two different districts. However, more extensive data collection was done at the state and district levels in the latter study. Both cases involved elaborate documentary analysis. Thus, data on the existing practices with respect to decentralized management of primary education and regarding the involvement of the community in decision-making were collected through analysis of documents and observation of the field reality. Perceptions and experiences of various actors involved in the decentralization and community empowerment processes were collected through questionnaires and focus group discussions.

A conceptual framework was prepared for systematically analyzing the dynamics of change involved in decentralization of the existing system of management in the two states. This is briefly discussed in the following section. The next section of this article deals with the presentation and discussion of the empirical findings with respect to various principles and factors related to decentralization and community empowerment. The last section attempts to highlight some of the critical questions and issues that remain unresolved in the ongoing efforts in the two states.

Conceptual Framework for Analysis

Central control or local self-governance is never an all-or-none phenomenon. It is essentially a matter of coming to terms with the sharing of power and authority between stakeholders at various levels. In fact, the contestation is not merely between the political representatives at the centre and the periphery. Rather, in the modern state, it is inevitably a three-cornered contest, the three parties being (a) the political power groups operating from the centre, (b) the representatives in the peripheral units of governance who are closer to the local community they represent, and (c) the bureaucracy which has become an integral part of the modern administrative set-up in all countries. Within a stable political set-up, even though the equations keep changing, all stakeholders come to accept a set of norms over a fairly long period of time. Thus decentralization, even if contested, is not seen as seriously threatening to the established power centres. In a way, this is what one finds in politically stable countries of the world, where the nation-state has evolved over a relatively long period of time through historical coming together of local power centres, more or less voluntarily[6] (see Figure 9.1).

Figure 9.1: Evolutionary process

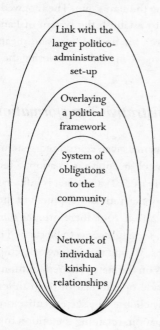

Link with the larger politico-administrative set-up

Overlaying a political framework

System of obligations to the community

Network of individual kinship relationships

In India, which became an independent nation-state through a decolonization process, the story of the relationship between stakeholders at various levels has been configured externally. Decentralization moves in India are, therefore, basically transformational and not evolutionary. As Laclau points out, decolonized countries such as India have assumed their present form of nation-state following an external logic, rather than acting in response to the internal growth of centres of hegemonic power.[7] Interestingly, even the linguistic division of states within India has come about on similar lines. Therefore, transforming the existing set-up to achieve a balance of powers between the central and the local self-government units, and reaching a state of relative stability is a continuous process of search. The question of what the capacity of the state/centre is to reform its own relationship and engineer the transformation process is not easy to answer. Perhaps it is quite limited, particularly if the operational space is occupied by well-entrenched political groups at the national/state level and the political space at the local level is occupied by traditional elements with vested interests in maintaining the status quo. The renewed efforts during the last five decades in India to establish the system of Panchayati Raj essentially represents such a search for finding ways and means of transforming the political–administrative set-up and empowering the local communities for self-determination.

Technical–administrative Transformation

In any effort to transform a given centralized system of management into a decentralized one, one clear option is to adopt a technical–administrative approach. This (see Figure 9.2) approach is influenced by the fact that the internal logic of the bureaucratic development of the state has been a powerful factor in centralization. And, therefore, the *transformation process begins essentially as a top-down technical exercise* to be carried out within the ambit of administrative reforms. Within this framework, empowerment of the local governments depends on the state. The redefinition of powers and authority can further be made operational through different mechanisms. The state government may choose to issue executive orders for the transfer of powers through delegation, retaining the option to abrogate the powers at its will. Alternatively, the changed framework of sharing of powers and authority between the state government and the local governments may be politically devolved through legislative action. In the latter case, withdrawal of power and authority requires the state to go through the legislative process and therefore makes it difficult to recentralize.

Figure 9.2: Technical–administrative transformation

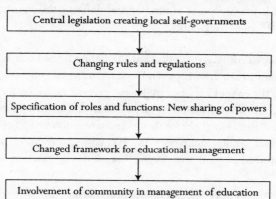

An alternative model of decentralizing the management framework is to begin from the other end, adopting a bottom-up approach. Here, even though the actions are carried out under the patronage of the central leadership and through the intervention of an external agent, primacy is given to the local community (i.e., civil society) in formulating the rules of the game. The approach, to some extent, tries to orchestrate the evolutionary process by building from below an organizational arrangement that should eventually get integrated with the framework of state-level administration. In the former model, the main scene of action is the centre, and the activity mainly consists of rewriting the books of rules, regulations and functional allocations. At best, this may involve consultation with the actors at the peripheral levels. In contrast, a bottom-up approach shifts the scene of action to the villages, and community members become the main actors. The basic purpose of adopting a bottom-up approach is the creation of endogenous factors of change that contribute towards increased equity and generate developmental dynamics at the grassroots level. As Marsh points out:

> Bottom-up in the state-initiated reform context focuses on school and teachers as the bottom....Important dimensions of the bottom-up strategy found in the dissemination literature: power equalization among decision makers at the bottom and an emphasis on a set of process steps featuring needs assessment, setting of site-relevant objectives,

searching for solutions, and implementing those solutions. The role of the state is primarily one of funding and defining the parameters of the local problem-solving effort.[8]

It is difficult to come across efforts at the national level which are exactly on these lines in any country, even though small-scale efforts and sectoral plans, as in the case of literacy campaigns, present examples for generating such grassroots-level dynamics. The problem with many of these efforts is that they are abandoned before they culminate, without incorporating the organizational arrangements into the formal–legal framework. They are generally treated as good innovations that cannot be taken to scale.

Figure 9.3: Social–political transformation

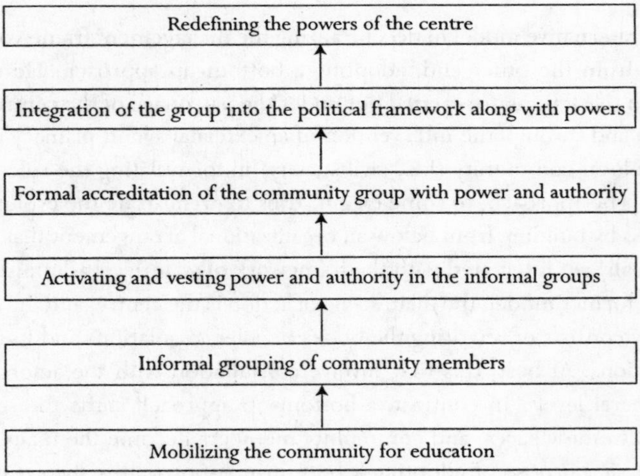

Viewed within the above conceptual framework, recent developments in Madhya Pradesh and Rajasthan present interesting cases with respect to the management of primary education. It can be hypothesized that Madhya Pradesh has gone for a top-down model of decentralization while Rajasthan, under the banner of Lok Jumbish, is attempting to decentralize primary education management by building it from below. Several questions have to be examined in both cases. For instance, in Madhya Pradesh, has the process of decentralization really empowered the community members in decision-making? Does Lok Jumbish attempt to orchestrate processes at various levels in a consistent manner for implementing a programme of transformation from below? Do the moves portend the emergence of a fully decentralized arrangement for managing primary education in the two states?

It has to be recognized that in both the states these processes of transformation have been initiated within an already operating system. Also, one cannot insulate these processes in the sphere of primary education from the developments in other social sectors. Further, elements of these two models may be operationalized in an overlapping manner. For instance, while advocating for people's mobilization at the grassroots level, the government may find it politically expedient to simultaneously initiate actions for the deconcentration or delegation of powers. Similarly, while rewriting the statutes to allow for greater power and authority to the Panchayati Raj bodies, the state government may initiate processes for community mobilization. Some of these actions may complement one another and promote effective decentralization. But some others may remain asynchronous and create more friction within the system. For instance, creating formal bodies, within a larger political framework or otherwise, at the periphery without adequate preparation among the stakeholders for self-determination may prove counterproductive. In fact, there are ample examples where governments have put forth lack of capacity and preparedness as an excuse and moved to recentralize power.

Decentralized Management of Primary Education—Situation in Madhya Pradesh and Rajasthan

As mentioned before, educational development has been quite unsatisfactory in both the states. Thus, providing basic education for all continues to be a priority task in these states. It is in this context that large-scale projects on primary education are in operation in both the states. The Lok Jumbish project which began in 1992–93 has expanded during the last five to six years to cover more than 100 blocks of Rajasthan. In Madhya Pradesh, the District Primary Education Programme which began in 1994 has grown even faster and covers more than 40 districts. Both the project documents underline the importance of decentralization and community participation for achieving the goal of education for all. Further, in both the states, these projects occupy centre stage in the process of decentralization.

The Madhya Pradesh Case

The Panchayati Raj in Madhya Pradesh had remained quite dormant and without much teeth in terms of powers and authority for the local governments till the beginning of the decade. The 73rd Constitutional amendment adopted by the Indian Parliament in 1992, making elections to the Panchayati Raj bodies mandatory, led to a series of measures by the Madhya Pradesh government. A three-tier system of local self-government was established and elections were held for these bodies. The structure created by the state government is almost completely in line with the model legislation proposed at the national level.

As mentioned earlier, the decision regarding the specific powers and authority to be vested in the local bodies, or those to be retained by the state machinery, is the prerogative of the state legislature. Accordingly, a number of notifications have been issued by the state government transferring several subjects to the control of the district-, block- and village-level Panchayati Raj bodies. The state government also set up a State Finance Commission to decide on transfer of resources to the district bodies. At present, 65 per cent of the funds received at the district level are provided to the village panchayats for developmental action. This has undoubtedly brought in a sense of self-direction among the elected representatives at the grassroots level.

One can easily recognize that the political space from the district level downward is now occupied by democratically elected representatives. But has it significantly changed the decision-making process? Do the members of the civil society really feel empowered for deciding on local action and determining their own future? As illustrated by the diagram on the management structure, the operational space, at least with respect to educational management, seems to be still clogged with bureaucracy.

Main Features of the Education Management Set-up

In the Indian federal set-up, state governments are responsible for internal administration including the Panchayati Raj. Therefore, effective decentralization depends on the willingness of the state government to transfer powers and authority to the local bodies. Several questions arise in this context: What powers and authority have been transferred to different local government bodies? Who wields the power within the panchayat set-up? What is the role of the existing education management personnel? What is role of the VEC/SMC in school management and what is its relationship with the village panchayat? Does the nature of power and authority transfer amount to political devolution? To what extent is primary-school management truly participatory? What is the relationship between the project management and the state department of education? Some of these questions were examined through empirical observations in the field.

Figure 9.4: Panchayati Raj and educational management structure in Madhya Pradesh

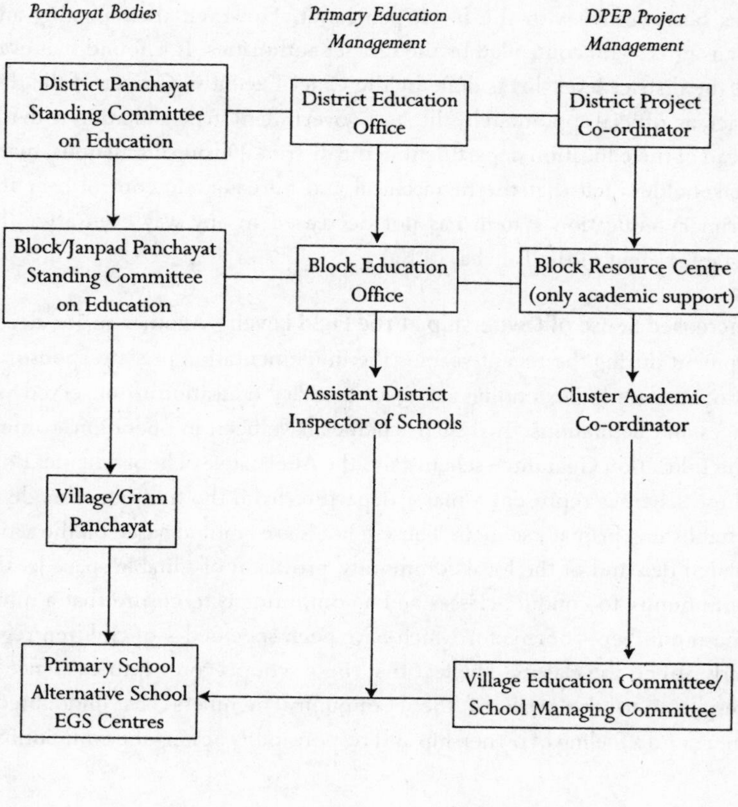

Transfer of Powers and Authority: Following the creation of Panchayati Raj, the state government transferred a few select subjects to the exclusive control of the local bodies. With respect to education, the Commissioner of Public Instruction issued a special notification transferring specific powers to the district, block and village panchayat bodies through an executive order. It is important to note that this only represented the delegation of select powers and functions, with the overarching power given to the state department to intervene in any matter.

Bureaucracy Continues to Reign: An important item of the delegated power (not presented in the chart) relates to the appointment of teachers. The procedure nevertheless requires that the local bodies only recruit and allocate but do not create any new post. This is essentially done at the district level. The authority for appointment of certain categories of teachers has been vested with the block panchayat. However, their posting and transfer is again controlled by the district authorities. It is found that even at the district level this is done by the Chief Executive Officer of the district, an official appointed by the state government in consultation with the head of the education department in the district. During discussions, many stakeholders felt that the hierarchical and bureaucratic control over the primary education system has not decreased in any way even after the establishment of the Panchayati Raj.

Increased Sense of Ownership at the Field Level: Another major development during the recent years is the implementation of state-sponsored programmes for extending access to primary education to unserved villages and habitations. Two such schemes have been in operation, namely, the Education Guarantee scheme and the Alternative School scheme. Both these schemes represent a major departure from the traditional mode of establishing primary schools. These schools are granted based on the articulated demand of the local community, provision of suitable space by the community to conduct classes and a commitment to ensure that a minimum number—norms for which have been specified—of children regularly attend the classes. The fact that these schools come into existence in response to the wish of the community members has undoubtedly increased a feeling of ownership and responsibility among the community.

Table 9.1: Devolution of functions/delegation of powers to the three-tier Panchayati Raj institutions by various departments of the Madhya Pradesh government, and their basic functions and duties, 1998

Activities of the State Sector	Activities of the Local Self-governments		
	District	Block	Village
1. Recognition of schools	1. Management and running of schools	1. Inspection of all schools falling under village self-governments.	1. Establishment, management and conduct of primary, secondary and senior secondary schools
2. Specification of curriculum and textbooks			
3. Planning and conducting examinations	2. Arrangement of school buildings, etc.	2. Advocacy, publicity for literacy campaigns	
4. Assessment of students' educational levels	3. Duration of study and vacation in schools	3. Construction, extension and maintenance of primary school buildings	2. Collection and distribution of textbooks and school material
5. Preparation of annual academic calendar	4. Purchase of teaching material		
6. Approval for starting new courses in schools			3. Construction, repair and maintenance of secondary school building costing upto Rs 5,00,000
7. All co-curricular activities at divisional and state levels	5. Supply of free textbooks and Book Bank scheme	4. Supply of free uniforms to girl students	
8. Innovations in school-based activities	6. Distribution of free uniforms	5. Book Bank scheme	
9. All activities related to collection and analysis of educational data	7. Non-formal education programme	6. Conduct of formal school programmes	4. Distribution of scholarship
10. Implementation, supervision, and monitoring of central and centrally sponsored schemes	8. Mid-day meal programme	7. Total literacy campaign	5. Book Bank scheme
11. Responsibility for training of teachers and other staff; control over the staff of teacher training institutions such as DIET,* and BTI.**	9. Operation Blackboard scheme		6. Appointment of instructors and supervisors
12. Power for decision-making regarding opening of new schools and construction or extension of school building using funds provided by the state government; constitution of district planning committee according to the policies provided by the state government.	10. Distribution of freeship and scholarship		

* DIET: District Institute of Education and Training; ** BTI: Basic Training Institute

Community Participation: Yet to be Galvanized: The main indicator of empowerment is the proactive participation of the people in development activities that directly affect their lives. Thus, one should expect the community members to be actively involved in the management of the local primary school where their children study. There is, of course, a SMC/VEC set up for each school. However, the involvement of the community seems to be only marginal. Many of the people expressed that they felt inadequate to play any significant role in the management of the school except with regard to construction of the school building or finding temporary space for the school. This limited participation is not confined only to Madhya Pradesh. Studies in other parts of the country also reveal that the panchayat members mainly take interest in construction activities and expect the teacher and the state department to look after school management.[9]

A general feeling among the people is that the SMC is mainly meant for mobilizing resources for the construction of school buildings. Interestingly, wherever the state government or the DPEP establishes a primary school, the community is not required to contribute any resources, be it in cash or kind. In contrast, if the demand is from smaller habitations, which are invariably inhabited by poorer sections of the society, it is obligatory for them to find space for the school and offer local resources; the DPEP or the state does not fully bear the expenses. This anomaly may in the long run prove counterproductive.

DPEP Project is the Main Vehicle for Community Involvement and Decentralization: Though the state legislation on Panchayati Raj and notification on transfer of functions and powers do not refer to any project initiative, field-level analysis of the functions being performed at the decentralized levels appear to be mainly under the DPEP. For instance, at the village level, very little funds are available for the VEC or the SMC to promote school development activities, except for the small contingency amount provided under the DPEP project. Other activities in which the villagers are expected to take part, namely, (a) preparing proposals for getting a school under the EGS or AS scheme or a new primary school in the village, (b) construction of school building or classrooms and (c) purchase of school equipment, are all under the DPEP framework. It should be noted that about 75 per cent of children study in the regular primary schools in which the DPEP does not have such a significant role as in the EGS centres, alternative schools or new primary schools. In effect, community involvement and decentralization is also less prominent in the regular primary schools functioning outside the direct purview of the DPEP project. This raises serious questions regarding the sustainability of the level of community involvement currently achieved beyond the project tenure.

More Responsibilities Assigned than Powers Delegated: Apart from the fact that the transfer of powers and functions to Panchayati Raj bodies has been effected only through a process of executive delegation, even the list of transferred items does not signify true empowerment of the people in decision-making. The list mainly represents functions and responsibilities rather than powers and authority. In fact, most of the critical decision-making areas are retained by the state government. There is considerable vagueness and ambiguity in the items specified in the list. Two important factors have to be noted in this connection. First, no serious attempt has been made to restructure the management system operated by the department of education. Neither have the roles and functions of the existing functionaries been redefined nor has any systematic reorientation been given to them on the changed system of management. Second, two parallel systems of authority and management seem to be functioning simultaneously with regard to the primary schools. Added to this is the third operational wing functioning under the DPEP framework. For instance, responsibility for inspection of the schools has been vested with the block-level panchayat. But it is not clear whether a new system of inspection is being visualized or the existing Assistant District Inspectors of schools will continue with their traditional role. With the existing system of management remaining unchanged, and the roles of different functionaries not being redefined, it will be difficult for the decentralized system of management to take root.

Representational Politics Brings in New Dynamics in Rural Life: Legislation on the constitution of the Panchayati Raj bodies at various levels requires adequate representation of women and deprived sections of the population. For instance, it is obligatory that one out of three representatives in all the bodies be a woman. Similarly, seats have been reserved for scheduled caste and scheduled tribe candidates in all the bodies. Has this process of compulsory representation changed the traditional rural power structure and empowered the deprived sections of the community? The state has had only one round of democratic elections for the Panchayati Raj bodies. It is therefore too early to judge the potential of this process in empowering the poorer sections. However, discussions with different categories of stakeholders point to a high level of hope and expectation that this will, in course of time, change the power equations in the rural areas, provided elections are held under these conditions regularly.

Creating Public Access to Educational Information: A significant feature that could be observed in most of the primary schools, particularly those operating under the aegis of the District Primary Education Programme was the preparation of a concrete information base on the status of primary schooling in the village. For instance, a village education map clearly indicating the status of every household and every child of school-going age has been prepared. This pictorial representation of the status of participation of children, along with a register containing corresponding figures, is maintained in each school. These data instruments are readily accessible to every member of the school management committee as well as other community members. It is, of course, not clear whether these are creating any social pressure on the community for ensuring the participation of all children in the school. Further, it appears that the database was prepared by the teacher and not the community members themselves—which would have further heightened the sense of commitment of the community members towards participation of all children in primary education.

The Case of Rajasthan

In Rajasthan, the management of primary education in rural areas has been a subject of dual control involving the department of education and the panchayat and rural development department. Involvement of the panchayat department made no difference in terms of people's participation. It essentially meant an indifferent management by the bureaucracy. However, with the launching of Lok Jumbish (LJ), the state government initiated certain radical changes in the prevailing set-up. First, the state government almost completely handed over the task of primary education development to the Lok Jumbish Parishad, an autonomous organization created by the state government, which is the apex body of the LJ project. Second, departing from the tradition of keeping the district as the main level for planning and allocating tasks in primary education, the state government passed executive orders empowering the block-level body of the project to take decisions in this regard. With these moves the state government virtually made the state department of education as well as the panchayat and rural development department mere facilitators rather than planners and managers of the primary education programme. It should, however, be noted that LJ was not launched simultaneously in all parts of the state. It began its operations in a few selected blocks and has now come to cover more than 100 blocks in 13 districts.

Thus, decentralization and community empowerment in Rajasthan have to be examined from within the project framework. The state government has not taken any special legislative action to empower the Panchayati Raj bodies or any kind of local self-government. However, the Lok Jumbish project was launched as a "people's movement" at the grassroots level to mobilize support and participation of the rural community in primary education. It was not conceived as a project distinct from the existing programme of primary education. Rather, the objective was to revitalize the existing programme of primary education to make it more responsive and inclusive. The project was based on the assumption that the creation of a people's movement for primary education would generate a stimulus for human development which, in turn, would contribute to basic socio-economic change empowering the community as a whole.[10]

This approach of attempting to transform the existing management system operating from within a project raises several issues and questions. What are the implications of beginning with mobilization of people without prior specification of roles and functions to be performed by management bodies at different levels—district, block and village? Does the system point to a genuine move towards community involvement and empowerment? How will this process of building from below be institutionalized? And, to what extent are the various aspects of the system sustainable? As an evolving and expanding project, Lok Jumbish may be unable to provide final answers to these questions. It will greatly depend on the course that the state government takes as the project expands its activities. It further raises the question whether the project structures for decentralized operation would get smoothly merged into or transformed to operate in a larger developmental framework as and when the Panchayati Raj bodies get empowered and primary education becomes a subject of local control by elected representatives.

Basic Features of the Decentralized Framework under Lok Jumbish

Institutional Framework of Lok Jumbish—Block as the Critical Level: As was mentioned earlier, Lok Jumbish was conceived not as a project distinct from the existing programme of primary education. Rather, the objective was to revitalize the existing programme of primary education to make it more responsive and more inclusive. A unique feature that distinguishes Lok Jumbish from most other project initiatives in India is its effort to build a block (normally consisting of about 100 villages) as the critical level for project management and decision-making in contrast to the district level (generally consisting of 10 or more blocks) or the state level. A Block Steering Group (BSG) is set up in each project block. The block, for the execution of LJ, is divided into manageable clusters consisting of 20–25 villages. A small group of LJ staff function in each cluster, and act as the vital link between the people and the project.

A Block-level Education Management Committee (BLEMC) is constituted in each block with powers delegated to open new primary schools, upgrade primary schools to upper primary level, create posts of teachers, etc. The committee, normally headed by an educationist from within the block, consists of the block development officer, block-level education officer, the LJ project officer, teachers' associations, women activists, etc. The BLEMC members examine for approval all the village-wise proposals that come to them through the cluster functionaries. The village-level actions are formulated and co-ordinated by a small group called the core team consisting of 10–12 animators (men and women in equal numbers) who are known for their interest in education. These are set up by the cluster-level workers of LJ in each village after initial contact and environment building. The core team receives training, which includes, among other things, techniques of school mapping. A women's group and a building construction committee are also set up in each village.

Role Specifications evolve through Practice: While the powers and authority of the BLEMC are fairly well defined, the roles and functions of the functionaries at various levels are considered in an evolving framework as indicated in the figure (see Figure 9.5). It should be noted that transforming a system of management in the final analysis implies: (*a*) new actors such as members of the local community get involved in planning and management activities, and (*b*) new roles and functions get assigned to various people engaged in managing primary education programmes. If the purpose is to create a system of management where the community members feel fully empowered, the choice of what tasks they would like to perform should also be theirs. Thus, in reality roles and functions are acquired according to the needs and demands of the community, and not prescribed from outside. It is with this perspective that no rigid prescription is made regarding the functions and responsibilities of the various structures from the village to block levels. This perspective has also allowed for considerable variety in the field-level activities in different areas.

An apprehension at the field level is: "How would this freedom and flexibility regarding the roles and responsibilities of people at various levels of

Figure 9.5: Decentralized management set-up under Lok Jumbish

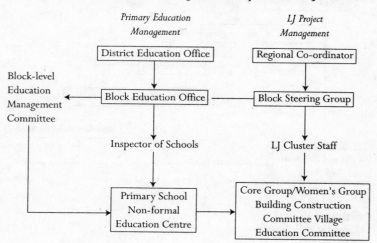

the management structure be sustained after the project period?" Obviously, this requires the state government to issue necessary legislations changing the existing rules and regulations.

Inclusive Participation and Empowerment of the Deprived Sections: If one goes by the level of participation of the underprivileged and the overall success in getting women to form their own action groups, Lok Jumbish seems to have made a positive beginning. After all, it has to be recognized that inclusive participation by the whole community in a still feudalistic and caste-ridden society as in Rajasthan is a long-drawn affair. Making the participation more representative of all sections gains further significance in the context of the emerging scenario of decentralized management through Panchayati Raj bodies. The participatory school mapping process, initiated under Lok Jumbish, has set the stage for introducing more direct participation of villagers in the management of primary education. This is a timely development in the context of the current move to transfer the responsibility for primary education to the Panchayati Raj bodies. As there is considerable fluidity and lack of direction in the roles and functions of these bodies, LJ efforts and experience in building

Figure 9.6: Process of redefining roles and functions

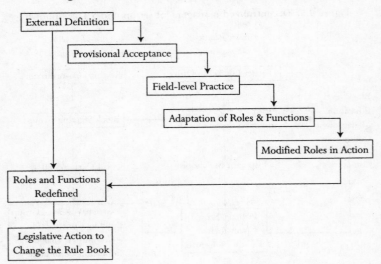

representative local groups should help clarify what community bodies could do. Lessons from LJ would also help in defining the roles and functions of the Panchayati Raj bodies with respect to primary education.

Organizing People at the Grassroots level—Paving the way for Decentralized Management: It is recognized that people's mobilization is not just "raising" them once and cannot always be orchestrated by external forces. If this has to be sustained and harnessed for educational development, it is essential that they be organized. Formation of core groups and women's groups under Lok Jumbish meet this need for the coming together of people *voluntarily* for a common cause. It is this voluntary organization of people that gives them a feeling of empowerment. However, organizing people can be threatening to the established power structure. The success of LJ in initiating such a process without inducing a feeling of threat and yet ensuring a transformation is particularly worth noting. It may be too early to conclude whether this will lead to a fundamental transformation in the existing social structure of rural Rajasthan. Nevertheless, changes observed with respect to women's participation in LJ activities in particular, and in village development activities in general, have to be specially taken note of.

Creating village teams and involving them actively in processes of educational development in the village seem to be serving another important focus of LJ. One can easily observe that the formation of village teams has laid the foundation for building a system of self-determination and decentralized management *from below*. The involvement of these teams has successfully imparted to community members the habits of rational decision-making with respect to primary education, in particular. In some of the older LJ villages, core teams are getting transformed into VECs, thus converting the informal organizations of people into formal, legitimate structures. These are significant developments in the context of the renewed effort made all over the country for establishing Panchayati Raj bodies for local self-governance. However, there seems to be no clear perspective on the process of formalizing the informal groups. Currently, these groups work with a voluntary service orientation, and incorporating them into the electoral process of Panchayati Raj, which operates under the framework of power to govern, will bring in new dynamics.

Participatory School Mapping as Core Component: The core component of Lok Jumbish is the participatory process of school mapping and micro-planning. Under this, it is the villagers themselves who carry out field surveys and prepare an education map of the village indicating the status of participation of every child. This participatory approach, coupled with the use of the map as a tool of advocacy with reticent parents, has undoubtedly heightened the sense of commitment and accountability of the community members. It is based on such participatory exercises that proposals emerge at the village level for improving the facilities available for primary education.

Training common villagers—A Unique means of Empowerment: In the rural setting, the training of any one person chosen from among the common people is altogether a new phenomenon. In particular, to consider that common people can do any constructive activity in the area of primary education, which has traditionally been the preserve of teachers and government officials, presents a new framework for self-perception to the villagers. This is viewed as an empowering process by the villagers and unreservedly welcomed by them. Needless to say that apart from instilling a sense of empowerment, such capacity building activities are essential if decentralized management has to become really effective and sustainable in the long term.

The State continues its Hold in Critical Areas of Decision-Making: In the final analysis, the extent of decentralization is determined by the level of control exercised by the central authority, in this case the state government. As was mentioned earlier, the state government has allowed for an unusual experimentation in public management by taking decision-making to the block level, down from the district or state level. Having provided for this, how well is the state machinery capable of facilitating this change? Field investigation shows that the state government still retains certain critical decision-making powers. For instance, the sanctioning of teacher positions to different primary schools is done by the BLEMC based on proposals—drafted on the basis of actual data—presented by the community. However, the appointment of teachers and their posting as approved by the block committee continues to be done by the state government. This splitting of powers between the sanctioning authority and the appointing authority highlights the fact that the state government continues to hold control in critical areas of management decisions.

Continuance of Parallel Structures of Management: It was clear from the field study that while the LJ management tries to influence all aspects of primary education, parallel structures of management have continued to persist. This continuance of parallel structures has not only created confusion among the school personnel, but also significantly affected the capacity of the project personnel to bring about positive changes in the functioning of the primary schools. This could have been overcome by integrating the two structures—or at least by establishing better interaction mechanisms between the two sets of personnel. In the absence of such efforts, continued existence of parallel management structures is likely to result in conflict of interests and even hinder the emergence of a stable system of decentralized management.

Positive Signals from the Field

Taking the Decision-making Process nearer to the Field of Action: Irrespective of the route taken, a positive development in both the states is the effort to move decision-making processes down the hierarchy. In Rajasthan, the creation of the BLEMC with power and authority to deal with several aspects of primary education marks a significant step forward in this direction. In the Madhya Pradesh legislation, though a bit cautious, the direction of the move is unambiguous as indicated by the transfer of several items from the state and district control to the authority of local self-governments at block and village levels.

Another important change observable in both the states is the involvement of the village-level community in demanding additional educational facilities and in implementing the follow-up action for creation as well as maintenance of the school. This again signifies an attempt to empower the community with respect to management of primary education at the local level. The process is more participatory in Rajasthan as compared to the situation in Madhya Pradesh. But this could be due to the fact that the actions are initiated through informal groups in the former while it is done through formal representative bodies in the latter. Which will survive longer, and serve the interests of decentralization and empowerment better is difficult to say at this stage. One has to allow for the systems to work for a longer period of time. However, there is undoubtedly a clear attempt to generate two important prerequisites for decentralized management—namely, participatory diagnosis and planning by the community, and reflection and self-direction by the community.

Access to Information and Public Accountability: In both the states, using the ongoing primary education projects as the vehicle, an attempt has been made to generate a concrete information base in the form of village education maps and village education registers. Further, for the first time, this information is being made accessible to the public at large. This is a complete departure from the traditional practice where educational information collection and consolidation had been the preserve of the teacher and other educational authorities. This transparency of information on school functioning and participation of children has instilled not only a feeling of control among the community members, but also a sense of accountability. In fact, the participatory dynamics has further heightened this feeling in Rajasthan.

Paradigm of School Provision undergoes Radical Change: Macro-level statistics show that access to primary schooling facilities is almost universal in both the states. But micro-analysis reveals that about 20–25 per cent habitations in the two states do not have any schooling facility. It is important to note here that most of these habitations form part of larger revenue villages and are invariably inhabited by poorer sections of the society. Again, girls have been the main losers as parents hesitate to send them out for schooling. This barrier has been broken in both the cases by providing alternate means of primary schooling within the habitation. A more significant development in this regard is the articulation of demand by the community members. It is no more the traditional norm-based supply of educational facilities. Rather, the building of schools is dependent on the articulation of demand by the people themselves and their commitment towards making the school function.

Positive Perception of Change: As noted earlier, renewed advocacy for decentralized management is not merely on ideological grounds; it is more so on the expectation that it will improve the efficiency of the management system. In the primary education sector, it is a question of whether the primary schools are becoming more efficient under the new arrangement. If the perception of the people is any indication, the general opinion is that primary schools function more regularly and effectively than before, more children are attending schools now than earlier, and even learning seems to be taking place more effectively. Of course, it is difficult to attribute this perceived positive change exclusively to decentralization and community involvement. Without any doubt, increased inputs and supervision by the primary education projects have contributed significantly. Nevertheless, it is important that we build on this positive perception of the community and make the change process more sustained.

New Leadership is emerging at the Grassroots Level: In a hierarchy-ridden community, empowerment can be quite deceptive, engendering further hegemony for the dominant groups. Elaborating on this issue in the context of India, Myrdal writes,

> Another hope inspired and initiated from the centre is that a system of locally elected bodies, the *panchayati raj*, better known under the label "democratic decentralization" or "democratic planning," will encourage the masses to participate in the management of local affairs and thereby weaken the power of the local political bosses.... The most conspicuous immediate effect of such efforts has been to strengthen the grip of the rural elite, the self-elected boss class, over the masses. Whenever locally elected bodies are given powers worth scrambling for, they are almost invariably run in the interests of the dominant caste in land and wealth. The system of *panchayati raj*, like the basic democracies in Pakistan, has not, in general, thrown up any new leadership in rural areas.[11]

How has this problem been tackled in the current round of decentralization? This has been a matter of primary concern in both the states.

The recent Constitutional amendment adopted in the national parliament clearly saw this problem and created in-built protection against such distortions. Following this pattern, the Madhya Pradesh legislation for constitution of the Panchayati Raj bodies ensures proportional representation to scheduled castes and scheduled tribes at all levels; it also reserves 33 per cent of seats to women in all the local bodies. In Rajasthan, though the creation of grassroots bodies does not have a legislative cover, guidelines issued for the constitution of the village-level committees such as the core team and the women's group ensures that the deprived sections of the society have adequate representation in these informal groups.

Empirical data shows that people at almost all levels are unanimous on the point that the dynamics of power is changing and a new leadership is gradually emerging, which is more inclusive and representative. A point that has to be noted in this connection is that the new leadership is currently dealing with a limited agenda, mainly riding on the back of a project initiative. As long as we are operating within the framework of an innovation, it is not likely to be questioned by the traditional stakeholders in the larger system. However, many components of such innovations may become a bone of contention when they move to the mainstream.[12] How do we minimize such frictions and human tensions that may affect the change process? Can the integration process withstand the opposition from within society posed by long-entrenched vested interests supporting the maintenance of the status quo? These are questions that need careful consideration.

Areas of Critical Concern

Problem of Entrenched Hierarchy: A centralized system breeds bureaucracy, leading to an entrenched official hierarchy, and the inegalitarian social set-up characterizing the rural areas tends to echo this and reinforce the hierarchical relationship. However, decentralization demands the dismantling of hierarchy. Is it really happening? Broadened and more inclusive participation of all sections of society in decision-making is the best antidote for hierarchical control systems. In Madhya Pradesh, this is reflected in the efforts within the DPEP project set-up. The legislative measures of reserving elected positions to representatives from deprived sections of the society also strengthens this position. However, the top-down reform model does not fully promote the ethos of non-hierarchical functioning in the lower echelons of decision-making. Discussions with teachers, headmasters, and even elected representatives reveal that decision-making and control still flows from above. This should not surprise anyone. Changing the long-practised behaviour of the people at the periphery takes time and it may be too premature to judge the efficacy of these measures.

In Rajasthan, chances appear to be relatively higher for generating a non-hierarchical system of decision and control. At present, decision-making within the LJ set-up is relatively less hierarchical. In this regard, not having a district-level decision-making mechanism seems to be playing a significant role. Separating project management and decision-making at the block level also seems to have introduced an element of transparency and public accountability.

The threat to the sustainability of this arrangement seems to emerge from the fact that project management is still parallel to the departmental set-up in both the cases. A point that needs more careful observation and analysis is whether the distribution of powers in the Madhya Pradesh legislation also reflects an element of hierarchical control. In the final analysis, what matters is whether a restructured decentralized set-up is used only as a strategy by the state authorities, or as a basic principle for overarching empowerment of the people at the grassroots level. This requires an examination of the actual functioning of grassroots-level bodies, to see whether the decentralized powers and authority are pervasive enough, covering all aspects of public life, or whether they are limited to achieving specific short-term goals of project implementation. This is important as in both the states, large projects of primary education development constitute the main instrumentality of changing the existing system of management.

Roles and Functions—Prescribed vs. Performed: It is the changed behaviour of management actors at various points of decision-making that will indicate whether a centralized system is getting transformed into a decentralized one. The managers are all basically trained to operate a centralized system. Will the mere prescription of a new set of functions and responsibilities succeed in changing the behaviour of the incumbents?

For this to happen, it is essential to create a convergence between the roles and functions prescribed for different actors, and their performed roles. In fact, every one will have to acquire new habits of behaviour under the new dispensation. Where has it been better promoted? Some amount of role ascription is inevitable in any transformation, whether the transformation is externally initiated in a project mode or through top-down legislative action. In this context, the scope for redrawing the contours and redefining the roles incorporating the expectations of the community is a critical requirement. Seen from this angle, the top-down prescription of roles and responsibilities as done in Madhya Pradesh is a disadvantage. In contrast, participatory processes initiated in Rajasthan require an evolutionary perspective on determining roles and functions, and therefore provide the incumbents opportunities for acquiring and internalizing the new roles.

Persistence of Parallel Structures: For any changed framework of management to take root, two factors are essential. First, the new managers in the changed set-up should acquire the knowledge and skills necessary for efficient implementation of planned development activities. Attempts are visible in both the states to equip the new managerial leadership through training programmes. However, this has to be accompanied by adequate space, and freedom for the new incumbents to practice the roles and imbibe attitudinal reorientation. Second, the existing management structure should be transformed to facilitate effective performance of new managerial roles. Unfortunately, no attention has been paid to this requirement in both the states. In fact, the study revealed that new structures have been put in place without dismantling the old ones or allowing for their integration. This has resulted in parallel management structures apparently managing the same system, leading to multiple control and inevitable conflicts of interest. The longer we allow for this parallelism, the more difficult will it be to rectify the situation. Experience shows that since the new framework is operating invariably on a smaller scale under the patronage of innovative projects, in the long run it tends to get distorted and incorporated into the larger one, defeating the very purpose of its creation. It is true that dismantling the old structure will lead to friction and discontentment within the system, but that is inevitable in any process of change—and more so where sharing of powers and empowerment of new stakeholders are involved.

Question of Sustainability—Moving from Project to Programme: It was pointed out earlier that in both the states, ongoing projects of primary education (DPEP in the case of Madhya Pradesh and Lok Jumbish in the case of Rajasthan) are the main vehicles facilitating the process of decentralized management. To some extent, this is a positive factor as it readily provides a framework for the people at the decentralized levels to get involved. However, this can also become a limiting factor if care is not taken to do advance planning for their transition from project status to programme status. Is this happening in the two states? One could not see much action in this direction in either of the states. At present, in both the states, the primary education projects attempt to put in place a new framework for management of primary education at decentralized levels that functions with considerable autonomy and attempts to involve the community in an active manner. Can this really lead to a system-wide transformation of the educational management set-up of the state?

However optimistic one may be, time-bound and project-based innovations cannot be equated with processes of social transformation at the system level. The former are mainly technical interventions while the latter inevitably involve serious political decisions. The critical question is: Can these be considered as harbingers of system-wide reforms bringing in an era of decentralized educational management? Or will they remain mere show-pieces of small-scale successes? Even under the best of circumstances, one cannot but wonder as to the proportion of these innovative efforts that can be scaled up to cover the whole system. A frictionless, smooth *transition from the project mode to the programme mode* cannot always be assumed. For instance, two critical issues have to be tackled:

(a) A smooth transition from project to programme mode depends on the way the concerned policies, rules and regulations are reoriented to accommodate the new initiatives. One of the common tensions that arise in this regard is with respect to project personnel and their integration into the system. This will be a complex question in both the cases, as the Projects have become operational with a relatively new set of policy guidelines only in some selected districts while the existing rules and regulations continue to be in force in the remaining. How do we overcome this problem of dual sets of rules and regulations and ensure smooth integration of the project with the regular programme?

(b) Adoption of the project initiatives in the regular programme cannot be seen as an "all or none" affair. All elements of the Project may not get integrated into the regular programme of primary education at all. Decisions on this will have to be made on concurrent analysis of each component element in the Project throughout the period of implementation. This will reveal not only the worthwhileness of retaining the project components in the long run, but also their financial viability in terms of cost effectiveness.[13]

Need for Convergent Legitimization: It is often assumed that within a liberal democratic set-up, the community fully vests all powers for structural changes in the hands of the bodies elected by them to rule. Does this imply that the state can bring about changes without the participation and involvement of the people? To believe so would be an oversimplification. In fact, history is full of many proposals for change legislated by the state remaining ineffective and unimplemented due to the apathy of the civil society.

Nevertheless, the centrality of state power cannot be undermined. Many changes at the micro-level brought in under the banner of civil movements have also withered away, in course of time, due to their rejection by the state authorities. Thus, any fundamental structural change in

Figure 9.7: Model of convergent legitimization

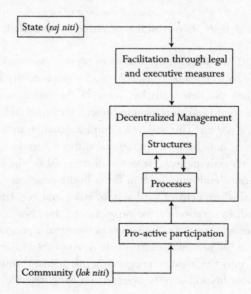

the socio-political organization of the society, such as decentralization of power, will have to recognize the existence of two poles, the state (*raj niti*) and the civil society or the community (*lok niti*). Viewed from this perspective, sustainability of changes initiated under decentralization requires a convergence of perspective, and legitimization by both the state and the civil society.

How do the developments in the two states measure up against this model of convergent legitimization? Rajasthan presents a favourable situation with respect to the requirement of pro-active participation by the community members. This is due to the extraordinary effort made under Lok Jumbish to mobilize people through participatory processes and capacity-building activities. But, does the state own the LJ philosophy and strategy of decentralization? The initial response of the state had been positive as reflected in authorizing the BLEMC to take vital decisions regarding planning and management. However, after the initial enthusiasm, the state has not shown any move to provide a legal status to this executive measure. When the time-bound project initiative comes to an end, will the decentralization process be rolled back? This is a real possibility as the coverage of the state under the project is not complete and the government is moving to implement a different project framework for primary education in more than half of the state.

The situation in Madhya Pradesh is quite different. In this case, the state has gone ahead with legislative measures devolving control and authority over a number of subjects to the Panchayati Raj bodies. The state department of education has followed up the legislation delegating a number of functions and responsibilities to the grassroots-level bodies. This is definitely indicative of the positive outlook of the state towards the process of decentralization and empowerment of the community. However, even this falls short of the requirement if one looks at the level of participation of the people in the management of primary education. Will mere representational politics ensure genuine participation of the people? Do people view the Panchayati Raj bodies as their own or do the common citizens view them as a mere extension of the state-level power politics to the grassroots level? These are critical questions that need more in-depth explorations. However, in a society used to a culture of silence, participation may have to be externally engineered till such time that people acquire the habits of self-direction and independent decision-making.

Postscript

What are the prospects that the ongoing developments will lead to a more permanent transformation of the system into a decentralized one with the empowerment of the people being more comprehensive, and not fractured in favour of the rich and the elite as is the case at present? It is difficult to answer this conclusively in either case. However, a silver lining is emerging in the rural horizon in the form of a new leadership configuration. Whether it is the informal participatory processes in Rajasthan or the representational politics of Madhya Pradesh, it is beyond doubt that these processes have unleashed a new dynamics in rural life and the contours of power equations have begun to change significantly. Field perceptions clearly show that if these processes can be sustained long enough, enduring changes in the management structure and processes will inevitably follow. This will, perhaps, be true at least in the project areas if not in the whole state.

The dynamics of transforming the centralized and hierarchical management structure steeped in bureaucratic rigidities into a people-friendly, decentralized system is not just a technical exercise of changing the rule book and issuing gazette notifications. Nor can one expect that a few rounds of exhortations to the community members through participatory processes will suffice. After all, this arrangement has served well to preserve the iniquitous socio-economic structure of the society. Changing the framework of power sharing can never be a simple process. It requires everyone concerned—the political personage, the bureaucracy and the common citizenry—to imbibe a new "world view" on human relations that underscores mutual trust and confidence in each other, and places the common good of the community before personal ambitions. When such a transformation of the system is linked to empowerment of the people through universalizing basic education, it makes it doubly complex and challenging. But there is no cause for despair—it rather calls for renewed commitment to strengthening the institutions of democratic governance that are already taking root in the country.

Notes and References

1. See "National Policy on Education: 1986 and 1992", and its Programme of Action, Ministry of Human Resource Development, New Delhi.

2. See Govinda, R. (1997), *Decentralization of Educational Management: Experiences from South Asia*, Paris: International Institute for Educational Planning, UNESCO.

3. See *CABE Committee on Decentralized Management of Education: Report* (Chairman: V. Moily), Ministry of Human Resource Development, New Delhi.

4. See Adamolekun, L., R. Robert and M. Laleye (1990), *Decentralization Policies and Socio-Economic Development in Sub-Saharan Africa*, Washington, D.C.: Economic Development Institute of the World Bank and Pan African Institute for development.

5. Misra, R.P. and Nataraj, V.K. (1982) "India: Blending Central and Grass-roots Planning" in W.B. Stohr and D.R. Fraser Taylor (eds), *Development from Above or Below?*, Singapore: John Wiley.

6. See Govinda, R. (1997) "Decentralized Planning and Management of Literacy and Basic Education Programmes", paper presented by the author at the UNESCO-ACEID International Conference on Educational Innovation and Sustainable Development, Bangkok, 1–4 December.

7. See Laclau, E. (1985), "The Hegemonic Form of the Political: A Thesis", in C. Abel and C.M. Lewis (eds), *Latin America, Economic Imperialism and the State: The Political Economy of the External Connection from Independence to the Present*, London: Athlone Press.

8. Marsh, D.D. and G.A. Bowman (1989), "State-Initiated Top-Down versus Bottom-Up Reform", *Educational Policy*, vol. 3, no. 3, p. 197.

9. See Varghese, N.V. and S.M.I.A. Zaidi (1999), *Local Bodies and Planning for Education: A Study of Aurangabad District, Maharashtra*, New Delhi: NIEPA.

10. See Govinda, R. (1999), *Reaching the Unreached through Participatory Planning: Study of School Mapping in Lok Jumbish*, Paris: International Institute for Educational Planning, UNESCO.

11. Myrdal, G. (1968), *Asian Drama: An Inquiry into the Poverty of Nations*, New York: Pantheon.

12. See Govinda, R., cited in note 1 above.

13. Govinda, R. and N.V. Varghese (1994), *District Level Plan Implementation Strategy with Particular Reference to School Improvement*, Paris: International Institute for Educational Planning.

10

Capacity Building for Educational Governance at Local Levels

R. Govinda

Contemporary discourse on education management in all countries is full of references to various concepts that directly or indirectly point to the need for shifting the system of educational governance from central to local levels. In the policy literature one finds this referred to in various ways as decentralized management, local school management, increased role for the civil society, community empowerment in school management, and so on. All these indicate to a process of transformation of the existing system of educational governance. But in reality, change on the ground is not keeping pace with the pronouncements made in policy and planning documents. Resistance among the central authorities to give up their powers is not unexpected. But the slow progress in transforming the system seems to be equally due to lack of understanding and capabilities among the new stakeholders to power at the local level on their precise roles and responsibilities.

In the traditional management framework, educational institutions such as schools are viewed as mere recipient bodies implementing the decisions made for the larger system. Changing this perspective and shifting the locus of control over education to the local level, possibly located in the school itself, demands a total change in perspective. But, how would this change be brought in? This throws a major challenge as governance at the local level requires a new set of skills and attitude among all the stakeholders.

Are the traditional programmes of in-service education of headmasters and school teachers geared to meet this challenge? In fact, local level governance of education brings a new kind of clientele to the forefront for capacity building, namely, community members. Do community members who would take up new roles for governance of education need special orientation? How should such orientation be organized? Do the existing institutional arrangements suffice to reach out to all of them? What would be the nature of inputs to be provided in such capacity-building efforts with respect to different groups of stakeholders from the school, the community and the education department? These are some of the important questions addressed in this article.

The Context

In fact, participation of the local community in education management has a long historical legacy. After all, the first schools were founded and even funded solely by local community groups. The state entered the scene much later in the history of schooling. Initially, the role of the school had been to wean the individual away from the emotional world of the home in order to socialize in the outside world, and to introduce young men and women to the rational world of knowledge and learning. With the onset of industrialization, along with the emphasis on compulsory schooling and education for informed citizenship, national governments began to take over the responsibility of funding and organizing school education. This, in some ways, set the stage for distancing the local community from educational governance. With the evolution of 'national systems of education', governments began asserting their authority and control over the system of schooling as fully legitimate. Today, all over the world, it is the prerogative of the national governments to determine the shape of the school system as a publicly funded phenomenon.

Seen in the above evolutionary perspective, the current focus on participation of the local community in school governance is actually an instance of "coming round full circle"—the return of the prodigal. Is it not paradoxical? Perhaps, one has to unscramble the backdrop and context to understand what this return of educational governance to the local community means, in rhetoric and in reality.

The Indian scene at the grassroots level presents too varied a picture to draw a generalized one of the context. As discussed in the introduction to this volume, while some states have gone a long way in transferring not only powers, but also a substantial proportion of state funds to Panchayati Raj bodies, some others have chosen to keep considerable control in the hands of the bureaucracy at the decentralized levels. Some states have gone for the establishment of quasi-legal bodies such as VECs and SMCs to oversee governance of education at the local levels, whereas several other states have yet to move towards such decentralized management structures. In some cases, not much progress has been made beyond galavanizing PTAs to take greater interest and participate in school-related activities. Each of these models also imply varying perceptions of the policy makers and planners regarding the value of decentralization and local governance. Designing capacity-building activities to suit such varying contexts presents a big challenge.

The move towards greater control over education at local levels, in India as well as elsewhere, seems to have been prompted by three contemporary developments across the world:

1. The recognition of "greater legitimacy of direct control by local stakeholders" over education and several other social sectors—as part of the democratic decentralization framework.
2. The expectation that "smaller management systems are more efficient and accountable"—as part of structural adjustment processes or restructuring public systems.
3. The assumption that quality concerns can be better met by focusing on individual school development than by bringing system level reforms— school autonomy coupled with enhanced accountability becoming a major feature of contemporary reforms for quality assurance.

These contextual parameters, though closely interrelated, present different rationale for establishing local governance systems, and therefore bring with them a special set of issues to be tackled in capacity building for different stakeholders involved in education at the local levels.

Critical Issues Related to Capacity Building

Adopting a Comprehensive Perspective: Who Needs Capacity Building?

Traditional thinking on capacity building focuses almost exclusively on launching training programmes, especially for community leaders who have to take up new responsibilities for governance of education. It is necessary to look beyond this narrow framework. Involvement of the local community in educational governance demands a radical transformation of the organizational culture of the public education management system. Greater involvement of the local community demands that the higher authorities agree to give up certain powers hitherto enjoyed. Also, school control by local stakeholders brings greater pressure on the school authorities to promote transparency and share perspectives with parents. The school authorities cannot merely meet the demands of remotely placed higher authorities and get away even with low efficiency in school functioning. Accountability to local masters is not something many school authorities are familiar with. Seen from this angle, there are at least three distinct groups which need special orientation to function under the changed framework of governance. Accordingly, capacity-building activities have to be designed at three levels—for school personnel, local/community level managers and state education department authorities.

One of the biggest challenges with respect to equipping people involved in local governance of education is the magnitude of the task involved.

What about Academic Supervision and Support Services?

It is necessary to examine the question of linking educational governance with local community control within the local political and developmental context. While the school governing council or village education committee or local self-government body could become the apex body or main body for decision-making with respect to general management issues, questions of academic and professional management have to be independently dealt with. The extent to which community members could be associated with academic decision-making cannot be a uniform prescription as it depends very much on the profile of the members constituting such management bodies, and the mutual confidence that the teachers and the members of the committee enjoy. Nevertheless, the question of building awareness among the local leadership cannot be ignored.

Further, this also highlights the need for bringing comprehensive reforms combining local governance with more academic autonomy and accountability to the school—the principal and the teachers. A piecemeal approach of transferring powers to local leadership without strengthening internal management of institutions may lead to undue interference and subject the schools to undue political pressure from parochial elements in the local community.

Drawing up a Relevant Curriculum: In What do we Train or Orient the Functionaries?

There are no generic formats for designing and implementing programmes for capacity building. Every programme has to be designed even within a country in a contextualized manner. In some places the need may be more for building social cohesion and interaction skills while in others it could be more professional and technical capabilities. It would also depend on the specific group being dealt with, namely, school authorities, the local leadership or the education department officials. However, certain broad aspects need specific focus in all such programmes. Some of these aspects are illustrated in the following discussion.

Knowledge of Changed Roles and Functions: Studies on decentralized management in many countries have shown that changed rules and regulations often remain only on books and only the central authorities become aware of the changes. People who have to adopt changed roles and functions feign ignorance and continue to follow instructions from above instead of using the powers vested in them. Proper dissemination of the changed framework and its implications for people at different levels is a basic requirement. In this connection, two points need to be borne in mind: (a) Such awareness-building exercises are needed for all, not only for the new comers to the field of educational governance, namely, parents and community leaders; and (b) The inputs should cover the roles and functions of stakeholders at all levels, namely, the school, the community and the education department; it is counterproductive to inform people only of the role they have to play without reference to what they could expect from others.

Special Focus on Institutional Management: Traditionally, schools have been at the receiving end of innovation and change in the education sector. Changes that bring about reforms in school education are designed on a system-wide scale and the role of the individual school is to implement these given change processes. In contrast, under local governance of education, the "individuality or uniqueness framework" will begin to replace the "standardized framework" applicable to all schools, with a provision for greater autonomy to the school and the introduction of "school-based management". In many countries, the "school development plan" has become a powerful instrument not only for setting the direction of change and improvement within the school, but also for receiving recognition and support from public funds and building a system of accountability. Thus linking management functions to school development will give a focus for designing the inputs and determining the expectations from different stakeholders.

Development of People Skills: Educational institutions in a centralized management system generally function under considerable seclusion, with the remotely placed state authorities having limited supervisory outreach. With local governance becoming a reality, the situation will change significantly. The school authorities as well as the local community of parents have to acquire new skills in human relations. Teachers and headmasters have to look to building relations beyond the four walls and the parents have to imbibe a sense of active partnership in managing the affairs of the school. Operations within the school have to become more transparent than earlier. Parents and the school authorities have to adopt a positive outlook in their mutual relationship. Mere technical and academic management capabilities will not suffice.

New Framework for Personnel Management: Local governance of education requires a new framework of personnel selection and management. The current practice of appointing teachers to the system and not to an individual school, prevalent in many countries, needs reconsideration. Also, it is necessary to evolve a new structure for teacher career prospects under the framework, as teachers would belong to a local school or to a smaller network of schools. In fact, studies show that in some of the countries adopting local management measures, teachers are complaining about lack of career opportunities. Designing and implementing appropriate approaches for teacher recruitment and their professional development requires special capabilities on the part of local level educational planners and managers.

Grievance Settlement—Need for a New Code of Conduct Framework: Under the centralized system, teachers and other personnel in the education department are subject to countrywide rules and regulatory procedures. A common framework governs grievance settlement procedures and disciplinary codes. With local governance coming into the picture, the situation is likely to change. Accountability to local authorities is likely to subject the school personnel to undue stress and uncertainty if the local governors of education are not properly oriented. This is important as in many countries, along with local governance, school personnel are coming under considerable fire from local communities, causing avoidable tensions and jeopardizing the interests of the school.

Capacity Building is Not Mere Delivery of Standard Training Packages

In most countries, innovations in management bring with them a series of actions involving development and delivery of standard training packages. Just as merely changing the rules and regulations by transferring power and authority to local bodies will not suffice, simply training people through standard packages will not do. It demands a changed mindset among all concerned. This is not easy to achieve in places where people have been nurtured to act only on the dictates of higher authorities. Developing new habits of self-determination is a slow and arduous process which has to be tackled with adequate provisions for direct practice, with technical support and professional guidance. Capacity building should, therefore, be viewed as a comprehensive process of facilitating the change-over from centralized management to a system of local governance.

Institutional Arrangement for Capacity Building: Where and Who will Train?

Shifting from central control to local governance opens up a vast new ground unexplored and unexperienced by anyone. In this context, questions of who is capable of imparting knowledge and skills related to local governance, and which institutions could carry the responsibility become very critical. In many countries, the institutional arrangements for planning and management are too few to meet the need. Further, many of them are too remotely placed to reach out to all peripheral parts of the country, nor do they have the requisite expertise to take up the task. Experience shows that decontextualized training given in the form of theoretical orientations on the new rules and regulations are not adequate. These orientations are often given by central authorities who themselves are unaware of the dynamics of implementing them in the field. Therefore, establishing an effective source of learning for the trainers themselves needs to be considered seriously.

Conclusion

While the need for capacity building does not require any special justification, the critical question to be dealt with is: *Should the practice of local governance wait for capacity building?* One of the biggest obstacles pointed out in many developing countries in implementing local governance measures is the low education development among the local population. It seems that the link between low scope for self-determination at local levels and low levels of basic education operates as a vicious circle thwarting the change process.

It is true that the field-level personnel in many countries seriously lack planning and management capabilities. But it is difficult to decide whether refusal to change the governance framework is fully explained by the apparent lack of management capacity at the field level. How could they acquire capabilities if they have no opportunity to practice them? It is important to recognize that decentralization represents a way of living and not just a technical strategy.

Transforming a system characterized by centralized decision-making to one where local stakeholders have a significant role is a complex task and is

Figure 10.1: Link between low scope for self-determination and low levels at basic education

bound to be a slow process. It is likely to disturb deeply entrenched power relations among different stakeholders. Also, such a transformation cannot be achieved wholly through external inputs and guidance. After all, even those who formulate the new policy framework have no direct experience of functioning in a system of local governance. In such an environment, changing the system requires inculcating the habit of participatory, collective decision-making among those who have been hitherto nurtured in a system of top-down decision-making and implementation. Therefore, new ways of functioning would essentially come through practice more than training. What is required is to accept the new framework for implementation, to allow for some trial and error as part of the learning process, and to simultaneously pursue capacity-building activities. In the final analysis, effective implementation of a local governance system and genuine empowerment of the people at the grassroots level envisages basic transformation in the organizational framework, demands the emergence of a new "world view" of power relations, and requires an abiding faith in democratic processes of decision-making.

About the Editors
and Contributors

The Editors

R. Govinda is Senior Fellow and Head of the School and Non-Formal Education Unit, National Institute of Educational Planning and Administration (NIEPA), New Delhi besides being a Visiting Fellow at the International Institute for Educational Planning at UNESCO, Paris. He has also served as a consultant for UNESCO, UNICEF, ACCU, NORAD, the World Bank and the Asian Development Bank. Dr Govinda has published several books as well as professional papers in Indian and international journals. He has done pioneering work in areas such as policy analysis, decentralized management, school mapping, participatory planning and school improvement planning, educational evaluation and basic education. His most recent book is *India Education Report*.

Rashmi Diwan is Associate Fellow at the School and Non-Formal Education Unit, NIEPA, New Delhi. She has contributed numerous research papers to national and international journals and articles to national dailies on topics relating to school education. Her work mainly centers around the application of critical issues and innovative programmes on school education from around the world to the Indian context. She has three books to her credit, the most recent being *Improving the Quality of Educational Research*.

The Contributors

Piush Antony is currently a Visiting Fellow at the Institute of Human Development, New Delhi. An M.Phil in Applied Economics from the Centre for Development Studies, Thiruvananthapuram, she earlier worked as a Research Associate at the Gender Studies Unit of the NIAS. Her areas of interest include decentralization, women and development, food economy, child labour, informal sector workers, and migration. She has conducted studies and published articles on the above themes. She has co-edited a book on *Social and Economic Security in India*.

M.D. Gayathri Devi Dutt is Director, Regional Institute of English, South India (RIESI), Bangalore. A post-graduate in English from Bangalore University with a teaching degree from the Regional College of Education, Mysore, she has worked as an administrative functionary as well as an academician during her career of 29 years. She has also developed and executed several training packages for the benefit of teachers, trainers, and community workers. She has been associated with the DPEP project and the Janashala programme in Karnataka.

Vinay K. Kantha is Professor, B.N. College, Patna University. He has worked on a wide range of issues like education, development, children, pure academics, and civil liberties, and is closely involved with the Children's Science Congress. He is Chairman of the EWES.

N. Shantha Mohan is presently Fellow and Head of the Gender Studies Unit, National Institute of Advanced Studies (NIAS), Bangalore. An educationist by training, she has for the past two years been active as a researcher, activist, and teacher on issues related to gender using social education, engendered governance, issues relating to violence against women, gender and irrigation, etc. She has published several books and articles, and has presented papers at both national and international conferences and workshops.

Daisy Narain is Reader, Department of History, Patna Women's College. As Secretary of the East and West Educational Society (EWES), Patna, she is involved with the Society's school and environmental education programmes and also coordinates the functions of its different units.

Anjali Noronha has been working with Eklavya—an organisation based in Madhya Pradesh (MP) that works in the area of curriculum development and pedagogical reform—since its inception. Having done her post-graduation from the Delhi School of Economics in 1982, she joined Eklavya to help develop the civics section of an innovative social science education program for middle schools. She has also helped develop Eklavya's primary education programme, and carried it forward for inclusion of child-friendly and pedagogically sound practices in the mainstream curriculum of MP. She continues to work with Eklavya, and is presently involved in giving shape to a community-based initiative with first-generation learners as well as an urban education programme. She has written a number of articles based on her experiences.

Vinod Raina was involved in pioneering work at the Hoshangabad Science Project before founding Eklavya, a well known NGO involved in innovative work in curriculum development and teacher training. He was a driving force in organizing several total literacy campaigns as part of the Bharat Gyan Vigyan Samiti. He is currently engaged in promoting a programme of continuing education called Jeevan Shala.

Vimala Ramachandran is currently Director, Educational Resource Unit, Jaipur. Earlier, as Director of the Mahila Samakhya Project, she was responsible for designing its innovative features. She is currently involved in a number of research and development projects related to health and education.

Sadhna Saxena is Reader, Faculty of Education, Delhi University (DU). A post-graduate in Physics and a Ph.D. in Education from DU, she has done extensive work as a senior member of the Kishore Bharati group for more than 17 years in the fields of science education in rural schools, non-formal education with school dropouts, and adult education among the deprived section of society. She has also been engaged in education research for the past decade.

P.K. Michael Tharakan is Associate Fellow, Centre for Development Studies, Thiruvananthapuram. He was recently Director, Kerala Institute of Local Administration. He has been associated with committees and councils in Kerala as well as other states. He was elected by the Governing Body of St. Anthony's College, Oxford University to the Senior Associate

Membership of the College for the Trinity Term 1997. He has also held a Special Chair in Development Studies for one year at the Institute of Development Policy and Management, Belgium. In addition, he has contributed extensively on the issues of population projections and its implications for education, agrarian relations in less developed countries, literacy campaigns, etc.

Index